MODERN DRUMMER® *Legends*

STEVE SMITH

For access to the digital files referenced in this book,
go to moderndrummer.com/mylibrary

Enter Code
WTH2PI-5VTHMN-JMXFMV

Modern Drummer Publisher / CEO - **David Frangioni**

President - **David Hakim**

Director of Content / Editor - **Mark Griffith**

Senior Art Director - **Scott Beinstock**

Music Transcription - **Terry Branam**

Editorial - **Michael Finkelstein**

Archivist - **Felipe Laverde**

Cover Photo Courtesy of Sonor Drums
Back Cover photo by Diane Kiernan-Smith

Published by:
Modern Drummer Media, LLC.
1279 W Palmetto Park Rd
PO Box 276064
Boca Raton, FL 33427

Modern Drummer always strives for the best possible content available.
There may be some photos in this issue that do not meet our highest standards.
We have included them for their historical significance, rarity, and importance.
Steve was kind enough to share these photos with us, and we wanted to share them with you.

Subscribe to *Modern Drummer*: moderndrummer.com/subscribe

For videos, visit and subscribe to the "Modern Drummer Official" YouTube channel

- CONTENTS -

Rick Malkin

- INTRODUCTION -

This issue of **LEGENDS** has been 25 years in the making. About 25 years ago, when I was first writing for Modern Drummer, Steve Smith called me (out of the blue) to ask me to write the liner notes for his upcoming record *Buddy's Buddies*. I was pretty excited. I did some research, went to the recording sessions, interviewed the guys in the band, and wrote the liner notes for that record. I guess I did a pretty good job because since then, Steve and I have worked on many projects together. He asked me to write the books that accompany his Hudson videos *The Sound of Brushes*, and *Jazz Legacy: Standing on the Shoulders of Giants*. I wrote the liner notes for a few more records, and we co-wrote some articles together. But most importantly, Steve and I have become good friends.

Our friendship has fostered hundreds of conversations, emails, and late-night talks. Along the way, (needless to say) I have learned *a lot*. Steve even *claims* that he has learned from me as well. But amazingly, I never "formally" interviewed Steve for Modern Drummer (we did do two interviews for Percussive Notes.) So, when it was confirmed that there would be a Steve Smith LEGENDS book, I knew it would be special! (Truthfully, I want **every** LEGENDS book to be very special!)

I think we have succeeded. For starters, I can't ever remember Steve being so candid and thorough when talking about his career. For anyone planning a career in music, there is some priceless advice here. Would you like to know how Steve creates grooves and writes tunes? Keep reading… And try to find another musician that references AC/DC's "Problem Child," Ahmad Jamal's "Poincianna," and The Mahavishnu Orchestra all in one interview. Lastly, listen to the included download of the solos from Steve's drum solo project "The Fabric of Rhythm." Just when we all thought that he had done *everything*, Steve has started to create and record a new repertoire of drum solo compositions. Check out his explanations of how he created these solos.

In preparing to interview Steve, I thought back on 25 years of our conversations. Believe it or not, there were actually some interesting subjects that we had never really gotten around to talking about. *Those should be a part of this interview*. Then I tried to recount the conversations that we had in which I have learned the most about: being a drummer, a professional musician, the history of jazz and fusion drumming, the music business, and being a student of the drums. *Those would have to be a big part of our interview*. I also remembered all of Steve's amazing gigs that I had seen that hadn't been "officially" documented or recorded, and there were some really good ones. *That is where we should start.*

Sure, I saw some amazing Vital Information gigs, and Steve's playing was always just ridiculous, but when you're a touring bandleader sometimes your mind is split in many pieces (travel, lodging, bandmembers needs, promotional stuff, dealing with clubs and agents, etc…) It was always great to hear him with Steps Ahead because he was in super-relaxed sideman mode. I even saw some Journey gigs early on, and in the last four years. He always played his ass off with Journey, but to me, Steve never seemed comfortable in the "rock star" setting.

It was the freelance gigs that Steve did as a sideman with Mike Stern, Hiromi, the many editions of the band Electric Miles, or the tribute gigs playing The Music of Coltrane or The Music of Ornette Coleman that were always the ones that excited me the most. I witnessed many of them. That is where Steve's role of the student of music, the over-prepared sidemen, and the fantastic drummer, all merged. Talking about, and watching Steve prepare for those gigs is when I learned the most from him. And I knew the readers would too.

This was not your typical interview. This was two friends having a long conversation about the past, present, and the future, and you are a fly on the wall. There are a lot of surprises in this **LEGENDS,** and there is a mountain of useful information. Steve and I had a lot of fun talking to each other, and hopefully you will have even more fun "eavesdropping" on us. We each learned a lot, and I'm *sure* you will too.

—**Mark Griffith**

Steve Smith Library

A NOTE FROM THE PUBLISHER

I remember the first time that I saw Steve Smith play, it was with Journey on the Escape tour. I had seen videos of Steve's playing, and had heard him on records, but seeing him live took it to another level. He was so precise, creative, and powerful, and had unbelievable chops. I followed his work closely from Journey to Vital Information and on his many other projects including awe-inspiring clinics, drum festivals, and his educational materials. I have seen Steve play many times and always learn something new from watching and listening to his drumming.

Years later, I had the privilege of working closely with Steve on two different projects. One was a 5.1 DTS surround sound remix of his Vital Information *Global Beat* album. The other was a drum loop library called *Rhythmic Journey*. On both of these projects, I heard Steve's playing at the most detailed and intimate level and it just got better every time! Seeing his work ethic, attention to detail and hands-on approach only solidified what we hear every time Steve plays: HE IS ON!

Here we are decades after my first Steve Smith live show, and you are holding a true work of drumming art: **Steve Smith Legends**. The word Legend is a rare classification for someone to earn in their respective field. You already know that Steve has *(more than)* earned it, he has lived it, and he continues to inspire us every day. Enjoy Steve Smith Legends!

David Frangioni
CEO/Publisher of Modern Drummer Publications, Inc.

Steve Smith:
Understanding, Following and Developing the Opportunities

By Mark Griffith

In looking back through all of the interviews that Steve Smith has done with *Modern Drummer*, most have been based around Vital Information or Journey. While those groups are both excellent examples to study Steve as a musician, his musical scope is far greater.

A passing comment on Steve's versatility would be an understatement. For example: There was a time from January to April 2016 where Steve Smith recorded a solo drum set album (*Fabric of Rhythm,*) a new Vital Information album (*Heart of the City,*) played live shows and recorded a new album with Steps Ahead and the famed WDR big band (*Steppin' Out – with WDR Big Band Cologne,*) performed straight-ahead jazz at Birdland Jazz Club NYC with the Groove Blue Organ Trio and the next week played Madison Square Garden with Journey! Who else does that?

Steve answered that question with a nice synopsis of his drumming approach, "Understanding what every gig requires is essential. Developing that understanding means living with a particular musical approach for a long time. Initially it's a case of studying the music and practicing the music, but then you have to immerse yourself in playing the music by being hired by someone that excels at that style. That way you get to play the music night after night and really embrace and inhabit the musical concept. I have been fortunate to have been hired for many different situations because the bandleader, or band, believed that I have

Lin Biviano Big Band 1975 Barry Kiener (keys) John Lockwood (bass) Bob Malach (tenor sax)

Steve Smith Library

the *potential* to do the gig. Then I put in the work to develop and try to become a *master of that gig* and of that musical situation. I have been extremely lucky to be able to go from Berklee to Jean-Luc Ponty to Ronnie Montrose to Journey to Steps Ahead to all of the various Indian musicians that I have been playing with. You can study a style of music with all your heart but studying can only get you so far. Hopefully, it will get your foot in the door, but the real learning starts when you go out and play the music. That's the real university."

Unfortunately, a lot of that development, and many of the gigs that Steve has immersed himself in have gone un-recorded or have appeared on very hard to find authorized recordings. But the times have changed.

Through the "wonder" of YouTube, unofficial recordings of gigs can be enjoyed by one and all. Bootlegs are no longer only traded amongst friends, and you don't have to scour dozens of record stores to find a hard-to-find recording that someone did in their past. On the internet you can find obscure U.S. or European TV appearances, rare and out of print recordings and artists filming their own gigs. It's all right there with a few keystrokes.

I will skip the ethics of YouTube, and INSIST upon the educational benefits of seeing music live, supporting your favorite musicians by buying their recordings, and NOT selling or posting any unauthorized recordings. That's what your favorite musicians advocate, and that is what helps them make a living.

But for historical and educational purposes, many one-time tours, and one-off gigs live on YouTube and can be learned from, studied, and enjoyed. Today, many musicians (like Steve) even document these gigs and post them on their own YouTube channels for exactly this reason. At least that way they can remain somewhat in control of what is seen and heard. For the sake of his Legends interview, I asked Steve if we could begin by talking about many of the gigs in-between Berklee, Journey, and Vital Information. That's where we began.

MD: In one way or another, and for better or worse, we are all a product of the gigs that we have done, not just the most popular gigs. For you, there have been lots of gigs and recordings that many drummers might not even know about, and many of those gigs have really helped you develop and grow into the musician you are today. So much has been written about Journey and Vital Information, and we'll get to those later, I would like to start by going through these gigs and explore your career outside of the big spotlight. But let's start by talking a bit about your experience at The Berklee College of Music. What, and who, were you as a musician when you got to Berklee as a student?

SS: Before Berklee I had taken nine years of private lessons with an excellent teacher in the Boston area named Billy Flanagan.
I played in the school concert bands and marching bands, various All-State and New England orchestras and during my last two years of high school I played with the Bridgewater State College Big Band in Bridgewater, Massachusetts. I had also played in many rock bands in high school. We played Led Zeppelin, Deep Purple, Grand Funk Railroad, and some original rock music.

When I was at Berklee, which was from 1972-1976, I did a little of everything: I played in the "ECM" jazz style, I was in an R&B "Top 40" band with bassist Neil Stubenhaus, and I played a lot of straight-ahead jazz and big band. At that time, the vanguard of the great jazz musicians were performing and recording fusion, but fusion hadn't really trickled down to what we, as students, were playing at school. I would

go to see Return to Forever with Lenny White, Billy Cobham's Crosswinds band, Weather Report, Herbie Hancock's Head Hunters with Mike Clark or The New Tony Williams Lifetime, but we weren't really playing that style of music in school. Most of the jazz we were playing was based on the 1960s Miles group with Tony Williams or the Coltrane group with Elvin Jones. I hadn't really developed what I would call "a fusion approach" to drumming. Bassist Jeff Berlin, guitarist Jamie Glaser and I would play with that fusion approach somewhat, but it was really undeveloped. Some of the playing we did then was more like the extended blues-rock jams by Cream. Jeff Berlin was a huge Jack Bruce fan and

Steve Smith Library

Steve playing with Lin Biviano

the Cream album *Wheels of Fire* that also featured Eric Clapton and Ginger Baker was influential to me and lots of musicians my age. Mainly I was working on developing my jazz concept and the musicians I played with were mostly acoustic players: upright bass, piano, saxophones, trumpet and the occasional guitar player like Mike Stern, Bill Frisell or Jamie Glaser. We were playing jazz standards in small spaces and not playing loud. I had to carry my kit around, rolling it down the street from one building to another on top of my trap case, so I tended to only use an 18" bass drum, hi-hat, snare and a ride cymbal.

Steve with Jean-Luc Ponty 1977

Steve Smith Library

An important point is that when I was in high-school I loved big bands like the Buddy Rich Big Band, Count Basie, Stan Kenton, Woody Herman and Maynard Ferguson. Fortunately, I got to see all of those bands. Sitting in front of a powerhouse big band was some of the most exciting music that I had ever experienced. Plus, I was into, what I considered, the great rock bands of the late 60s/early 70s and got to see Led Zeppelin, Mountain, Grand Funk and other rock groups live. Once I got to Berklee I was introduced to a huge world of jazz that I had never listened to. I was discovering the music and, at the same time, the drumming that fueled that music. It was a case of music first, then drumming. It started with Miles Davis' *Four & More* with Tony Williams, and continued with all the other Miles albums that Tony played on. Then I went back to embrace Philly Joe Jones on *Workin', Steamin,' Cookin,' and Relaxin,'* then Elvin and Rashied Ali with Coltrane. I was studying innovative drumming concepts with Gary Chaffee, more traditional jazz drumming vocabulary with Alan Dawson plus my peer group of fellow musicians at Berklee were very influential. I was discovering the depth of jazz music and that was inspiring! The music of Miles and Coltrane from the 60s wasn't even 10 years old when I dug into it. And most of the players who had spent time with Miles

were leading innovative groups that I got to experience live. Being in the room with those bands altered my DNA. It was a heady time and I felt like I was in the middle of it!

Some of the important albums for me that were being released around that time were the Chick Corea albums *Now He Sings, Now He Sobs* (with Roy Haynes) and *Tone's For Joan's Bones* (with Joe Chambers,) Miroslav

Steve in high school 1972

Steve Smith Library

on sax, Rich Appleman on bass, and Bob Gullotti on drums. There was a period when Bob was on a year-long tour and George and Rich asked me to play in the group. In The Fringe, one second I was playing free-time like Rashied Ali, and the next second we were playing up-tempo swing as fast as we could play. The main idea in that trio was to transcend time and space. We played ourselves into an altered state. Most of the time when we rehearsed, we turned off all the lights and played in total darkness. On gigs we would take the audience on a kind of acid trip. That's when I really discovered the beauty of the energy Coltrane had tapped into with his later groups and his album with Rashied Ali, *Interstellar Space*.

MD: You said in an old MD interview that "The ECM concept of playing wasn't working for you," what did you mean by that?

SS: What I meant was that the influence of Gary Burton was very strong at Berklee, the ECM concept of free-flowing implied-time was really popular. When I was at Berklee there were many different drumming concepts that were hip at the time. The ECM concept, which meant playing very freely in the style of Jon Christensen, Jack DeJohnette, or Bob Moses (like on the Pat Metheny album *Bright Size Life*), was a popular way of playing. You can also say that a prototype for the ECM school of drumming came from Tony Williams and some of the albums with Miles but especially Tony on the Herbie Hancock album *Maiden Voyage*, which was an important album for me. I had enough technical

Vitous,' *Mountain In The Clouds* (that album has also been released as *Infinite Search*) (with Jack DeJohnette,) John Abercrombie's *Timeless* (with Jack DeJohnette,) Ralph Towner's *Solstice* (with Jon Christensen) and Steve Grossman's *Some Shapes to Come* (with Don Alias.) Also, Airto was a big influence on me and most of the drummers at that time. The way he played the jazz-samba on the first two Chick Corea Return to Forever albums (*Return to Forever* and *Light As A Feather*) was imitated by everyone! And there were the albums that featured the two studio kingpins of that era, Steve Gadd on the East Coast and Harvey Mason on the West Coast plus all the Berklee musicians loved Tower Of Power with Dave Garibaldi.

To get back to some of the playing I was doing at Berklee, I also played avant-garde free-jazz in a trio with bassist Rich Appleman and saxophonist George Garzone called The Fringe.

MD: That's the same band that existed for almost 50 years with drummer Bob Gullotti, George Garzone, and bassist John Lockwood right?

SS: Yes. The original line-up was George

Steve Smith/Joe Casano Big Band 1974

Steve Smith Library

background and could understand the concept to adapt my playing to that approach but I never went on tour with anyone that embodied that approach. Had Gary Burton ever hired me to tour, or someone like ECM artist Eberhard Weber, then I may have gone in that direction and mastered that concept. It's not that I didn't like that style of playing, I did. In fact, there are a number of tunes on my early Vital information albums that are in that ECM style, it's just that I was not hired to do that. Instead, I was hired by Jean-Luc Ponty to play in the fusion style. It was a case of following my opportunities.

When I got the gig with Jean-Luc Ponty, I knew about that concept of fusion playing, I had played along to Mahavishnu's *Inner Mounting Flame* and Return To Forever's *Hymn of the Seventh Galaxy* albums but hadn't really played that way live. I'd say the young jazz musicians of that time thought of it as the new way of playing jazz, we called it jazz-rock. Some of the big band charts I had been playing had a jazz-rock approach and on some Boston gigs the groups would stretch in the jazz-rock concept. I used to rehearse with keyboard player Barry Kiener and bassist John Lockwood, with Barry on Rhodes and John on electric bass, and we'd play jazz-rock. We were the rhythm section for the Lin Biviano Big Band and we would occasionally jam in my parent's basement at their Cape Cod cottage.

Once I was hired by Ponty I really applied myself to learn how to develop that style. It pulled together many of the styes that I had already played. Like I said, I had played rock and big band in high school plus jazz and R&B with very good musicians at Berklee. Fusion playing wasn't a stretch because it was a combination of all of that music. What is interesting to see from a current perspective is that, when I was at Berklee in the early 70s, the musical environment wasn't about playing fusion. It wasn't until I was actually in Jean-Luc Ponty's band that I adapted myself to that style of fusion drumming. You can see me playing my second

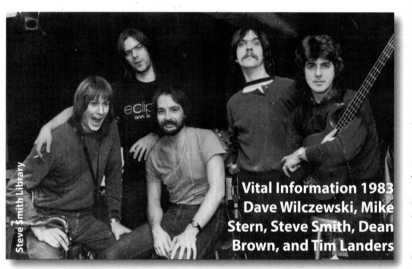

Vital Information 1983
Dave Wilczewski, Mike Stern, Steve Smith, Dean Brown, and Tim Landers

gig with Jean-Luc on a YouTube video of the PBS TV show called *Soundstage*.

MD: You told me a while back that you had done a European tour as a young man with guitarist Philip Catherine, and bassist J.F. Jenny Clark. I had never heard about that, and you have never mentioned it. Was that before the Ponty gig?

SS: No, that was during my time with Ponty. When I toured Europe for the first time in 1977 with Jean-Luc Ponty, we played in Holland and Thijs Van Leer came to the gig. He is the flute player and the organist for the Dutch band called Focus. Thijs invited me to come back to Holland later that same year to record with Focus on a record called *Focus con Proby* (with singer P.J. Proby.) There were two guitar players in that band: Eef Albers and Philip Catherine. I had met Philip previously because he and Larry Coryell had a guitar duo called Twin House that opened for Jean-Luc Ponty. And Eef would later play in Vital Information. After I did the record with Focus, Philip asked me to do some gigs with his trio. The fact that Philip asked me to do that tour after playing on the Focus record was very good for my confidence, because Jean-Luc was playing fusion, the Focus record was more of a rock thing, and Philip's gigs were straight-ahead jazz gigs.

MD: While this might seem insignificant, this is how careers get started. A tour with Jean-Luc leads to a recording with Focus which leads to a straight-ahead tour with Philip. There was even a tune on that Focus record that you later recorded with Vital Information, right?

SS: Eef's tune "Orion" was the title tune of the second Vital record. Another unrecorded gig of that time was a band called *Not Bad for White Boys*. That band was an annual get-together that bassist Tim Landers and sax player Dave Wilczewski and I would have at a Boston club called Jack's. Tim, Dave and myself met playing in the Bridgewater State College Big Band, though all three of us were high-school students at that time. Once we became working pros and were touring with various bands, we would get together once a year and play with a different guitarist. One year we had Daryl Stuermer because he and I were playing together with Jean-Luc. Dean Brown played one year and Barry Finnerty another year because Tim was playing with them in Billy Cobham's band. That band evolved into the first edition of Vital Information. We did those gigs for fun, but a lot of the music that we did on those gigs became the music that was on the first two Vital Information records.

MD: You moved to Los Angeles because the Jean-Luc Ponty gig ended, and that led to the Ronnie Montrose gig. Those Ronnie Montrose gigs on YouTube are unbelievable, you can see that that band was on fire.

SS: There is footage of a gig in New York from a venue called The Palladium, which was a 3,500-seat theater. There was a big difference between the earlier band called Montrose with Sammy Hagar on vocals and Denny Carmassi on drums and the Ronnie Montrose band that I played in. When it was billed as Ronnie Montrose it was more of a jazz-rock or maybe better described as a rock-fusion band. Ronnie had made a record called *Open Fire* of instrumental rock that was influenced by Jeff Beck's direction. That's how I ended up in his band, Ronnie wanted a rock-fusion style of drummer.

MD: Was this at the same time that Ronnie was recording with Tony Williams, Herbie Hancock, and Billy Cobham.

SS: Yes, but for some reason Ronnie didn't pursue that instrumental direction for too long and he wound up forming a rock band called Gamma with Denny Carmassi playing drums.

I didn't walk away from Ronnie's gig feeling that I learned a lot, but it was a really fun gig. The opportunity presented itself, and I decided to go in that rock-oriented direction because I was enjoying playing a big kit in the fusion style. The guys in the band were very good rock musicians, but I was coming from a jazz

Steve Smith Library

Steve Smith and Philip Catherine

background, so I didn't have a whole lot in common with them musically. We all got along and had fun but I learned more in Jean-Luc's band because the players were coming from a jazz point of view.

MD: That Ronnie Montrose band went on tour opening for Journey on a triple bill that also includes a young Van Halen as an opener doing their first tour, and after that tour Journey asked you to join the band.

SS: The transition from Ronnie Montrose to Journey was a more interesting transition for me. I really had to adapt to become the right drummer for the individuals in Journey.

I have a certain ability to intuitively understand, see, and hear, what a musical situation requires. I've listened to a lot of music and I can adapt myself pretty well. When I play with rock musicians they usually consider me a rock drummer and when I play with jazz musicians they consider me to be a jazz drummer. That's because I have an intuitive understanding of what they need to make their music work. I don't know where that ability came from, it's just something that I've always had. It goes back to when I was in high school, continued at Berklee, and has been a thread throughout my entire career.

MD: How do or can you determine what a musical situation or style "needs?"

SS: Good question. Styles usually exist within styles, and it's all within a musical context. For example, last week at Birdland we were playing Coltrane music, and we played the tune "Like Sonny." Billy Higgins played a Latin groove on the head on the original recording, but we did the whole tune with a Latin feel. So "Latin" is a style, but it's a style within the context of small group jazz. So that's how I approach "Latin styles." I am not going to go into a musical situation and try to play authentic Latin grooves. I play "Cu-bop" Latin, which is a jazz interpretation of a Latin time feel as interpreted by Kenny Clarke, Art Blakey, Elvin Jones or my version of that idea.

For "Like Sonny" I transcribed Billy Higgins' beat on that tune, and learned it. That helped expand my musical vocabulary. Then I got loose with it and was inspired by what was happening on stage around me with the other musicians in the band. That's the process of spontaneous improvisation while being inspired by the music. You have to allow yourself to respond to what is happening around you, I think that's what we are all trying to get to. You have a musical idea, and then you find the musical language, or vocabulary, to express that idea, and it's the same no matter what type of music that you are playing.

MD: You told me that your first gig/audition for Journey was a live radio broadcast that can now be heard online on San Francisco author and music critic Joel Selvin's website. That sounds like a lot of pressure to be under while you are *finding the musical language and vocabulary to express ideas.*

Steps Ahead 1986 Michael Brecker, Mike Mainieri, Darryl Jones, Mike Stern, and Steve

https://opensourcemusic.com/journey-superjam/
SS: After the Journey-Ronnie Montrose-Van Halen tour, Journey manager Herbie Herbert asked me to come to San Francisco to rehearse with the band and play some gigs. They had already heard me play with Ronnie Montrose, so there was no need for a formal audition process. After some rehearsals, my debut public performance with Journey was on *The King Biscuit Flower Hour Journey Super Jam* on October 19, 1978 for a live radio broadcast. Some older readers might remember that show. In 1941 a radio show called *King Biscuit Time* featured early blues musicians and was sponsored by King Biscuit *Flour*. In 1973 a new syndicated radio show picked up on that name and, with some 60s "Flower Power" influence, they called

it *The King Biscuit FLOWER Hour*. At the Super Jam we played some songs from *Infinity*, and we did a variety of rock and soul songs like "Crossroads" with Tom Johnston from The Doobie Brothers, Steve Perry wanted to do "Good Times" by Sam Cooke and some other R&B classics, plus The Tower of Power horn section played with us.

MD: That was live to tape for broadcast so there were no fixers right?

SS: No fixers. We played in the studio with all the musicians playing and singing live with no overdubs. That recording is a good example of me being a fairly quick study of seeing what kind of drummer that they wanted for the band. Although I did my share of overplaying on the Ronnie Montrose gig, it was pretty obvious that Journey didn't want me to overplay. But they did like having a drummer with some chops to play their older instrumental tunes and stretch out when they wanted to extend some songs. But mainly they wanted an R&B-rock drummer.

MD: It's interesting to listen to those Ronnie Montrose gigs, and then listen to that first Journey broadcast because it doesn't even sound like the same drummer.

SS: What you're hearing is discipline. In Journey I was playing with a lead singer, and up until then, I hadn't worked with a singer. That was a very interesting and educational process. And because Steve Perry was a drummer, he really helped and coached me through that transition.

After I started with Journey in September 1978, I moved to the San Francisco Bay Area. Shortly after moving there, I met bassist Randy Jackson at a jam session and he introduced me to Tom Coster who had recently left Santana. Tom had played with Randy in Billy Cobham's band and the three of us really hit it off personally and musically. Eventually we became The Tom Coster Band and played some local gigs and recorded two albums. That was a very free, high-energy and reckless band, we had a lot of fun playing together. Later, Tom joined Vital Information, and Randy remains a friend.

There was a point later in the 80s when jazz-fusion began to become more disciplined with emphasis put on playing difficult music with a high degree of accuracy. But before that, what I heard from jazz-fusion bands like Billy Cobham's bands or The New Tony Williams Lifetime was more over-the-top, with extended soloing, and what I would call "playing with reckless abandon." Those bands were going for a certain kind of energy. I related that to the energy that John Coltrane used to generate with his quartet in the 60s with Elvin. That's what we were getting into with Tom and Randy. The playing was a vehicle for spiritual transcendence, a kind of out-of-body experience, and the players and the listeners had to surrender to that kind of overwhelming energy. It's the same idea I talked about playing with The Fringe.

When I saw The New Tony Williams Lifetime band with Allan Holdsworth, Tony was not holding back at all, his playing was very creative and free, occasionally making mistakes and not playing "perfectly," and I really dug that. He would go for different fill ideas and sometimes they didn't come out right at the end of the phrase. When that happened, he would have a look on his face, you could tell that he was upset with himself. Yet as much as he played these amazing fills and phrases that did come out "correctly," I found it just as interesting and equally inspiring when his phrases did not come out where he wanted them. I saw Billy Cobham play with that kind of freedom as well. That's what I mean by recklessness.

MD: One of my favorite Tony Williams quotes is him saying, "I don't trust musicians who don't make mistakes."

SS: That's great! That first generation of jazz-rock-fusion was different from what developed later when there was a lot of emphasis put on precision and perfection in jazz-fusion. Put on the Tony Williams Lifetime album *Emergency!* or the Mahavishnu album *The Inner Mounting Flame* and you will hear exactly what I am talking about. The raw energy of those bands is undeniable! Although with later fusion something was gained with the precision and perfection, something

was lost with that loss of freedom, expression and recklessness which could generate a feeling of spiritual/emotional transcendence.

Tom, Randy, myself, and guitarist Joaquin Lievano would push ourselves to play in the high-energy spirit of the ground-breaking fusion bands. We made two records as The Tom Coster band, the first is called *T.C.* and then we recorded *Ivory Expeditions*. Those albums are a good documentation of our music when we were playing live around the S.F. Bay Area, but of course, the live gigs were much more high-energy than the records.

MD: From 1978 to 1985 you were very committed to Journey and there is no reason to rehash those years. Then Vital Information went from a side project to a serious recording and touring band which has been working for almost 40 years. However, in 1986 or 1987 you played with jazz piano legend Ahmad Jamal. That seemed to be a real departure for you. But looking at your background, maybe it really wasn't?

SS: I had joined Steps Ahead in 1986. The Ahmad Jamal gig came about because producer Milan Simich heard me at a Steps Ahead show at The Bottom Line in New York. That was the Steps band with Michael Brecker, Darryl Jones, Mike Stern, and Mike Mainieri. The musical stretch from Steps Ahead to Ahmad Jamal is pretty wide, but Milan told Ahmad's manager about me. When Ahmad needed a drummer, I got the call. I wasn't terribly familiar with Ahmad Jamal's music at the time, but I quickly went to work learning it. I discovered how important he was in jazz history. I learned his new music which he had recorded with Herlin Riley, and of course I learned "Poincianna," but I learned it wrong. Now I know that drummer Vernell Fournier played that classic beat with the left hand on the hi-hat and his right hand played the snare and floor tom.

MD I think Vernell was the first open-handed player. But we'll get to open-handed playing later.

Tom Coster Band 1981
Joaquin Lievano, Tom Coster,
Steve Smith, and Randy Jackson

Steve Smith Library

SS: My first gigs with Ahmad was a week at the original Catalina Jazz Club in L.A., and he was very complimentary of my swing feel, he dug my pulse. Playing with him was a great experience. He's the real deal. He had a set of hand signals that he used. There was a signal for the top of the tune, a different signal for the bridge, and a signal that told you to lay out. Ahmad was creative and spontaneous. In each set that we played, the tunes had different arrangements, based on his hand signals, and the tempos of the tunes varied from night to night. James Cammack was the bassist, and for the short amount of time that I played with Ahmad it was quite inspiring.

During the week at Catalina's Jazz Club in L.A. with Ahmad I also rehearsed with Joe Zawinul for a jazz showcase at a CBS record convention in Vancouver, Canada. I was signed to Columbia Records at that time and Dr. George Butler, head of the Columbia jazz department, organized a Columbia all-star jazz group to play at the convention. The line-up was Joe Zawinul on keyboards, Nancy Wilson on vocals, Grover Washington and Ronnie Laws on saxes, Abraham Laboriel Sr. on bass, and me on drums. There were some other performers as well but at this point, I don't remember who they were.

Since I happened to be in L.A. I was contacted by Joe Zawniul and the two of us planned on getting together for a jam and a rehearsal at his home in Malibu, and that first rehearsal would just be Joe and I. Since we were going to play Grover Washington's "Mr. Magic" at the CBS Showcase, Joe asked me to stop at Tower Records in Hollywood to pick up a cassette of the tune on the way to his house. Amazingly, he had never heard "Mr. Magic" before. Joe put the tune on his stereo, and in his inimitable style said, "That's some sad shit. We'll have to hip that up!" Joe came up with a hip new way to play "Mr. Magic," with a pretty elaborate drum beat that he sang to me. He didn't want me to play any 2 & 4, only syncopated type beats. That was just the beginning of an interesting afternoon with Joe. When I first started playing, he stopped me after only a few bars to tell me to lower my right shoulder. I had my right shoulder raised up to get my right stick on the hi-hat and my left shoulder lowered to play the snare with traditional grip. He told me that I needed to play with both shoulders even, "Like a boxer." He stood up and demonstrated, I said "*Okay,*" and did my best to retrain my shoulder

angles on the spot. Every so often he would look my way and move his own shoulders to remind me to even out my shoulders. Then he told me to play the hi-hat more open and legato, he didn't want me to play staccato on the hats. He also had me play mainly my China cymbal as a ride versus my main ride. He was very specific in what he wanted to hear from the drums. When I related this experience to Peter Erskine, Peter told me that Jaco used to call Weather Report soundchecks, "The drum lesson," because Joe would continually be giving Peter direction of what and how to play the drums.

MD: Peter and I discussed the Zawinul "drum lessons" in our Legends interview.

SS: After the rehearsal, and "drum lesson" with Joe, I drove back to Hollywood and played two sets with Ahmad! The full CBS Records All-Star Jazz Group rehearsed a few weeks later in Vancouver and everyone in the group deferred to Joe as the bandleader, though there really wasn't a leader per se. Joe had a presence and gravitas that was undeniable. We played a fantastic show to a packed house. Grover loved the new arrangement for "Mr. Magic." We also played an updated version of Joe's tune "Mercy, Mercy, Mercy" that was very cool. I brought in the Vital Information tune "Johnny Cat," written by Tim Landers, and Joe turned that into a Weather Report tune. When I returned to Vital Info, I had a cassette tape of the gig with Joe and played "Johnny Cat" for the band. We started playing the tune with Joe's "arrangement," which was basically play the head and then improvise. You can hear this approach to "Johnny Cat" on the Vital Info album called *Vitalive!*

MD: In 1988 there was another unrecorded band that can also be heard on YouTube, called Superband: Jazz Explosion 1988.

SS: That was with Stanley Clarke, Allan Holdsworth and Randy Brecker. Airto played percussion on some of the gigs as well. A promoter put that band and tour together. That was an "all-star" band that was really fun, but I don't think we really gelled as a group. Everyone got along well, but sometimes all-star groups gel, and sometimes they don't. We each brought a couple of tunes to the band and we played together very well but the music never really took off.

I learned a few things in that band. Every night Allan would be really negative about his own performance.

I have since learned that he was like that no matter who he played with. After a while, his self-depreciating negativity got to be a drag, and then it turned into a running joke. So much so, that Stanley would eventually beat him to the punch after the gig and jokingly tell Allan that he didn't play well, even though he sounded amazing every night. I can be self-critical of my own playing, so I understood what Allan was feeling, but I learned that it's probably best *not* to voice those feelings to the rest of the band. I also learned that it's

After that tour was over both Allan and Randy invited me to go on tour with their own bands. I was leaning in the direction of playing more straight-ahead jazz so I chose Randy's tour, but it was a hard choice. I've been playing with Randy, over the years, ever since.

The first tour I did with Randy was a State Department tour of Eastern Europe where we played a lot of straight-ahead jazz from Randy's record *In The Idiom* that he recorded with Al Foster. We also played some Brecker Brothers tunes, which was great fun. That band

Steve Smith and Ronnie Montrose

Steve Smith Library

best to focus on the 90 percent of the gig that went well instead of the 10 percent that didn't go well. It's no fun to walk off stage and travel with someone who was constantly singing the blues about their own playing. My favorite part with that gig was the encore. If I remember correctly, we played "Invitation" as a medium swing with Stanley on upright bass. Playing swing with Stanley on upright was, for me, the highlight of the evening. He swings his ass off on upright!

was Dave Kikoski on piano, Barry Finnerty on guitar, Dieter Ilg on acoustic bass and Randy on trumpet. That tour was back in 1988 before the Berlin Wall came down, and the world was a very different place.
MD: You mentioned Steps Ahead, how did that come about and how did you prepare or adapt to that gig?
SS: When I first joined the band, it happened pretty quickly and there wasn't time to prepare. I was doing a drum clinic tour shortly after leaving Journey in 1985

and one of the clinics was in Pennsauken, NJ with Peter Erskine, Lenny White, Kenwood Dennard, and Gerry Brown. Peter had been in Steps Ahead for a while but he was preparing to leave and join Joe Zawinul's new band called Weather Update, which was basically Weather Report without Wayne Shorter. Mike Brecker and Mike Mainieri had called Lenny White for the gig but Lenny turned it down. Backstage at that clinic I sat with both Peter and Lenny, when Peter said he was leaving Steps and Lenny said they just called him, I told them "I'd love to do the Steps Ahead gig!" Lenny called Mike Mainieri and recommended me. The next day, I got calls from both Michael Brecker and Mike Mainieri asking me to come to New York and join the group. After that clinic tour I went to New York and started to rehearse with them.

They gave me their new recording called *Magnetic*, I wrote out charts and completely learned that record. It was a crash course. I had heard all of their previous recordings but I had never played the tunes. I had to learn all of that music very quickly, and the way I did it was to write my own charts.

That version of Steps Ahead with Mike Mainieri on vibes, Darryl Jones (or occasionally Victor Bailey) on bass, Mike Stern on guitar and Michael Brecker on sax and EWI was together for about a year. After that, Mike Mainieri disbanded the group while Mike Brecker went out with his own band with Mike Stern, Jeff Andrews, Joey Calderazzo and Adam Nussbaum. After a few years, Mike Mainieri put Steps Ahead back together with saxophonist Bendik Hofseth, bassist Tony Levin, guitarist Steve Khan and myself. We recorded the album *NYC*. When the group went on tour, we added pianist Rachel Nicolazzo and Victor Bailey joined on bass.

That was the around time that everybody started to get into the more precise way of playing jazz-fusion which was influenced by Dave Weckl and Chick Corea's Elektric Band. That was a very different way of playing jazz compared to the more reckless-abandon type of fusion that I was playing with The Tom Coster Band and Vital Information. So that was another case of me adapting to the musical environment. Playing in Steps Ahead during the years of 1989 through '93 was a good example of that new musical environment because Mike Mainieri was using a Fairlight (sampling workstation) a lot. I also adopted that new musical environment and style of making music when I had Jay

Oliver produce the Vital Information record *Fiafiaga (Celebration)*. That approach to playing doesn't have any wiggle room when it comes to subdividing the beat. We were playing with sequences and live musicians at the same time, so everything had to be really precise. That was a transition that took some time for me because we didn't play with a click in Journey, nor did I use a click on any of the Vital Information records before that. But around the time of Steps' *NYC*, *Yin Yang*, and Vital's *Fiafiaga* that way of playing became the way that music was being made, so I adapted and went with it. Playing in Steps Ahead is where I first met bassist Jeff Andrews and he would later join Vital Information. In retrospect, I was probably a little too analytical of every note that was being played during that time. By 1997 I had decided to get back to playing looser and not be so locked into that kind of quantized perfection.

One thing about me is that once I get to the point where I have something really in my grasp, it no longer interests me as much. Therefore, once I understood that precise way of playing, and I became very good at it as I had made myriad pop and fusion records under that kind of microscope, it became less interesting and less fun to play like that. In fact, it made me want to play much looser, open and more relaxed. One time when I was with Freddie Gruber and we listened to some music that was played very "correctly" he said to me, "That was so right, it was wrong."

MD: Back to when you were transcribing Peter's drum parts for Steps Ahead; Were you charting out the tunes in a lead sheet approach, or were you transcribing his parts?

SS: I transcribed a lot of Peter's drum parts verbatim. The way that Peter played on tunes like "Beirut," "Pools," or "Oops" is essential to the tune. So are Steve Gadd's earlier parts on the Steps tunes like "Young and Fine" and "Sara's Touch." I transcribed the specific beats on all of those tunes so I could understand both *how and what* they were playing. When I played with the band, most of the time, I wouldn't stray too far from what they played, because it was the right part.

For that type of jazz-rock music, the specific beat is important. There are varying degrees of what is jazz and what is rock in those tunes. In the rock parts and when the melody is being played, the beat is important. In the jazz parts, the solo sections, the time-feel and the interaction is what's important. But for learning that type of music, I transcribe the exact beat the drummer plays on the recording as my starting point.

MD: How do you transcribe?

SS: With Ahmad Jamal, I had a little book of basically cheat sheets. I try not to overdo it and write in too much detail, if I can help it. For gigs that are more jazz-rock I start by writing down the main beat of the tune, from there I will start to write down the number of bars in each section. If there is a specific transition section or fills that need to be exact, I'll write those rhythms

Chambers, Terri Lyne Carrington, Al Foster, and many others. I have absolutely no attitude about learning drum parts that were created and recorded by someone else.

For example, here's a chart of a Mike Stern tune called "One Liners" that Jack DeJohnette played on. You can see that I wrote out the rhythm of the melody, it's an up-tempo swing tune based on rhythm-changes, so there's no specific beat to play, it's about knowing the melody and then playing the form.

Stuart Brinin

out too. Over the years, the process of transcribing drum parts for many different gigs and many different drummers has really helped my drumming expand.

For instance, let's talk about a gig like playing with Mike Stern. I have done lots of Mike Stern gigs throughout the years. In preparing for a Mike Stern gig, I listen to, and have transcribed tunes and drum parts played by Vinnie Colaiuta, Dave Weckl, Dennis

If you look at the tune called "Big Neighborhood," Dave Weckl played on that. It's really rockin' so I wrote out the way Dave played the bass drum and snare. I usually don't write the hi-hat parts unless they are super specific. If a tune has some odd groupings or unique phrases, I'll write out those rhythms so I can catch the phrases. I keep all of my charts in one book and stay organized with it. So, when I get a call from Mike Stern for a gig, I reach for my Mike Stern book.

However, whenever I make a pop record, and the producer wants the part to be like the demo, I write out a very detailed chart of the entire tune and exactly what's on the demo. It makes the recording process go much faster.

MD: In a past Legends interview Kenny Aronoff and I talked a lot about how he prepares charts for gigs.

SS: I've seen Kenny's charts, he writes really good and pretty detailed charts. I do something similar to that for my rock/pop charts.

MD: I remember when you recorded the Police tune "Synchronicity II" with Neal Schon and Arnel Pineda, you sent me the chart that you had written for yourself. I was surprised that you had written a chart with lots of repeats and codas. In my career of writing charts for gigs, I (strangely) had never thought of writing repeats and codas, I just wrote them straight down, and sometimes had to deal with some pretty long charts.

SS: That tune was really long and it had a very long coda section.

MD: But lots of rock tunes do, I had just never thought of writing rock charts that way. You're always teaching me something.

SS: Joe Bergamini wrote a really good book on how to write out drum charts you should check it out.

MD: It seems that one of the constant gigs for you throughout the years has been playing with Mike Stern. But there has never been any other official documentation of your playing with Mike. So again, we must go to YouTube and see the many incarnations of Mike Stern bands that you have played in.

SS: Mike and I go way back, we played together at Berklee in the early 70s, he's on the first and third Vital Information records. I have toured with Mike as a trio with Tom Kennedy, as a quartet with Randy Brecker and

Steve Smith Library

Janek Gwizdala, as a quartet with Tom Kennedy and Didier Lockwood, as quartet with Bob Malach and Anthony Jackson plus lots of one-offs at "The Dump," (which is the 55 Bar in NYC.) It's always fun playing with Mike. He likes hearing a strong pulse, and he likes to hear the drummer outline the form, where some musicians really don't.

MD: Really?

SS: For instance, I did a Canadian tour with saxophonist Mike Zilber's quartet with Dave Liebman as a special guest. Mike and I made a jazz quartet recording called *Reimagined, Vol 1: Jazz Standards* and we were playing that music. After a few gigs, Liebman asked me not to play so "literally." He didn't want to hear me clearly marking the top of the tune or the bridge. He wanted me to just play and keep the time going without any markers of the form. He told me, "If I get lost, I'll keep playing until I know where I am." I got what he was saying, and I love that type of playing, but some musicians I play with don't want that. A musician has to be very self-contained to be able to always keep the form internally without any indication of "one" every so often.

For me, the best example of that kind of playing is the Keith Jarrett Trio recordings with Jack DeJohnette and Gary Peacock. Jack plays through the whole performance of a tune and never plays a "one" to mark the top of the form, because Gary Peacock and Keith Jarrett are so strong internally. They get a beautiful flow generated and I feel those trio albums are some of the highest-level jazz-playing ever recorded.

MD: So, to go from a situation where someone didn't want to hear "one," to a situation where (almost) everything resolves on a "one" (eventually,) where did your relationship with Zakir Hussain begin?

SS: He played for one day in the studio on the *Yo Miles!* recordings, and we had fun, but I had no knowledge of

Indian rhythms at the time. My baby steps in learning about Indian rhythms began in 2001 when I did a tour with a group led by tabla player Sandip Burman. That group was Victor Bailey (bass,) Howard Levy (harmonica,) Jerry Goodman (violin,) Randy Brecker (trumpet,) Dave Pietro (alto sax,) and Paul Bollenback

phrases were throwing Howard and that's how he wrote it down. I was really intrigued, I wondered… *Is this what Indian music is all about?* That tour ended on 9/11. We did play that evening but all the remaining dates after that were canceled.

A year later I was teaching at a drum camp in

Steve Smith Library

(guitar.) Howard and Jerry recommended me for that because we had done a record together called *The Strangers Hand* and they knew I could handle a lot of odd-times.

There was a tune that we played with Sandip that Howard had transcribed with all of these bars of odd times and odd phrases. After we had played it for a while, I sat back and listened to it, and I figured out that it was actually in 4/4. It was just that all of the Indian

Marktoberdorf, Germany and that's when I started studying the basics of south Indian rhythms with a teacher named Karuna Murthy. In 2003 Larry Coryell had a gig in the S.F. Bay Area and he called George Brooks, Kai Eckhardt, and me to be his band. That's how I met George. After the gig George said he was putting a band together and asked if I was interested. I said, yes, and that was the band called Summit with Zakir Hussain. The band was Zakir on tabla, George on sax,

Fareed Haque on guitar, and Kai Eckhardt on bass. At that point George, Kai, Fareed and I had a little bit of knowledge of Indian rhythms. George had studied the Indian ragas a lot and was writing all of the tunes, which were great to play. For a few years Summit did a lot of gigs and tours, and while we toured, we all learned a lot about Indian music because Zakir loves to teach, and we were all eager to learn.

He liked to "take me to school" most nights in front of the crowd when we were trading. Sometimes we would go up the rhythmic scale and we would trade by playing polyrhythms over four. I'd start by playing 5 over 4, then 6, 7, 9, 10 and I'd skip 11 over 4 and go directly to 12. Zakir came off the stage and said, "What happened to 11?" I told him that I'd hadn't worked on 11. So, of course, the next night everything we played was 11 over 4. I had no ego about that because I knew I was in the presence of a great musician that I could learn a lot from, so I allowed myself to be vulnerable and learn. (To hear Steve play the rhythmic scale, ascending and descending, listen to track #6, Infinity Knot Pt. 1 on the *Fabric of Rhythm* recording.)

In time I learned about Konnakol, Tihai's, Korvai's and other Indian musical concepts. George Brooks started to incorporate more of these Indian devices in his writing, which was really cool. Kai and Fareed eventually brought some of that information back to their group Garaj Mahal too. When we did the first Summit recording, I set up opposite Zakir and played my little Sonor Jungle Kit, with two flat rides, and two splash cymbals, with bundles and brushes – no sticks. He was impressed by how quiet I could play without losing the intensity of the music.

While watching Zakir solo each night, I witnessed what could happen in an extremely virtuosic drum

Steve and Zakir Hussain

Steve Smith Library

solo. One of my takeaways was that the audience could *appreciate* what he was doing although they didn't *know* or *understand* what he was doing. I decided to never play down to an audience, especially when playing a big rock show. Of course, I might use some stick tricks like Sonny Payne did, but that's entertainment, and there's no shame in that. That philosophy really worked during the four years I toured with Journey from 2016-2019. I played virtuosic solos every night and the audiences really responded.

Throughout the years I have learned from a lot of Indian musicians, and most of them are very good teachers. I was fortunate to have played with Mandolin U. Srinivas before he passed, his music taught me a lot. My tours with guitarist Prasanna were educational and I have continued learning about Indian rhythms from Vikku Vinayakram, Selvaganesh and Pete Lockett. As many of the readers probably already know, I use the south Indian vocal artform called Konnakol in Vital Information currently.

MD: In 2005 you bought a place in New York City. At the time you told me that you had always wanted to live in New York City and be a "New York City Jazz Drummer." I found that really interesting. You made it sound like Journey was a detour in the road that you took because it presented itself, but that you were returning to continue what you considered to be your original career plan.

SS: It's true that I went to Berklee because I wanted a career as a jazz drummer, though in those years I didn't have a clear career plan in mind, I just went with the flow and followed the work. I can say now that my "career plan" at first was simple; become a good musician, play with other good musicians and play interesting and exciting music. In the early years of my career, I was open for any kind of music with all types of players. While playing with Jean-Luc Ponty I enjoyed playing a big double-bass kit and being on large stages with lights and sound systems. That's how I became open to playing with rock musicians like Ronnie Montrose and Journey. After I had gotten to the point of playing with Journey, leaving Journey and joining Steps Ahead, I started to see that I had more options. Was Journey a detour? No, it was part of my path of following musical opportunities, and I learned a lot about music and the music business with that group. But ultimately, I decided I was not interested in playing with rock players on tour. I was available for rock and pop sessions but not touring, I was only interested in touring with great jazz players. For me, the creative part of rock drumming takes place in conceiving and recording the drum part for a song. To play those songs night after night on tour takes a certain skill, and I've developed that skill, but it's not what I want to do with my time. Playing jazz on tour leaves the door open for fresh ideas and an opportunity for the unexpected to happen. Also, the ongoing backstage and traveling conversation is more interesting touring with jazz musicians. Being a bandleader became more important to me over the years and by the late 90s I started to turn down most session work in favor of being available to tour with my own groups: Vital Information, Buddy's Buddies, Jazz Legacy, The Raga Bop Trio or the Groove Blue Organ Trio. Also, playing sideman gigs with great jazz players became more important to me than pop session work. As a working drummer I was making better money as a sideman than a bandleader and there was less stress to being a sideman and the music was always good.

MD: When you were young, was becoming a bandleader something that was even on your radar?

SS: That's a very interesting question! The answer is no, I didn't have aspirations in becoming the leader of my own band. But as I look back now, I can see that even at a young age, I *was* a bandleader. I organized my first band called The Roadrunners, and we played the music of Herb Alpert and the Tijuana Brass. Eventually, I co-lead a big band with trumpet player Joe Casano. Then while I toured with Jean-Luc, Ronnie Montrose, and Journey, I would organize yearly reunion gigs with Tim Landers and David Wilczewski. That eventually became Vital Information, and I was the leader. So, it's always been a part of my persona, but it wasn't an early goal.

MD: So, in 2005 the "NYC Jazz Years" begin.

SS: My wife Diane and I decided it was time for a change. By that time our kids had grown up, moved out and were developing their own lives. I had a good run of being a session player in the S.F. Bay Area and I made a lot of albums at my home studio, including most of the Tone Center albums and Vital Information albums from 1984-2005. We downsized by selling the house in Marin County, bought a smaller home in Ashland, Oregon, and bought a condo in New York City. That began our lifestyle of moving between residences. Having an NYC place was also very convenient for all of the international touring I was doing. It was easier to commute to Europe from New York than San Francisco plus it was easier to travel to east coast and mid-west cities too.

After I moved here, I reconnected with Milan Simich, the jazz producer-promoter who recommended me to Ahmad Jamal. As a jazz producer and impresario, he comes up with gig concepts and he sells those concepts to clubs. They are usually a tribute gig in the style of a jazz great. It's very educational and satisfying to be a part of those gigs.

Every year we do "Coltrane Revisited" at Birdland the third week of September, celebrating Coltrane's September 23rd birthday, and each year it's a slightly different lineup. Lonnie Plaxico usually plays bass. Lonnie always learns the music and he's very easy to play with. Joe Lovano and Mike Mainieri did it one year, which was great. Eric Alexander and Jaleel Shaw have both done it a few times and they are both killin'. Steve Kuhn did it for a few years which was cool because he was a member of Coltrane's first quartet.

Steve Kuhn gave me very explicit directions on how and what to play from day one. Before I ever played a note with him, he approached me and said, "Never change ride cymbals behind my solo, and never play brushes behind my solos." After we had played a few sets, he pointed to one of my three ride cymbals, and said, "Play THAT cymbal behind my solos." Eventually, there were some nights when Steve Kuhn, Lonnie Plaxico, and I were playing that it was just effortless. Steve Kuhn's sense of swing is impeccable, and when the time is that good, you don't really have to do much. You just get out of the way and don't interrupt the flow.

With the Coltrane Revisited gigs, every year Milan puts together a different set list based on music Coltrane played in his own group or music he played as a sideman. So, every year I am checking out different drummers that played with Coltrane, and it's not always Elvin Jones. Sometimes it's Art Taylor, Jimmy Cobb, Roy Haynes, or Philly Joe Jones.

MD: Maybe even Pete LaRoca who played drums with Steve Kuhn in Coltrane's first quartet, or even Rashied Ali who played with Coltrane late in his career.

SS: Absolutely!

MD: How do you hear all of those guys, what do you hear as similarities and contrasts between them?

SS: Firstly, it's not like learning the jazz-rock stuff that we discussed earlier, it's not about learning beats. I am really listening to how those different drummers play behind the soloists, and what their time feels like. The more I listen to drummers like Art Taylor, Jimmy Cobb, and Philly Joe… The more I start really tuning in to (bassist) Paul Chambers. He was amazing! I hear that those drummers were what I call conversational within themselves, but not necessarily interactive with the soloist.

MD: That's a very interesting difference to hear.

SS: The big difference is that those three guys had different comping vocabulary and styles between their snare and bass drums. Finding those differences is fun. What they have in common is, they all play a super-swinging ride beat. By the time I get to the gig, I've listened to, and played along with, the records. I've listened to the different drumming approaches and I've learned the tunes. That means that by the time that I get to the gig I've done my homework. Then I can get out of the way and let the music happen. I never really try to sound like any of those drummers, I just play what I feel sounds right with who I am playing with at that time. In my mind, I have references, but I allow the music to "be," and I play how I play.

During the pandemic Eric Alexander, Donny McCaslin and I filmed a 55-minute improvised performance at Birdland based on some of the later music of Coltrane, mainly *A Love Supreme* and *Ascension*. It was just two saxes and drums. Preparing for that gig I started exploring the tonalities and possibilities of integrating my Zildjian gong into the kit. I brought the gong to Birdland and played it with sticks like a ride cymbal and used different mallets to create various atmospheric effects. It's a nice legato sound, and fits especially well with music that is more rubato and open. There are a few of my "From The Practice Room" videos where I integrate the gong into the kit.

SS: I have also been doing Milan Simich's "Electric Miles" gigs for 7 or 8 years now, those gigs focus on the electric music that Miles played in the 70s. Those bands usually include Randy Brecker and Jeremy Pelt on trumpet, Lonnie Plaxico on bass, and Paul Bollenback on guitar. Oftentimes that core band will be augmented by other guitarists or a sax player. Like always, when Milan plans these gigs, he sends us a setlist of tunes. My homework is already spelled out. I listen to that music and start writing charts. That means listening to a lot of the Miles music with Al Foster playing drums. Al's playing with Miles is, in my opinion, some of the most overlooked drumming in jazz-rock fusion. Especially his playing in the 70s with Miles, there was a way that Al played with his open hi-hats and a big wide-open rock groove that implied a feel between half time and double time. That type of groove really opens up the music for the soloist, I wound up using that approach a lot in Vital Info, and I think it's really a cool approach. I usually film all of these Milan Simich gigs and post some tunes on my website.

By playing many years of the Electric Miles gigs I have had a chance to develop that kind of playing. For Electric Miles, Milan tells us specifically that he doesn't want any breaks between the tunes. That means there has to be some kind of an organic improvisation to join the tunes together without a break, which can be challenging.

MD: Do you work out those transitions at the rehearsals?

SS: What rehearsals!?!? Everybody does their homework, and we let it happen on stage. Milan insists on that.

MD: But that wasn't the first time that you had been involved with playing some of Miles' electric music. In 2004 you were in a band called *Yo Miles!* And those records (*Sky Garden* and *Uprising*) are amazing! I think that is some of your best fusion playing on record.

SS: That was a band in San Francisco that was organized by guitarist Henry Kaiser. Wadada Leo Smith was the trumpeter and the band included Greg Osby (alto sax,) John Tcichai (tenor sax,) Karl Perazzo (percussion,) Michael Manring (bass,) Mike Kenneally (guitar,) Tom Coster (keyboards,) and Zakir Hussain (tabla.) That was a fun band, and I agree those are very good records. There is some footage of us in the studio on YouTube. We also played some live gigs with that band which were fantastic.

After the recording I also played a duet show in San Francisco with Wadada, just trumpet and drums. Wadada's charts are actually quite beautiful pieces of artwork. They have shapes and lines and an indication of how long, in minutes, to play a certain shape, density, airiness, crescendo or decrescendo. The "chart" is a suggestion or guide for the players to create on the spot but it does not look like traditional notation. Fascinating and very creative.

Yo Miles! is when I began doing my homework on

Andrés Forero

the electric Miles music and Al Foster's playing in the 70s with Miles. I also began exploring the music that Jack DeJohnette played with Miles on the *Live at the Cellar Door* box set, and (what is now called) Miles' Lost Quintet with Jack, Dave Holland, Wayne Shorter, and Chick Corea. I also got into what Ndugu played with Miles' band when he had bassist Michael Henderson, Gary Bartz, and Keith Jarrett.

MD: I have been listening to that band a lot recently, that band that is mind-blowing!

SS: What probably helped is that I saw Al Foster play live with Miles at the Boston club Paul's Mall with the

70s electric band with Michael Henderson on bass and the two guitarists Reggie Lucas and Pete Cosey. When I saw that band, it was brand new, and I had never heard anything like it. I didn't really understand it, but I knew that I liked it.

MD: That's a really important idea to explore and emphasize. Seeing (or hearing music) that you don't understand, and liking it although you don't know *what* is going on.

SS: I saw a few gigs like that, when I was still in high-school I saw Elvin Jones' band with Gene Perla, Dave

Liebman, Steve Grossman, and Don Alias and I didn't understand that at all. It was heavy duty music, but I knew I liked it. After my ears developed more, I could understand what was going on, but at first, I had absolutely no idea what was happening.

MD: There have been some other Milan Simich gigs too.

SS: We did a week at Birdland called "The New York Jazz Masters Play the Music of Ornette Coleman" with Donny McCaslin on tenor, Tom Harrell on trumpet and Ben Allison on bass. Before that I had listened to Ornette's music, but it's one thing to listen to it, and it's another thing to learn the tunes and play them. Some of that music was hard to play, and not because it's complicated, but because it had a lot of starts and stops and went in and out of time in different sections. Some of the stuff that Shelly Manne played with Ornette on *Tomorrow is the Question!* was really difficult. And then Billy Higgins was on the next record called *Something Else!!!!* I had to listen to how they played Ornette's music before I even got to the Ed Blackwell records.

Most recently there was a "Bouncin' With Bud" Bud Powell tribute with pianist Helen Sung and Lonnie Plaxico on bass. For that I listened to a lot of Art Taylor because Bud used Art Taylor in the studio a lot. There were tunes and entire albums where Art played brushes throughout. He was a really strong timekeeper and had a strong groove. Bud Powell wrote really difficult music that had little intros, endings, segues, and some specific beats. So, I wrote out some pretty detailed charts to prepare for that gig, especially since we had no time to rehearse. I hope we get a chance to develop that trio and music some more.

MD: Has Milan ever told you what it is about your playing that he likes? I know his favorite drummer is Idris Muhammad.

SS: There is a quality in my playing that he resonates with. Milan has told me that he hears me coming out of drummers like Shelly Manne, Frankie Dunlop, Art Taylor, and Idris. Those are all drummers that play with a strong pulse. He likes my pulse, which goes back to what Ahmad Jamal told me, he liked my pulse too. And it feels good to hear guys say that.

MD: Since you mentioned that. I want to ask you about something that you said in a very old *Modern Drummer* interview. You studied with Peter Erskine at a Stan Kenton camp when you were young and you mentioned that Peter had a really unique way of explaining time and pulse, can you tell me what that was?

SS: I remember Peter talking about playing a very clear and swinging quarter note pulse on the ride cymbal. He has been talking about that throughout his whole career, but at that point I had never really heard someone talk about it. He came from the perspective of "Hey guys what are we doing here? We're playing TIME so the band can feel the pulse of the music. Here is the typical jazz ride cymbal beat, but it begins with a strong quarter note pulse." Each student at the camp would play time with the Kenton bassist, and it was a revelation to me. At the time, I had heard a lot of great jazz drummers, and I had taken a lot of lessons, but no one had ever said to just make the ride cymbal pulse feel great. And in order to do that you had to get that quarter note pulse to swing really hard. That was a turning point for me, and it really helped me focus.

MD: Unfortunately, when many people teach jazz drumming, they start with the ride cymbal beat, and immediately go on to comping and breaking up the beat without letting the weight of the quarter note pulse really sink in for a while.

SS: Good point. The fact that Peter pointed it out, stressed it so strongly, and made it so important, is what

---

Jazz Producer Milan Simich on Steve Smith

MD: Why do you hire Steve Smith for so many of your projects?

Milan Simich: When I first heard Steve with Steps Ahead in 1986 at the Bottom Line, I realized that he was a professional, and like Idris, he's clear that the job is to make everyone on stage look and sound good. And that's what he's doing on my gigs. He takes direction well, shows up prepared and has a sense of how to perform and entertain a live audience. Steve, like Idris, can play rock, funk and jazz, which is what I like. When I hire Steve for a gig, I can relax and know that he will take care of business.

really stayed with me. That message came to me at the right time. I was willing to listen which is important too.

I make a distinction between time and pulse. Pulse is the feel, and everyone in the band needs to connect and agree on the pulse. That's what makes music swing and feel good. Whether or not the time is steady is a different question. The pulse is the feel, and the time is the steadiness of the pulse.

I've spent years listening to the Miles records *Workin'*, *Cookin'*, *Steamin'*, and *Relaxin'*. They all had Philly Joe Jones playing drums and Paul Chambers playing bass.

MD: It might be telling that the word "pulse" is a very human word, and the word "time" relates to inanimate things like clocks and machines. Do you think this applies to straight eighth music as well as jazz?
SS: Yes. If you listen to The Beatles or Zeppelin or Cream the pulse is always right, although the time or tempo might fluctuate. If the band moves together and keeps the pulse and the feel, it works, and it's beautiful!

In today's musical world I know it's necessary to be able to play with precise time because we are playing and overdubbing parts with clicks and loops which are

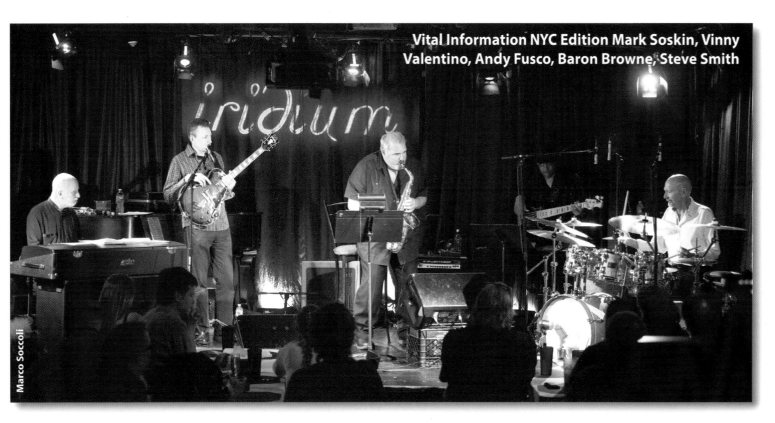

Vital Information NYC Edition Mark Soskin, Vinny Valentino, Andy Fusco, Baron Browne, Steve Smith

Marco Soccoli

I've played along with those tunes often too. If you get to the end of the song and then start it over again, you'll notice many of them slow down a little bit. A few may speed up. The time might not be perfect, but the pulse IS!!! The fact that the pulse is so strong means that you don't register the fact that the time might move a bit. I think pulse supersedes time. A classic example of this is "The Sermon" by Jimmy Smith with Art Blakey on drums. The tune has a very strong swing/shuffle pulse throughout but if you start the tune over once the twenty-minute track is over you'll hear they started much slower than they ended, but it grooves like crazy the entire take.

created in perfect quantized time. But you also have to learn how to generate a strong pulse by playing with living, breathing musicians. You can't learn to do that in any other situation besides doing it. That's why it's so important to develop that live side of your playing by playing with other musicians. That is what helps you develop your pulse.

Recently I re-bought the Chet Baker record *She Was Too Good To Me* which has Steve Gadd playing drums. The way Gadd plays on that record is so swinging. His time has such a strong quarter note feel. It's sort of coming out of Elvin but Steve has his own vocabulary and his drum sound is so unique.

MD: Elvin's time was very quarter note-y. Especially when he played with organist Larry Young. Those are my favorite Elvin recordings.

SS: Gadd plays like that on the old Steps records too!

MD: And on Jim Hall and Art Farmer *Big Blues*.

SS: I'll have to check that one out.

MD: Another gig that wasn't documented "officially" but lives on YouTube is the gig with Hiromi. How did that happen?

SS: After Hiromi did *The Trio Project* recording with Anthony Jackson and Simon Phillips, she started to book dates and Simon couldn't make all of them, because at that time, he was still in Toto. Hiromi and I knew each other casually, and she asked Anthony about me. His reply was, "Call him!" I had toured and recorded with Anthony and pianist Ayden Esen years before, and that's how Anthony knew that I could do that gig because Ayden's music was, like Hiromi's, very difficult.

When she sent me the recording and the charts, I was pretty freaked out. Some of the tunes were up to 10 pages long! There were bars of odd times all over the place, unexpected phrases, long forms, it's really hard music. I learned all of Simon's parts and gained a whole new respect for Simon. He sounded so good on that music. His parts were compositional masterpieces unto themselves, I had no idea that he could play that kind of music on that level.

Hiromi's trio is a different kind of trio because the drums are the second soloist in the band, unlike most other piano trios where the bassist is the second soloist. Anthony only solos once a set, he really doesn't like to solo much.

I had to develop some specific things for that gig. I worked on my soloing in odd times, because so many of her tunes were in odd times and there are drum solos on most of the tunes. Plus, many of Simon's parts were constructed around his open-handed approach. That meant that I had to start to develop some real open-

Steve Smith Library

Steve, Hiromi and Anthony Jackson

handed facility.

MD: But you had already played some open-handed stuff with Journey that we'll talk about later.

SS: That was simple open-handed playing, what Simon does is on a whole different level. Hiromi's work ethic was different than anyone that I have ever played with before or since. With Hiromi, every day at 5:00pm we had a rehearsal. And I don't just mean running through some stuff at soundcheck. I mean, full intensity, playing the music while working out details and honing the music, REHEARSAL. I found it really refreshing, so I started doing that with Vital Information. There was some grumbling at first, but eventually the guys found that it was helping everybody get deeper inside the music. That meant that we could take the music even further every night. That process makes it possible to make the music both *looser* and *tighter* at the same time.

A good thing about the Hiromi trio was, as long as I knew where I was, they knew where they were. And sometimes they knew where they were even though I was lost! There were never any restrictions on how abstract things could be on that gig, because Hiromi and Anthony are so strong and self-contained in their perception of the pulse and the time. I didn't have to give them markers of where "one" was even on extended odd-time improvisations. There were some really cool things that came out of that gig that have stuck with me. I did that gig from 2011 to 2015, I learned and played many of her earlier compositions plus every song on her Trio Project albums *Voice*, *Move* and *Alive*. That was a lot of work but very rewarding.

MD: In general, do you like to rehearse?

SS: Yes, but with so many of the situations that I have been in, there has never been any rehearsals except for the soundcheck before the first gig. I always do my homework and come prepared because so many musicians don't like to rehearse.

MD: I know that she made everyone (Simon, Anthony,

and you) memorize the music, do you have any advice on memorizing music?

SS: I tend to memorize things in short chunks and then put them together. Sometimes with her music it was two or four bars at a time. But something else about me is that I like to over-prepare for a gig. That means that sometimes I actually practice the music for a gig so much that I actually get a little tired of it. But then I

the real point of that practice? In my case, and I think for many drummers, we practice to become good improvisers.

When I play, I want to be in the moment. I think to be a good improviser means to be "in flow." To me, that is when I am in a mental space where I am present and in the moment. I'm connecting with the other musicians that I am playing with, and I am able to follow my own

Steve playing open-handed

Steve Smith Library

know that once I get on the gig that I'll be really ready.

MD: How have you learned to improvise and what do you practice to develop that musical skill?

SS: I think in the drum world there is a lot of attention paid to *what* do you practice, and *how much* do you practice, and in some ways, there isn't enough attention paid to *why* do we practice what we do, and what is

ideas through, with some real-time mental editing, without interrupting the flow of those ideas. As a drummer you are not only improvising as a soloist, but also as a timekeeper. If you think about what jazz drumming is, it's establishing the pulse and playing a time feel that is improvised in the flow of the music while listening, responding and offering ideas. The key is to be in flow. That means to have a good stream of ideas flowing that feel good within the context of the music. That goal remains the same if you are playing time or soloing.

My practice tends to include the practice of phrases and concepts, not exercises. I spent my early years practicing exercises, for instance I practiced out of *Stick Control* a lot, and I developed specific exercises that developed independence that grew from the Ted Reed *Syncopation* book and the Jim Chapin book. When you actually play jazz, your approach and vocabulary goes far beyond the basic coordination that you can develop by using those books, they are simply starting points. I find that it serves me best to not practice a lot of exercises, because I don't want to sound like I am playing exercises, I want to play flowing melodic and rhythmic phrases. Therefore, for the last 20 years or so my practice has had very little to do with exercises.

MD: Do you have a practice routine of how to develop flowing melodic and rhythmic phrases at the drum set?

SS: There is really no routine, other that the fact that I like to practice almost every day, five or six days a week. My practice will evolve depending on what gigs I have, what ideas I want to develop, and what I feel I need to work on to keep myself interested in my own playing and in the music that I am playing.

Here's how I tend to practice my melodic vocabulary on the drums: I start with a phrase, and that phrase could come from anywhere. It could, for instance, be a phrase that I transcribed from a Max Roach solo. I start by learning that phrase verbatim, exactly as Max played it. Then I will alter the phrase so it sounds like a question-and-answer type of phrase. If it is a phrase that goes from high to low, I'll reverse it and practice it from low to high, to create that question-and-answer effect. Then I break up the rhythms from the initial idea into two and three beat ideas. I practice those initial two and three beat ideas independently over and over until they become fluid, and then I start to build different phrases with them. I will also practice them in different rhythmic rates like eighths, triplets, or sixteenths. Then I start to elongate the phrase by combining those two and three beat ideas into various longer phrases of four (by combining twos) five (by combining twos and threes,) six (by combining the threes,) seven (four plus three or three plus four) and nine (four plus five) as well. That's where some influence of the Indian

rhythms comes in. The Indian musicians have a clear way of developing phrasing ideas that I know are going to work out mathematically and musically. I put those ideas in a musical context like eight, twelve, or thirty-two bar phrases, or other song forms. That's how I really get comfortable with the ideas, by playing them within a musical form. I'll do this at different tempos, and with different feels too. Then, hopefully, I can tap into those ideas effortlessly without interrupting the flow of the pulse or time.

However, the idea of breaking phrases into twos and threes isn't necessarily an Indian idea, there is a book by Jack DeJohnette and Charlie Perry called *The Art Of Modern Jazz Drumming* where Jack talks about phrases of two and three as applied to the ride cymbal. When I went through that book many years ago, it answered many of my questions regarding the jazz ride cymbal phrasing of Roy, Tony, Jack, and Elvin. I've heard recordings of Shelly Manne where he was breaking up the ride patterns into twos and threes back in the 1950s.

MD: Do you ever find that some ideas are both time keeping and soloing ideas?

SS: There are lots of ideas that can start as solo ideas that can be broken down into comping phrases behind a soloist or vice versa. An initial musical idea can become anything. Drumming is drumming, what changes is the music that surrounds it. I could play those solo ideas with Journey, and I did. You can say there are rock ideas and jazz ideas, but in my world, my ideas and vocabulary are fluid. I can play most of them in any setting from a straight-ahead acoustic trio to fusion to rock. My vocabulary is adaptable, and what makes it that way, is in the intention of how it's played, where it's played within the beat, how long the phrase will go, and the sound of the drums.

If I am in a rock situation where the musicians are not self-contained and might need more direction rhythmically to keep them from getting confused or lost, I'll make sure my phrases are short and to the point, and not go too far over the bar-line. Or maybe not go over the bar-line at all. The more self-contained the players are, the more I can develop longer phrases and ideas within the music.

MD: You mentioned being inspired by ideas that you transcribed from Max Roach, but where else can these ideas come from?

SS: They can come from anywhere. I can be inspired from any recording or live performance that I have seen or heard. Here's an example. During COVID I have been working on some ideas that I saw my old friend Vinnie Colaiuta play. He was playing groups of five r**L**rll with the accent on the second note. I usually play fives **R**l**R**ll with the accents on the first and third notes. So, when I heard Vinnie do that, it inspired me to try it. I also saw him adding a bass drum at the end of the five and it becomes a nice phrase of six, rLrllF (F for Foot). Here is where I went with the phrase of six: If I play the six in an 8th note triplet rate, rLrllF is two 8th note triplets. If I play rLrllF in even 8th notes it's a three, or six even 8th notes. That way you can combine the same pattern to be a phrase of five if you play it once at an 8th note triplet rate and once as even 8ths. That is just one simple idea, but you can do so much with it. That might seem like an exercise, but I see it as developing vocabulary. Sometimes it happens in reverse. I might start with a phrase that I am playing on the drums that I like the sound of, but I'm not sure what it is. I'll slow it down, figure out how many notes I'm playing and then work out how I can develop the idea beyond the initial way that I played it. Why do I say that's different than an exercise? Many times, drum exercises can be "tongue twisters" designed to develop dexterity, or challenge your technical ability. It's true that I have developed some vocabulary from that approach. But if I hear a phrase that sounds good, lays on the kit naturally and may actually be easy to play, that is an idea that can be learned and developed into vocabulary that can be adapted to a variety of applications.

MD: In the two examples that you have talked about (the Max and the Vinnie ideas) both have been very short ideas. Do you find it easier to learn short ideas and lengthen them, instead of learning long ideas and reducing them?

SS: I don't think I have ever tried to learn a "long idea." I always learn short ideas, and eventually the phrasing can be elongated. Smaller ideas can go so many different ways.

When we first learn drumming, in many cases we learn the rudiments which are short ideas. The rudiments are great for developing even-handedness, meaning having your right hand and left hand being equally developed, but I generally think of the rudiments as single strokes, double strokes, and embellishments. And the rudiments are the many different ways of combining those three elements.

MD: I always teach beginners that there are three sounds: singles, doubles, and buzzes. And then we develop those three core sounds into longer different sounds called rudiments.

SS: Cool! But instead of, as you say, "sounds," I'll take it a step further. I hear all of the rudiments as melodies or at least potential melodies. There are times when you want singles and doubles to sound the same; But I think the obsessiveness to develop your doubles and singles to sound perfectly even can become counter-productive because I want the different sounds, stickings, accents and melodies to come out.

MD: I agree, I enjoy having a right hand and a left hand that don't sound *exactly* the same.

SS: I recently began hearing the melody of paradiddles in Art Taylor's playing. He plays the paradiddle accenting the rights: RlRR lRll with the right hand on the high tom playing the accented notes and the left hand on the snare playing the unaccented notes, and then moves the right hand to the floor tom and plays the same pattern which creates a nice rhythm and melody. (A.T. paradiddle notation on page 31.) In fact, I heard Mitch Mitchell play similar paradiddle melodies, many drummers have used that idea, and it's still a good one.

MD: Speaking of places to find new ideas. You have also recently started to re-investigate Charles Wilcoxon and George Lawrence Stone, how did that happen?

SS: Before COVID, much of my practice time usually went to learning new music. With all of my touring canceled I wanted to take the opportunity to go back and review certain things. I started pulling out my old drum books. I wanted to spend time working on some things that I hadn't worked on for a while. I wanted to re-investigate some things, and Wilcoxon's *Modern Rudimental Solos for the Advanced Drummer* was the first thing that came to mind. At the beginning of that book, he goes through the 26 rudiments with all sorts of variations, so I spent some time on those and I found that there were certain rudiments that I had completely forgotten; for example, Flam Accents. I relearned them and started orchestrating them around the kit. Then I learned and made a video of the Wilcoxon solo "Rhythmania," posted the solo online, and was contacted by the people at *The Wilcoxon Challenge* and decided to take "the challenge." It was good for my chops and good for my reading, because for the last few years I haven't been reading much. Then I took certain phrases from the Wilcoxon book and orchestrated them around the kit in different ways. It has definitely helped me develop some new vocabulary.

MD: Then you started emailing me about the George Lawrence Stone book.

SS: The book is called *Technique of Percussion* and it's a collection of Stone's articles that he wrote for the *International Musician* from 1946-1963. His columns have been very helpful to me. For example, one of them had to do with tempo and the fact that the "ancient" rudiments were played at 110 "steps per minute." That was news to me because I learned that 120 BPM is the accepted metronome marking for rudiments. I had independently come to the conclusion that a lot of the

Wilcoxon solos swing more when they are played a little slower. For instance, I recorded the "Rhythmania" solo at 109 BPM because it felt good there. After I read what Stone had to say about the ancient rudiments, it confirmed my own ideas. Legend has it that Philly Joe Jones worked out of that book and mined it for ideas.

MD: As did Elvin!

SS: That brings me to the Steve Gadd *Gaddiments* book. That book is made up of really nicely composed etudes based on certain rudiments. His etudes help with moving those rudiments through different subdivisions of 8th notes and 16th notes, then he starts the ideas on the different parts of the beat. The phrases that Steve comes up with are beautiful and feel good to play.

MD: After seeing many of the solos that you performed during the last four years of Journey (which are posted on vitalinformation.com), and after listening to your recording *The Fabric of Rhythm*, which are unaccompanied drum solos that is a download with this book, can we talk about how you develop a solo?

SS: There are many types of solos. Some examples are: unaccompanied stand-alone solo drumset pieces, open solos as part of a song, solos within the context and form of a song or solos over a vamp. Last week at Birdland we played "Mr. P.C." in every set, and I took a solo each time we played it. I have posted one of the best performances of that tune on YouTube. "Mr. P.C." is a blues, so my soloing would be contained within a 12-bar form and the tempo that we were playing that night. My vocabulary would have to fit that tempo and that form.

When I played the solo with Journey, I would play it off of the tune "La Do Da." That tune has a shuffle feel and a certain tempo, but the solo was open. In that case I took the challenge of keeping the tempo consistent throughout the main body of the solo. I allowed myself to change feels, or do metric modulations, but it would all relate to the original tempo, and the solo would come back to the original tempo and shuffle feel in the end. I would play half-time, or double time, or play off of the triplet… I think people could relate to it more when it all related to the original tempo, even if they don't understand what I'm doing. But even in that context, I am still relating everything to eight and sixteen bar phrases, which creates a sense of form and structure.

MD: In that context, are you creating or thinking about different phrases or ideas ahead of time, or is it spontaneous?

SS: In my warmup, I'd come up with ideas for my solo on my practice pad kit backstage. I would try to come up with something different every night. My process was this: I knew that I would make a video of my solo every night, and if I liked it, I would post it on-line. So, I would create and work on a new idea, or ideas, for the solo while warming up. I spent about 40 minutes doing essentially, the same ideas the next night. I'd keep working on the ideas in the solo until they worked. When the solo "worked" then those ideas where documented and I would move on to another idea or concept within the solo.

MD: How many shows would it take a specific idea to work before you "retired" that idea?

SS: Sometimes an idea would last for two or three

Christine Vaindirlis

that. Then I'd go for those ideas during the solo. I would have to have the equanimity to remember what those ideas were, and then I'd have the challenge of creating a flow of ideas that felt good, sounded good, made sense and communicated with the audience.

MD: Did that process always work?

SS: Sometimes it didn't work, then I would try, shows. So over four years of between 60 and 70 shows a year, I worked through a lot of ideas, and they are all posted on-line. Sometimes I would nail an idea the first night, but that was rare. Of course, I had different parts of the solos that stayed consistent. There was the beginning shuffle groove which led into the main body of the improvised solo followed that. There was usually a "question-and-answer" section between hands and feet, but what I actually played was different each night and proved a challenge to the video director to stay with me for the "foot cam" moments. There was a "stick-trick" section in the middle of the solo that worked because I knew there were cameras on me so the audience could see what I was doing in those quieter moments, and then there was an ending which was the same each night so I could cue the band to come in. Having made so many videos for Hudson Music I knew how to place the cameras on my kit so the audience could see the details of my playing, which helped them appreciate what I was playing.

MD: So, you weren't completely improvising before 40,000 people every night? You had a plan for your solo every night, right?

SS: Yes, I did have a plan for each night though, each solo rarely went exactly as planned! I think most of the ideas that we musicians play, we have played before, but probably not in the exact same order. Occasionally, there are moments when you play something that you have never played before. Those moments when something totally "new" comes out might only be for a short period.

When I was a student at Berklee, there was a naïve and idealistic way of thinking that you could only "truly improvise" by only playing ideas that you had never played before. Of course, I tried that, but I found out that it was unrealistic, and more of a "student point of view." That point of view led to me being wildly inconsistent in my performances.

But maybe that type of improvisation is possible, it's just that I'm not there yet or haven't done it enough. When you listen to the Keith Jarrett *The Köln Concert*, it appears that's an example of total and pure improvisation. At the time of that concert Keith had years of study in jazz and classical music, so he had a deep well-spring of vocabulary to draw upon. I

Steve's Journey warm-up kit

Steve Smith Library

have listened to Keith Jarrett a lot over the years. My interpretation of what I am hearing in the *The Köln Concert* is a young optimistic man who has yet to live through the vicissitudes of his life. However, when I listen to his later improvisations, I hear the toll that life has taken on him. And that would likely be true for all of us.

My transition away from my idealistic way of thinking about improvising happened when I toured with Jean-Luc Ponty. I saw our band of wonderful improvisors play very consistently every night. But I also noticed a similar vocabulary from tune to tune. I started to hear and observe that it was necessary to have that approach to be consistent and professional. Much later, when I toured with Steps Ahead with Mike Mainieri, Mike Brecker, and Mike Stern, I saw unbelievably great improvisors who occasionally had those breakthrough moments of genius, but who had a high level of consistent vocabulary that was well-practiced and well-rehearsed. This was especially true of Michael Brecker. I watched him play every night, and I saw a musician who was so self-contained, that even when the musical environment was not optimal, for instance sitting in with a high school big band, he could walk on stage and sound truly amazing. He inspired me to try to become that self-contained in my approach.

I have walked on stage and completely improvised. That is what I usually do in drum clinics. But even then, sometimes I like to have certain ideas that I would work towards and work out of. I view drum clinic solos like playing a set of solo drum compositions, or themes, with segues between them. I've used drum clinics as a platform to develop my solo drumming.

MD: You have used the phrase "self-contained" a few times, what do you mean by that?

SS: By self-contained I mean, that I want to be able to play music in a way that I am not relying on listening to the other musicians to keep the form or to know where "1" is, for example. I always want to know where I am in the beat and in the form of the song no matter how involved the playing, or improvising, becomes. In addition, I mean that I want to sound good even if the musicians I am playing with are not highly developed. When I was coming up, if all the musicians I was playing with were on my level, then I usually had a good night. If they were not that developed or had a bad night themselves, that would affect me. I wanted to move beyond that and become strong enough that even if

the other musicians were not well developed, or didn't play well, I would still play at a high level and feel good about my performance.

After I left Journey in 1985, I took that break in my recording and performing schedule to do a lot of clinics. I did the same thing after Steps Ahead went on a hiatus in 1987. In those years many drummers were playing to pre-recorded tracks in their clinics. I decided that I didn't want to do that, I wanted to use the clinic platform to develop my solo playing. And that is where I really started to develop my ability to be self-contained. I thought, that a solo doesn't have to be that different from playing with a group, it's just that people are hearing only the drums and not the other instruments. If I were to play with a group and the other players drop out, the audience is left with the drums, but I continue to play as if I'm playing with a group. That was my starting point for solo drumming. It doesn't sound strange when I say it like that, but in general, when a drummer knows it's time for their solo, they start to play harder, louder and busier. There are a lot of problems with that. One, by playing harder and louder, they are cut off from being able to play with the main body of the chops and technique they have developed because when you play loud there are only so many things that you can play because of the tension in your body which translates to lack of finesse on the kit. And two, by playing busier, or faster, they are greatly limited to the story they can tell while soloing. I decided that in my solo drumming, I would play exactly the way that I play in a band, just without the band playing around me. I'd have the same dynamic range and the same concept of playing spaciously or densely.

When I did clinics, and I played solo, there were times that I would hear the sound of a band in my head, and I would play along to that. I'd keep the form of a song in my head, imagine playing with a good bass player and accompany the playing that I was hearing in my head. That harkens back to my lessons with Alan Dawson when he would have me solo while singing the melody of "Stella By Starlight," for example. Or I may think of the Buddy Rich Big Band playing "Love For Sale" and just play along to it. Then I started to learn the Max Roach solos like "Drums Unlimited," "The Drum Also Waltzes," or "For Big Sid" and I would use those drumset compositions as my solo drumming themes. I had seen Max play solo concerts a number of times and he really inspired me to develop the ability to play solo concerts.

Through that approach, I was becoming very "self-contained" as a musician. Therefore, if I was playing with a high school or college big band that wasn't that good, I could still sound good by not relying on what I was hearing around me. Of course, I always listen to the musicians around me but I was no longer brought down if they were not great. Inversely, if the musicians around me are exceptional, then there is the potential for my playing to transcend what I can conjure up on my own.

MD: I think Michael Brecker was the perfect example of a musician being self-contained. I always got the impression that he could sound exactly the same if he was playing with Jack DeJohnette or with a simple click track…

SS: …or in the band that he was in with Herbie Hancock, Roy Hargrove, John Patitucci, and Brian Blade.

MD: The record that they made called "Directions in Music" is surreal.

SS: In the best bands, like that one, all the musicians should be self-contained, or very close to that ideal. If everyone in a band is self-contained, they will collectively become greater than the sum of their parts because the musicians can play without any fear that they will lose the other bandmembers. The music that they produce will potentially be of the highest level and inspire each player to go beyond what they can do as an individual. That experience of transcendence is one of the main reasons that we play music.

MD: I think many young musicians practice as if they are performing, and perform as if they are practicing. For you, what is the difference between playing and practicing?

SS: I think I've been describing my playing concept already, but when I practice, I have a particular goal in mind, and I can stop and start. There are times when I practice improvising where I want to play with the same concept as performing; developing ideas, following one idea with the next logical statement that builds on the previous idea, and getting in-flow. But when I practice new ideas, I am NOT trying to sound "good." As a musician you have to be okay with that. When I practice, I am trying to learn something new, and develop new ideas slowly and incrementally. I know that I have a high tolerance for very slow, deliberate practice, and that has been important in my development. I think

it is crucial to be able to play a new idea without any mistakes, even if that means playing that idea at a VERY slow tempo. Eventually when I practice something enough, I'm no longer aware of the technical aspects of the idea, it becomes a sound, and when I want to hear that sound, my body is able to execute the components necessary to create that sound.

When I am in New York City, and feel the need to practice on a real drumset, versus the low-volume kit in my apartment, I'll book three hours at The Collective. However, when I do that, there are always a few students standing outside the practice room door expecting to hear some *great shit*. Meanwhile I'm in there practicing an idea really slow, making mistakes, stopping and starting. I have to say to myself, *"Okay, I'm NOT going to perform for them"* and stay focused and actually practice. I hope hearing me *actually* practice inspires them, and they don't walk away thinking, *"He's really not that good."* But, of course, I'm sure that happens too!

MD: I love the Tony Williams quote, *"I don't trust musicians who don't make mistakes, they're just not trying hard enough."* Talk about the importance of making mistakes, and not always trying to "sound good."

SS: I like that too, it's a fantastic epigram. If you don't push yourself and make mistakes, I doubt you'll get to that transcendent place that I referred to. And you aren't being creative as you can be. But it's all in context, if you are playing drums in the band at the Grammys you can't make mistakes. But if you are on stage with a jazz group, you don't *want* to make mistakes, but you *can*. The main thing is, when you make a mistake, you don't want to look in the rear-view mirror. If you are running and you trip, and you look back to see what made you trip, you are probably going to fall on your face because you aren't looking ahead. The analogy is: Don't dwell on your mistakes, let them go, and keep moving forward.

MD: When people hear you play, I don't think that they hear you making mistakes.

SS: They definitely happen! There is always a transition when an idea that you have practiced makes its way into a performance, and that transition isn't *always* smooth.

MD: In the past you have talked about your relationships with great teachers like Gary Chaffee, Alan Dawson, and Freddie Gruber. In older interviews you have also mentioned the great relationship that you had with your first teacher Billy Flanagan. However, you have mentioned to me (in passing) a few others. Namely Louie Bellson and Pete Magadini. Can you explain about the mentorship that you got from Louie and the lessons with Pete?

SS: I became intrigued with Pete Magadini by hearing about his book called *Poly Cymbal Time*. I first met him while I was touring with Journey in 1980 in Toronto. While we were in town, I set up a meeting and a lesson with him. Years later, when I was living in Novato, California, Pete moved to Novato as well, I contacted him and asked if I could take some lessons with him and go through the *Poly Cymbal Time* book with him, so we did weekly lessons for a while. His ideas were based around how to play time in a jazz setting using different subdivisions of the beat. I got some great ideas by studying with Pete in person. I wouldn't have gotten the ideas had I just gone through the book on my own, because I got to hear him play and explain them. One of the main ideas that I took away from the lessons was based on super-imposing 3/4 jazz time off the quarter note triplet pulse in 4/4 time. When I had played a "three-over-four implied-metric modulation" idea previously, I played an evenly subdivided 6/4 over 4/4. But when Pete played it, he played the super-imposed time in ¾, like a waltz. That helped me develop the ability to play a very clear 3/4 over 2/4 polyrhythmic pulse in my jazz playing, instead of a more "rock" 3 over

Steve Smith Library

2 approach. The way Pete explained it clarified what was written in the book. He feels it in 9, so it's actually like playing 9 over 2. That was brand new to me, and it works on gigs with people because you aren't playing over the bar line, it's all within the bar. Other musicians don't get "uncomfortable" when I do it. I think that idea may have originally come from the Bill Evans trio with Scott LaFaro and Paul Motian or Joe Morello with Dave Brubeck.

MD: So, he is taking the quarter note triplet, and playing three inside of every note of the triplet, and playing that pulse in three? That is what becomes the 9 over 2?

SS: Yes, you got it. Pete has remained a friend, and I have integrated that valuable idea from lessons with him.

MD: How about Louie Bellson?

SS: He showed me some very specific crossover patterns to play on the cymbals. I saw him play them and asked him how he did it. Playing even 8th notes, it's an eight-note pattern played like this: Starting with the right hand on the right cymbal and the left hand on the left cymbal, play RL, then RL with the right hand moving "over" the left as the right moves to the left cymbal and the left moves "under" the right hand to the right cymbal, then play RL in the original position, and finally RL with the right hand "under" and the left hand "over" the right hand. He would also play the double bass drums in unison underneath it. I thought it sounded and looked cool, so I asked him to teach it to me. That's part of my repertoire now. I really loved his snare drum technique and the beauty of his press roll, it was so special to observe him playing up close. Louie and I did a number of clinics together over the years. He was a complete gentleman and we would always have

loved that he just came out and said what he observed in a straight-forward, matter of fact manor. He was completely correct and since then I have mastered feathering the bass drum and the difference in my overall sound is profound. I have a wonderful memory of hanging with Ed Thigpen and Terry Bozzio at the Marktoberdorf drum camp in Bavaria, Germany where we were teaching. One night we snuck away from the students, came up to my teaching room, where I had a few drum kits setup. The three of us improvised some wonderful music together that night. We were all listening, playing with respect, and found a common musical meeting place to communicate with each other

Vinny Valentino, Tony Monaco and Steve Smith: The Groove Blue Trio

Steve Smith Library

great talks about drumming and music. Hearing first hand stories from Louie about playing on 52nd Street in NYC or jam sessions at Minton's Playhouse in Harlem were priceless.

Another teacher/mentor that I received some valuable guidance from was Ed Thigpen. Of course, he showed me his brush playing techniques but I got something more from Ed. He listened to me play jazz in the early 80s and told me I had no bottom to my playing. He said I really needed to learn how to feather the bass drum in order to get a fuller sound on the kit. I

in a beautiful way.

MD: I think it is really nice that you still talk about your first drum teacher as well.

SS: I am so fortunate that my parents found Billy Flanagan as my first teacher. He was from the swing era, and because of his influence I got instruction that reaches back to the foundation of swing era. He was a very good all-around drum instructor.

MD: So, what do you consider to be a good all-around drum teacher?

SS: Billy had me learn the rudiments, proper snare drum

technique, fundamental drumset coordination, we read a lot, but he really focused on sight reading, so every lesson would involve some sight reading.

MD: How did he teach sight reading?

SS: He would always have me sight read the next lesson before I went home and practiced it during the week. I think that is a great teaching technique. I'd be working from two or three books at the same time, and for the first three years based on snare drum technique only, all of the classic drum literature like: *The Bower System for Percussion*, *Progressive Studies for the Snare Drum, Vol. 1, 2 and 3* by Carl E. Gardner, *Modern School for Snare Drum* by Morris Goldenberg, *Variations of Drumming* by Ralph Pace, *Adventures in Solo Drumming* by William Schinstine, *Portraits in Rhythm* by Anthony Cirone, one of the many Wilcoxon books, Stone's *Stick Control* and *Accents and Rebounds* of course, Louie Bellson's *Modern Reading Text in 4/4* and *Odd Time Reading* Text. And eventually, books applied to the drumset like "The Chapin Book," lots of Sam Ulano's books like *Bass Bops* plus various ways of playing Ted Reed's *Syncopation* like the long notes on the bass drum and the short notes on the snare. I studied *Syncopation* again with Alan Dawson once I got to Berklee. Alan took those concepts to a whole new level!

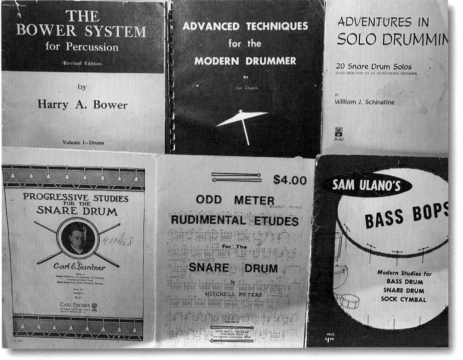

With Billy Flanagan we never did any specific pedal technique except for the fact that he had me learn the left foot "heel-toe" rocking technique on the hi-hat where your heel rocks back on 1 and 3, and your toe closes the cymbals on 2 and 4. I'm glad I learned that.

MD: Why?

SS: It feels more grounded to play that way rather than always playing heel up. Plus, that technique allows you to play the jazz swing beat on the hi-hats. You can't play that beat if you only play heel up.

MD: The circumstances surrounding how and why you began and developed your open-handed approach relate directly to who you were playing with, and some special circumstances. Let's talk about that.

SS: That's a long conversation. I played a few specific things in the 80s open handed: "Don't Stop Believin'," for the tom and cymbal bell melodies. The other Journey tune I played open-handed was "Dead or Alive" (from *Escape*.) I did that because my right hand felt too "refined" and I wanted a more "punk-ish" approach to that song. Playing open-handed provided that punk feel because my left hand on the hi-hat, at that tempo, was pretty jagged sounding. I also played "Where Were You" open handed when we played it live. Any tunes that I didn't have to play anything jazz inspired or intricate on the ride I would sometimes play open-handed. But I never specifically "addressed" open-handed playing back then.

Around 2006 I started to lose some cartilage at the base of my left thumb in the CMC joint, there was some bone touching bone. I did a lot of research on that injury and I don't think it was caused from gigging, but I do think it was caused from practicing too many hours without breaks while playing traditional grip. I had been pushing myself and practicing beyond the point of fatigue which is not a good thing. I had some PRP (Platelet Rich Plasma) injections in the CMC joint of my left thumb, and then started to develop my matched grip, because it didn't hurt when I played matched grip. But I found my matched grip technique to be severely limited. I didn't have the dexterity with matched that I had with traditional, so I had some work to do. I found that the best way to work on my matched grip was to play the jazz ride cymbal beat with my left hand. My right hand technique was highly developed and one of the main reasons for that was years of playing the jazz ride beat. To develop my left hand matched-grip, I played jazz time with both hands, in unison, in front of a mirror, and worked on matching the grips and motions that my right hand was making with my left hand. I tried to have my left hand learn from my right hand, that's what got me started playing open-handed and taking that concept to a new level. That is when I noticed, and started to develop, the four versions of matched grips that I discuss in the Hudson Music *Pathways of Motion* book/video. To be clear, I wasn't developing matched grip to be the only way that I played drums. I saw matched grip as a way of giving my traditional grip a break. Even though I've invested hours of practice -- and gig time -- with matched grip, my left-hand traditional grip is still better, but at this point I am not experiencing any pain in my left hand at all. And there have been some benefits to playing open-handed.

In 2011 I started subbing for Simon Phillips with Hiromi in her group called The Trio Project, and a musical need for open-handed playing developed. I had to play Simon Phillips' drum parts in that group. On most of the gig I could play the way I normally play, but some of Simon's orchestrations of the Hiromi music required me to further develop my open-handed approach. After that I started to play some Vital Information tunes open-handed. For example, with Vital Information NYC Edition we played Tony Williams'"Sister Cheryl" and Herbie Hancock's "Chan's Song," which were both reminiscent of Vernell Fournier's "Poinciana" groove with Ahmad Jamal, I played them open-handed, because Vernell played the "Poinciana" groove open-handed. Also, I had more options for tom melodies with the open-handed approach. When I went on tour with Journey in 2016, I relearned all of the Journey tunes open-handed.

MD: But you didn't play them all open-handed live.
SS: I could if I wanted to. At first, I did it as a coordination exercise, but then I found that the option of open-handed playing gave me three options of how to play each tune, or part of a tune: Traditional grip, matched grip, or matched grip open-handed.

MD: Jim Keltner expressed that same idea to me a while back.
SS: Cool. Some tunes worked as matched-grip, some worked well open-handed. But I found that there were certain tunes that felt best with traditional grip. I would try and create that same feeling open-handed. Now we're getting into subtleties. A good example is the song "After the Fall." That tune has a real strong R&B feel, and on the original recording I played a lot of ghost notes with my left hand on the snare and with my right hand I played a "jazz-ride" rhythm on the hi-hat with a strong accent on the "&'s" plus some open-hat syncopations. I needed to work on certain subtleties of my open-handed playing to be able to play that groove with my left hand on the hi-hat and right hand on the snare. Eventually I started playing the tune alternating between traditional grip and matched grip/open-handed, depending on which snare drum I was playing. I played my deep-tuned side-snare to the left of my hi-hat on the verses using traditional grip. For the chorus' I played open-handed so I could play my main snare, which lifted the song. You can see what I'm describing in the DVD *Journey Live in Tokyo 2017: Escape and Frontiers*.

MD: Because you had two snares set up to the left of the hi-hat for the Journey gig?
SS: Yes, there was a 14x5 ¾ deep tuned snare just to the left of the hi-hat and a 12x5 high-pitched snare to the left of the deep tuned snare. The result of my recent training is, now I can save the use of traditional grip for when I really want to use it. I can break up the grips now, so nothing gets overused.

For me there is also something very "yang-yang" in playing open-handed. When you are playing with your dominant hand on the cymbal and your non-dominant hand on the snare, there is a "yin-yang" see-saw between your right foot and your left hand. But with open-handed, if you are right-handed, it's all dominant hand and dominant foot, with the right foot on the bass drum and right hand on the snare. It's a very strong sound, and possibly the strongest way of playing, which works for a lot of things but, for me, it doesn't work for everything.

MD: In the past we have talked about the origins of some of your Journey fills and feels, and there were some real surprises. Can we discuss some of them?
SS: Obvious influences are Charlie Watts, Ringo, Mitch

Mitchell and John Bonham, plus there are many more, for example Billy Cobham, Narada Michael Walden and Terry Bozzio, they all inspired me in different ways.

You can see Billy's influence was the big, multi-tom, double bass kit, the "upside-down" China cymbal and, in general, striving for a virtuosic approach of playing the kit.

Terry Bozzio's playing in Group 87 was the inspiration for the "Don't Stop Believin'" grooves. He played some very creative "industrial" type beats on the Group 87 record. He included melodic tom ideas and incorporated the bell of the ride cymbal on the tune "Sublime Feline." What Terry played made an impression on me to develop a different side to my playing in a rock context. "Don't Stop Believin'" isn't the only song on *Escape* and *Frontiers* that I used those ideas. If you listen closely, you can hear those concepts on some of the other songs.

The intro drum groove for "Party's Over" was inspired

I first moved to the San Francisco Bay Area, I took some lessons with Narada, and he showed me the intro fill that I played on "Where Were You."

MD: That's a cool phrase.

SS: While on tour with Journey in the 80s I tended to listen to a lot of music while we were travelling and the cassette tapes that I listened to constantly were *Visions of the Emerald Beyond* by The Mahavishnu Orchestra with Narada Michael Walden and *Standards Volume 1 and 2* by the Keith Jarrett Trio with Jack DeJohnette.

The fills on "Open Arms" were inspired by the Joe Cocker recording of "With A Little Help from My Friends" from the Woodstock recording. I listened to the Woodstock triple album a lot when I was in high school and when we were rehearsing "Open Arms," before we recorded it, those fills came to me. My reference was the Joe Cocker recording, though I didn't go back and listen to it for exact fill ideas, it was the overall impression of what I remembered that inspired me. I also liked

"To develop my left hand matched-grip, I played jazz time with both hands, in unison, in front of a mirror, and worked on matching the grips and motions that my right hand was making with my left hand. "

by Steve Gadd's hi-hat work and the fill in "Separate Ways" that people always ask me about (at 2:43 on the original recording) was borrowed directly from Steve Gadd, although John Bonham played almost the identical fill in "Stairway to Heaven," (at 6:22) but I didn't notice that until later.

When I first heard Narada with Mahavishnu, his approached seemed more rock and R&B than Billy Cobham's. I absolutely love Billy's playing but I felt that I could adapt some of Narada's playing ideas to the Journey music, and I did. I was thinking of Narada Michael Walden's concept when we were recording "Mother, Father." The opening fill is identical to a fill that I heard him play. There is triplet fill toward the end of that tune (at 4:40) that I stole from Narada from one of the albums that I heard him on, could have been Allan Holdsworth's "Velvet Darkness" or Alphonso Johnson's "Moonshadows" or any number of other albums. When

Nigel Olsson's big ballad fills with Elton John, and on Nigel's own solo records, which I owned and listened to frequently.

Steve Perry had an influence on my Journey drum parts too. With Steve coming up as a drummer, he would suggest a lot of ideas, and he would occasionally sit down and play a feel that he wanted to hear. I never let my ego get in the way of that, I found it instructive and gave me some direction. He gave me some great advice once that really stayed with me: "When you play a fill, make sure you give every note it's full value." I had never heard anyone say that, it made sense and really stuck with me. It's a great way to think about not rushing during a fill, especially on a rock ballad.

MD: I like to ask each of the Legend artists about longevity in the music business, because in my opinion, that is the ultimate compliment and goal.

SS: As I was coming up in the early part of my career,

I saw myself as a working musician and I considered myself a jazz musician, though I was open to playing any kind of music. I didn't have aspirations to be in a rock band, or to "make it" in a band, it wasn't even on my radar because coming out of high school I wanted to play with Stan Kenton, Maynard Ferguson or Woody Herman. My aspiration was to become an employable sideman-musician. My early training gave me the skillset to become employable. I achieved a reasonable success at a young age because I could read, play a variety of styles, and had good time. Those skills don't go out of style, they are necessary for a drummer to develop a long career, as an individual, in the music business. After I worked around the Boston area, I was asked to play with Jean-Luc Ponty, Ronnie Montrose, and then Journey. Becoming a Journey "band member" didn't cause me to change my approach to my overall career as an individual. I learned a lot and enjoyed many aspects of being in a band but ultimately, being a life-long member of a rock band is not what nourishes me musically. Most of the musicians I encountered while touring with Journey seemed to want to be "band members." The "band experience" seemed to be more important to them than it was to develop the skills to become an employable individual musician that could work for a lifetime. I encountered a lot of rock drummers along the way who played in the different bands that Journey would tour with, but the only drummer that I knew from those years, who is still an employable musician working today, is Kenny Aronoff, who I met when John Mellencamp opened for Journey. All the other drummers seemed to *live and die by the band*. I know that Kenny and I have some overlapping skillsets, and he worked hard to develop a similar approach to his career. I was fortunate that I became a royalty participating member of Journey, which allowed me a financial cushion. That opportunity helped me gain some musical freedom. It has been important to me to protect that freedom and make good choices financially so I could be selective musically.

In the early part of my career, I became known as "the drummer from Journey." Although it was a good launching pad for my career, to me it seemed limiting and gave me inspiration to prove that I was capable of much more than only playing that music. I spent years diversifying my gig choices, which was interesting for me and helped me grow musically, but it also let people know that I was capable of playing a wide variety of different music. The greater the variety of music you play, the wider the range of musicians that you work with, the more versatile you become and ultimately more employable. I think keys to longevity in a music career has to do with abilities, plus how you conduct yourself when it comes to the business of music. When you asked producer Milan Simich why he hired me, he said it was because he knew that he could relax and I would take care of business. I'm reliable.

In the early years of my career, I stayed as busy as possible by saying "yes" to pretty much every gig I was offered, and I took each gig seriously. I said "yes" for many years as it seemed necessary to get myself established. The other side of that equation is learning when to say "no" once you have more options. Being selective and pacing yourself is important to sustain your health and emotional well-being for the long run.

Louie Bellson and Roy Haynes are beacons of light for me regarding having a long career. Both have been sidemen and bandleaders, played on many albums and tours. Louie also had a career in music education with books, clinics and videos, that inspired me too. To see Roy Haynes playing with all of these fantastic young musicians and being the elder on stage inspires me as well.

At this point in my career, I'm the elder, and I'm surrounding myself with outstanding younger players. But also, as an elder I'm even more selective in what I do and don't do musically.

MD: Is that because of the physical requirements of playing drums?

SS: No, not really, but addressing the physical challenges of a long career in drumming could be a long and detailed answer.

MD: Let's get into it. You mentioned your thumb injury earlier, have there been any other injuries that you felt were drum related?

SS: I've always resisted talking about injuries, and I know it's an important subject, so okay, I'm glad you asked. About ten years ago I had a tear in my right rotator cuff, to treat that I did the opposite of what all the doctors recommended, and I consulted with three doctors in NYC before I made a decision. All three wanted to shoot me up with cortisone to reduce the inflammation and it was possible I needed surgery.

Instead, I went with a combination of PRP (Platelet Rich Plasma), physical therapy, and yoga. The idea is that the PRP can possibly help with healing instead of the cortisone which would only reduce the pain and inflammation. For me the combination of PRP, physical therapy and yoga has allowed the tear to heal without surgery.

Last year, I had a back surgery for a herniated disc between L4 and L5. That was a very serious surgery called a laminotomy. I did a lot of research and got a lot of input from my drumming peers and different doctors about my back injury. In the end I couldn't avoid surgery and found a great surgeon at the Hospital for Special Surgery here in New York.

MD: Was that a drum related injury?

SS: Yes, that was a *very* drum related injury! A lifetime of drumming causes compression of the spine. I wasn't always aware of the best posture or seat height in the early years of my career, and that didn't help. But I think it mainly had to do with fifty years of moving heavy gear, carrying cymbal bags and trap cases, setting up and breaking down drumsets and pulling suitcases off luggage carousels at airports after long flights. Drumming and touring can be a physical hazard if you are not aware of how to move and aren't in shape. Thankfully, I can say that every

time I had a physical problem or injury, I have taken the time to re-educate my body so I could learn a better way to move, both at the drums and elsewhere, to try to avoid any more injuries.

With my left thumb injury, I used that to investigate and develop my matched grip and open-handed playing. When I had the rotator cuff issue, I lowered my cymbals and re-addressed how I move on the kit. And now with the back surgery I'm working on my bass drum technique again and changing the type of drum-throne that I use.

MD: What have you found?

SS: The first thing my physical therapist recommended was a tractor-type seat. He believes the tractor seat is better for your back. I've gotten pretty comfortable with it right away. I also have a tractor seat with a slight split down the middle and that's pretty comfortable too. The idea of the split seat is your tailbone is suspended which can help reduce the spinal compression that occurs when you sit for a long time. One of the main reasons I needed surgery is that I had extreme nerve pain down my right leg into my right foot. As a result of that, I lost some range of motion with my right foot. It has taken a while to get that back.

MD: How did you work on getting that back?

SS: I started with a lot of physical therapy, which

Steve and Baird Heresy

Steve Smith Library

helped. I continue to do many of the PT exercises, they are part of my daily routine. About a month after the surgery, I started on the drums again. If you saw any of my "From The Practice Room" videos from my NYC apartment, that's when I started my drum rehab. I started slowly, just playing quarter notes, feathering the bass drum, playing along with records that had Paul Chambers playing bass on. His quarter-note swing pulse was incredible and inspiring to play with. I started off with slower tempos and gradually played faster tempos and expanded my range of motion. I practiced the "constant release" pedal technique that Freddie Gruber showed me in the early 90s. At first, I could only play for a few minutes before my foot and ankle were fatigued. Over the course of about six months my bass drum technique came back, and at this point, it may be better than it was.

The real test was a recent recording session that I did. I got a call from Baird Heresy, a guitarist and bandleader that I hadn't heard from in about 40 years. I occasionally played with his group called *The Year of The Ear* in Boston in the mid-70s. He reminded me that I had played with him when I was preparing for the Jean-Luc audition. Baird asked me to record five tracks on his new album called *Chapters*. The music is high-energy instrumental jazz-rock with excellent compositions. I was inspired to accept the invitation plus I wanted to test myself after my surgery. I was very up front with him about that, and he was completely okay with that. I spent about a month working on the music with a focus of getting my bass drum chops up. I did the recording in Woodstock New York and it went very well.

I also just played a week at Birdland in New York with the Coltrane Revisited group as well. That went great, in fact it felt like some of my best jazz playing ever. Plus, it was my first live gig in 18 months! After taking my time to recover and not pushing myself too hard during nine months of rehab, and those two musical "tests," I feel good and ready to start gigging again.

MD: You are very lucky to have had the time to do all of that rehab and reinvestigation during the lockdown. That afforded you the time to really take your time to recover.

SS: That's true. I am also very lucky to have a great life-partner in Diane to help me through the medical issues and my career as well. It's very difficult to have a long career as an individual, and I am very fortunate to be married to my wife Diane, we have been true partners in life for almost 30 years. That has been another key to my longevity and my long career. We are truly partners, we help each other in our collective life, and in our individual lives. Her wisdom and guidance helps me. I talk over literally every situation with her and she gives me great and honest feedback. She also takes care of the finances too. I can't imagine what it would be like to have a career as a musician without her.

MD: I can relate. Having a supportive relationship with my wife has been crucial in my career too.

SS: My career is a family business, and it's going well, but both of us run the business. We have a small team with Janet Williamson as my booking agent, Steve Orkin who takes care of my website and social media, and Christian Grassart who edits my videos. Occasionally, I'll hire a publicist, but that's it, that's the entire team. But it all starts with a supportive life partner, that's been an important component in my longevity.

MD: What would you like to say about touring with Journey from 2016-2019?

SS: When I was asked to come back, I signed up for two years, and I stayed four years. I enjoyed playing the Journey music and performing for the Journey fans and witnessing their joy at hearing some music they love. There were a lot of enjoyable moments with the band and crew over the four years. Particularly memorable was performing the entire *Escape* and *Frontiers* albums, in their original sequence, for an audience in Tokyo, Japan. We never played many of those "deep cuts" live, even with Steve Perry, so it was interesting for the band to re-learn and play all of those songs. We released a very good DVD/CD of that show called *Journey Live in Tokyo 2017: Escape and Frontiers*. There are some great moments on that DVD, especially the encore jam of "La Raza del Sol." Later that year we were inducted into the Rock and Roll Hall of Fame which was exhilarating. The six-month co-headlining tour with Def Leppard in 2018 was also a standout for me. In the end, the four years on the road with the band were valuable to me for many reasons. The playing pushed my chops to a new level and invigorated my drumming. The experience brought that chapter in my musical career with Journey to a conclusion. I'm proud of my contribution to the band and that body of work.

And back to the question that you had about why I'm being even more selective in the gigs I decide to take: During lock-down I have enjoyed being home immensely. I have a new granddaughter born this year and between Diane and I collectively we have five grandchildren. Being grandparents has been a very enjoyable part of our life together. I look back at my schedule, even before 2016-2019 Journey tours, and I was working way too much. I recently looked at my 2015 schedule, and I don't know how I did it, and I don't know how Diane did it either. I was gone for three weeks, and

Baron Browne. That's the end of an era for my Vital Information group. I will be organizing a new line-up but with the pain of loss and COVID still threatening live performances, it will be a while before I move forward with that. I do have a desire to make new music and play with great players, that's a drive that remains strong. I've been doing some jamming and seeing what it feels like to play the Vital Information music with some different musicians, which has been interesting. But

From left, Baron Browne, Steve Marcus, Andy Fusco, and Steve Smith in Buddy's Buddies.

Clayton Call

then home for two days, then back out for a month, home for a few days, back out for a few weeks… I've kept that type of schedule for decades. So, I am scaling back, and I'm enjoying the freedom that creates. Also, I'm in touch with the fragility of life. I lost my father this year, which was difficult. Herbie Herbert, the original manager of Journey, recently passed. We had developed a closer relationship in the past two years, so that has been hard. Two of my dearest long-time musical collaborators passed this year, saxophonist Andy Fusco and bassist

Vital Information music isn't a static set of songs. Vital Information is my platform to collaborate with individual musicians who inspire me to make music in a particular direction, and that direction changes over time. Each incarnation of the band creates its own repertoire, the process is organic and I'll give it time to happen.

I've never been one to rest on my laurels, I still practice most days and my ideas are flowing. I live with a great deal of gratitude and look forward to whatever the future brings.

STEVE'S CHARTS

In this issue of Legends, Steve mentions transcribing the Journey drum parts when he toured with the band from 2016-2019. He recalls, "When I started touring with Journey again in 2016, it had been thirty-two years since I played live with the band. We did the album *Trial by Fire* in 1996, but we didn't play any of the old songs like "Don't Stop Believin'" or "Who's Crying Now." I didn't remember any of those songs because I hadn't listened to them for a long time. I approached the Journey gig like any other gig that I get called for. I transcribed a big list of songs that the band wanted me to learn, I transcribed them note-for-note, exactly what I played on the albums.

Rick Malkin

The parts were looser than I remembered them being. Looser, as in the parts were not completely etched in stone for most of the music. I noticed that I had a verse groove, but I wasn't super-strict with it. For a chorus, I had a part, but it wasn't always an exact part. I made decisions about where to be loose with the fills and where to play verbatim what was on the record. It became a creative project for me… As long as the music felt right."

Marco Soccoli

In another part of this Legends book, Steve mentions creating charts for the Mike Stern gigs. Steve recalls, "For instance, let's talk about a gig like playing with Mike Stern. I have done lots of Mike Stern gigs throughout the years. In preparing for a Mike Stern gig, I listen to, and have transcribed tunes and drum parts played by Vinnie Colaiuta, Dave Weckl, Dennis Chambers, Terri Lyne Carrington, Al Foster, and many others. I have absolutely no attitude about learning drum parts that were created and recorded by someone else."

Steve even breaks down how he writes out different charts, saying, "For example, here's a chart for the Mike Stern tune called "One Liners" that Jack DeJohnette played on. You can see that I wrote out the rhythm of the melody, it's an up-tempo swing tune based on rhythm-changes, so there's no specific beat to play, it's about knowing the melody and then playing the form. If you look at the tune called "Big Neighborhood," Dave Weckl played on that. It's really rockin' so I wrote out the way Dave played the bass drum and snare. I usually don't write the hi-hat parts unless they are super specific. If a tune has some odd groupings or unique phrases, I'll write out those rhythms so I can catch the phrases. I keep all of my charts in one book and stay organized with it. So, when I get a call from Mike Stern for a gig, I reach for my Mike Stern book."

As musicians we all have to prepare for different gigs, and many times (like Steve) we do that by listening and preparing charts. I even talked about this important subject extensively in a past Legends book with Kenny Aronoff. So after hearing Steve (or Kenny) talk about preparing their own charts for their own gigs, listen to the songs and read along with their hand-written charts. Notice how they read and *interpret* the music on the page. This might help you prepare for your own gigs. Nothing beats learning from a Legend.

La Raza Del Sol

Mother, Father

Indian Rhythms for
Western Drummers

By Steve Smith (contributed to Modern Drummer in 2005 & 2006)

I've been studying Indian rhythms for the past four years, and it's been a lot of fun for me. By working with some basic Indian theory and exercises, I've been able to really expand my phrasing and rhythmic vocabulary. I believe that the Indian rhythmic systems are largely an untapped resource for Western drummers. I truly feel that if you become adept at learning these concepts, you'll greatly increase your knowledge of rhythm and, in turn, improve your drumming. We'll go over some of these fundamentals in this series on the basics of rhythms from India.

One of the cornerstones of Indian music is learning to recite rhythms with your voice. That way you get a very clear picture of the rhythms you'll be playing. I find it very interesting that all Indian musicians do this, not just the drummers. As a result, Indian musicians have a very high degree of rhythmic awareness.

In South India, the language of vocal percussion is called **konokol**. This first lesson will be learning the konokol syllables that we'll use for the basic building blocks of rhythm.

Use "Dhaa" for beat one. For two beats in a row, as in two 8th notes or two 16th notes, use "Ta Ka." Three beats in a row, as in a triplet or a phrase of three 8th notes, is "Ta Ki Ta." Four beats in a row is "Ta Ka Di Mi." Five beats is generally phrased two plus three, which is "Ta Ka Ta Ki Ta."

Six beats is generally phrased three plus three: "Ta Ki Ta Ta Ki Ta." Other common phrases for six are four plus two: "Ta Ka Di Mi Ta Ka," or "Ta Ka _ Ta Ki Ta," where the second beat is held one beat longer.

Seven is generally phrased four plus three, "Ta Ka Di Mi Ta Ki Ta," as well as three plus four, "Ta Ki Ta Ta Ka Di Mi." Eight is "Ta Ka Di Mi Ta Ka Jo Nu." Nine is generally four plus five, "Ta Ka Di Mi Ta Ka Ta Ki Ta." That's as far as we'll go, though obviously you can continue to ten, eleven, twelve, etc. There are many more syllables available, and we will get to a few more during this series. But this is a good place to start.

The first exercise to work on is getting comfortable with the subdivisions from two through nine using only the vocal sounds. This will give you practice with the syllables, and you can begin to internalize the various sub-divisions of the beat. Repeat each rhythm over and over until you get more comfortable with them.

You'll find that you can recite these syllables much faster than you can recite the corresponding numbers. Be sure to memorize each phrase rather than continuing to read them. The Indian tradition is an oral tradition, and memorization is very important—especially when putting together longer phrases.

Let's start with a phrase of two, work our way up to nine, and end on one, so you get used to resolving the phrases to Dhaa.

2: Ta Ka
3: Ta Ki Ta
4: Ta Ka Di Mi
5: Ta Ka Ta Ki Ta
6: Ta Ki Ta Ta Ki Ta
7: Ta Ka Di Mi Ta Ki Ta
8: Ta Ka Di Mi Ta Ka Jo Nu
9: Ta Ka Di Mi Ta Ka Ta Ki Ta
1: Dhaa

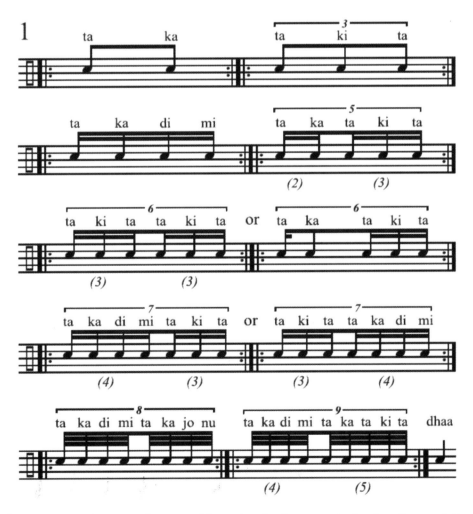

Pete Lockett and Steve

Marco Soccoli

The next step is to work on **reciting** the rhythms and **playing** them at the same time using the following **sticking patterns**. I came up with these stickings to approximate the sound and feel of the spoken rhythmic phrasing. Of course, there are many different stickings that you can come up with, but we'll get started with some of the stickings that I use. Start with the snare drum and then adapt them to the drumset.

Indian Rhythms for *Western Drummers*

I feel that learning konokol has added a lot to my drumming and my awareness of rhythm. I suggest that you memorize the syllables and the rhythmic phrases. This will be helpful as we move forward and put together some of those shorter building blocks into longer, more involved phrases.

We will start by taking some of the basic building blocks and arranging them, so they construct longer phrases that have a logical symmetry. Rhythms that have symmetry are a very common feature of Indian music. We'll start very simply so you can try out some of your new skills. The first example takes phrases of three and five in 8th notes and arranges them over eight bars of 4/4 time.

I have written this out in Western notation, but the best way to do this—and to use the Indian conception—is to memorize the sequence of phrases and play it from memory. The sequence is: 3+5, 3+5, 3+5, 3+3, 5+5, 3+3+3, 5+5+5, and then it resolves to beat 1.

First identify the formula. This will make it easier to memorize. The first rhythm, 3+5, is repeated three times, then the 3s are repeated two times and the 5s are repeated two times, then the 3s are repeated three times and the 5s are repeated three times. Now that you've identified the formula, it should be easy to remember the entire piece.

I've written out the stickings and the konokol syllables in Example 1, which may be helpful while you memorize the piece. Start with only the konokol, and once you're comfortable with that, play the rhythms on your snare drum and recite the syllables at the same time. Notice that the stickings used are consistent: RLL for groups of three and RLRRL for groups of five. You can put accents at the beginning of each phrase of three and five; this will help you begin to make music out of the phrases.

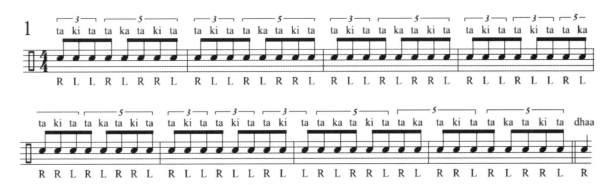

Example 2 employs the exact same formula, except it uses phrases of seven and nine over sixteen bars of 4/4 time. Here's the sequence: 7+9, 7+9, 7+9, 7+7, 9+9, 7+7+7, 9+9+9, and then it resolves to beat 1. Again, I've used consistent stickings—RLRLRLL for groups of seven and RLRLRLRRL for groups of nine. The 7s are phrased 4+3 and the 9s are phrased 4+5.

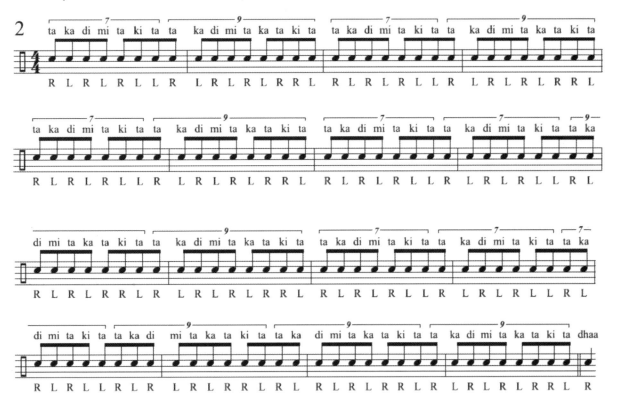

Indian Rhythms for *Western Drummers*

One of the great advantages of konokol is that you can practice rhythms away from the drums. You can recite the syllables while walking down the street or driving your car. (You may have to be careful about who hears you, though, so you're not locked up in the nearest asylum!)

Once you've mastered the konokol, play the stickings on the snare drum while keeping quarter notes or half notes on the hi-hat. After a while you'll begin to hear ways of including the bass drum, cymbals, and toms into the rhythmic phrases. These rhythms have been traditionally played on Indian drums, not the drumset, so their application to the drumset is largely unexplored territory. Let your imagination be your guide.

An Indian rhythmic concept that I have found to be especially useful in Western drumming is the **tihai** (pronounced TEE-high). The function of a tihai is to mark the end of a passage of music with a pronounced cadence. To do this, you play a rhythmic phrase that repeats three times in a row with a smooth resolution to beat "1." I will focus on two of the most common tihais that I have encountered while playing with Indian musicians.

Think of an 8th-note groove with a medium-slow tempo (approximately quarter note = 80 bpm), slow enough so that you can comfortably play fills using 16th notes. In a four-bar phrase, you'll start this first tihai in the fourth measure. The rhythmic phrase itself starts on the first 16th note after beat 1.

Example 1 uses five phrases of three 16th notes, which resolves smoothly to beat 1. Using "_" to designate a 16th rest, the konokol syllables for tihai #1 are: _ Ta Ki Ta Dhaa _ _, Ta Ki Ta Dhaa _ _, Ta Ki Ta Dhaa. In Western notation it looks like this:

Note that the phrase markings in Example 1 are not triplets, but are actually 16th notes in phrases of three. Also note that I've included suggested stickings and accents as a way to get the rhythms started with a Western approach.

The next step is to play the entire tihai three times in a row before it resolves to beat 1. In Indian music this serves the purpose of marking the end of a musical passage in a more dramatic way than it appears in Example 1, and it invites the other players to join in on the tihai. All Indian instrumentalists are familiar with these phrases. When they hear the soloist (or the drummer) playing the tihai rhythm, they recognize the phrase and can usually catch the rhythm the second or third time through. That creates an exciting resolution to a solo or a peak moment in a solo.

Note that the *extended* version of this tihai starts in the second measure of a four-bar phrase, because it takes three measures for it to resolve to beat 1. It is very important to start the tihai in the correct place so it resolves to beat 1 of a logical phrase. For instance, if you were playing in eight-bar phrases, you would start this tihai in measure six.

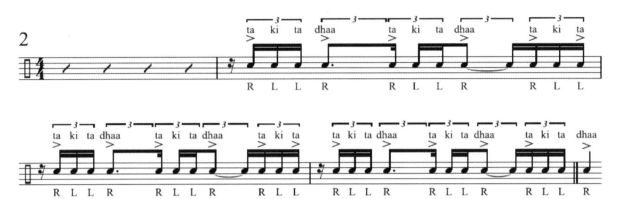

Another very common tihai uses three phrases of five 16th notes, which resolves smoothly to beat 1. Note that both tihais use fifteen 16th notes, therefore they have to start on the second 16th note of the measure so they resolve to 1 without adding or subtracting any notes. The konokol syllables for this tihai are: _ Ta Ka Ta Ki Ta, Ta Ka Ta Ki Ta, Ta Ka Ta Ki Ta, Dhaa.

The extended version of this tihai also starts in measure two of a four-bar phrase. In the extended version of both tihais, notice that you do not play beat 1 in the third or fourth bars, but wait until the end of the four-bar phrase for the big "1." This helps build excitement and tension before the release. You can enhance this drama by putting an accent on the last 16th note of measures two and three. This sets up the "gap" on beat 1 of measures three and four.

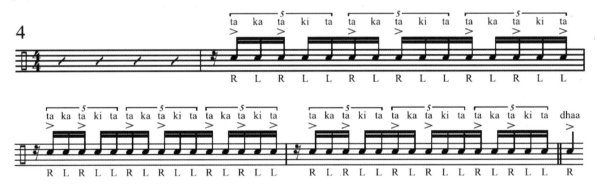

To hear examples of these tihais, listen to "Mad Tea Time" on the Magna Carta release *Modern Drummer Presents Drum Nation, Vol. 1*. On this track Zakir Hussain and I play both of these tihais in various parts of the piece. In fact, guitarist Fareed Haque uses the extended version of the first tihai to cue the end of his solo. He is embellishing the basic rhythm by playing two 32nd notes for each 16th note.

Embellishment of these basic rhythms is a way to "dress up" the rhythms and make them more interesting. To embellish the three-note phrase Ta Ki Ta, play two 32nd notes in place of the middle 16th note. The konokol syllables are Ta Ki Ta Tom. This introduces a new syllable—tom, sometimes spelled Thom. It's pronounced as a low sound with a bit of emphasis on the letter m, "Tomm." In Western notation:

Indian Rhythms for *Western Drummers*

Also note that if you're using a three-note sticking of RLL, you keep the same sticking and add a right between the two lefts. If we now play tihai Example 1 with the embellishments, it looks like this:

Using the embellished three-note phrase in a group of "five," phrased 2 + 3, looks like this:

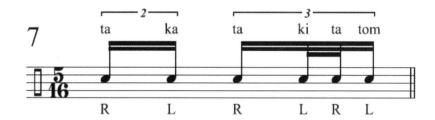

With the embellishments, the tihai made up of three groups of five 16th notes looks like this:

Be sure to take these ideas and memorize the konokol syllables first, then use the stickings and play them on a snare drum. Take your time and let these ideas enter your drumset playing gradually.

I suggest listening to some music that uses these concepts. Try some recordings by Shakti, the East meets West fusion group featuring John McLaughlin on guitar and Zakir Hussain on tabla. They use a lot of Indian concepts in their music. You can visit Zakir's Web site www.momentrecords.com. Or Ganesh Kumar's website www.ganeshkanjira.com. He is a kanjira virtuoso from South India.

The **repetition** of a rhythm three times in a row is a regular part of Indian music. Therefore, when playing with Indian musicians I've found it necessary to be very familiar with how to play common rhythms three times in a row and have them resolve to beat 1. By common rhythms, I'm talking about phrases of "3s" up through and including phrases of "10s."

Starting the rhythms in the exact place so they resolve to beat 1—without adding or subtracting any notes—requires math and memorization. I've done the math for you in this lesson; it's up to you to memorize where the phrases start.

In addition to these rhythms being helpful when playing with Indian musicians, I've also found them to be very powerful ways to end musical phrases when playing with Western musicians. The difference is that while the Indian musicians know what you are doing, the Western musicians don't—but they usually like the sound and feel of the rhythms.

I've written these rhythms in a series of two-bar phrases. It's easier for us Western musicians to read two bars of 4/4 rather than one bar of 8/4. But I want you to count the two bars as 1, 2, 3, 4, 5, 6, 7, 8, and memorize the rhythms and where they start in the eight-beat cycle. Most of the time, when Indian musicians are playing in what sounds like 4/4 time, it is really 8/4 time, or what they call "Adi Tala"—an eight-beat cycle. As Western music has names for certain scales or modes, like Ionian, Lydian, etc., Indian musicians have names for the beat cycles. For example, Khanda Tala is a five-beat cycle, and Misra Chapu Tala is a seven-beat cycle.

I've written the rhythms in Western notation, which for "3," "4," "5," "7," and "8" isn't a problem. When we get to "6," "9," and "10," the rhythms look different depending on where they fall in the measure, even though they're the same rhythm repeated three times in a row. This is a potential problem in that the written notation becomes difficult to read. Since Indian music is an oral tradition, I usually take that approach, learning where the rhythm starts and then playing it three times in a row, resolving to beat 1. The phrasing that I've written for the "6s," "8s," "9s," and "10s" are standard ways for Indian musicians to phrase these "numbers," though they are slightly unusual for Western players. However, I find them interesting, and I like the way they sound. They're a good example of how learning Indian rhythms can expand your playing vocabulary.

The "8" is subdivided 3+5 (with the 5 phrased 2+3), the "9" is 2+2+5 (with the 5 phrased 2+3), and the "10" is 3+2, 2+3. Note that in the "8s" and "10s" the (LL) are ghost notes that can be played with the left hand.

Indian Rhythms for *Western Drummers*

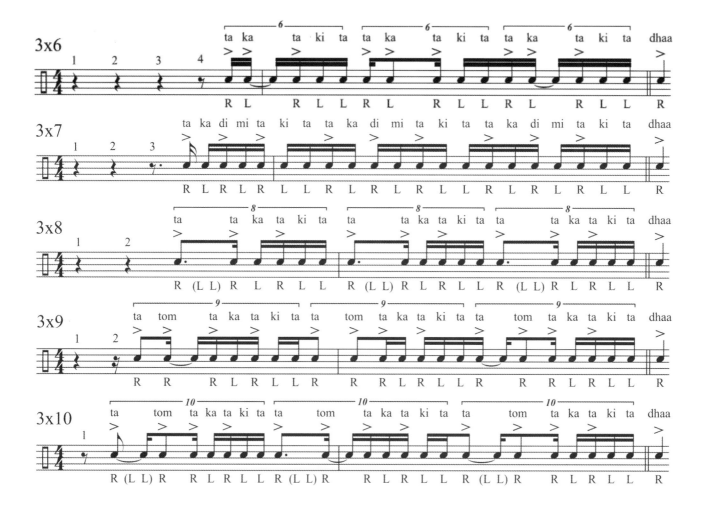

I first learned this sequence of rhythms when playing a duo gig with the South Indian guitarist Prasanna. He improvised melodies to these rhythms and expected me to catch them with him. The concept of putting melodies to specific rhythms in an improvisation is typical of Indian instrumentalists. After the gig I had him explain to me what he was doing, and I've been using the rhythms ever since. Check out his Web site: www.guitarprasanna.com.

An Indian rhythmic concept that I enjoy using is called a **reduction**. There are countless applications of this idea. One approach is to take a group of notes and alter their value so that each time you play them, they sound "faster."

Let's start with a group of five notes. The first time we play the five notes they will each have the value of a dotted quarter note. Immediately follow that by playing five quarter notes, and finally play five 8th notes. As you can see, the value of the notes are "reduced" each time the phrase of five is played, so it sounds like it's speeding up.

In Example 1 I wrote out the rhythm over four bars of 4/4 time. We had to start on beat 2 of the first bar so that the entire reduction resolved to beat 1. Notice that when you allow all of the notes in the first set of five to have their full value, the second set of five are all upbeats. Sometimes when I show someone this idea, their tendency is to not give the last note of each five its full value. If that happens, they will start the next group in the wrong place and the phrases won't resolve to beat 1.

When I'm learning Indian rhythms I don't always write them down using traditional Western notation. To me, Western notation can make many Indian rhythms look more complex than they really are. I've come up with a notation system that helps me memorize the rhythms. In my "modified Western shorthand" notation, I would write Example 1 like this. (See Example 2.)

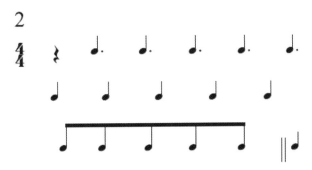

As long as I keep a steady pulse, know where to start the reduction, and give each note its full value, it will come out on the 1. If we take the same rhythm and cut every note in half, we have this. (See Example 3.)

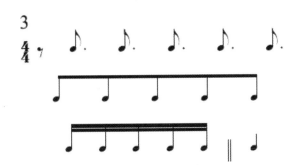

Indian Rhythms for *Western Drummers*

In Western notation, Example 3 looks like this:

On the Vital Information recording, *Come On In*, we used the reduction concept on a tune we wrote called "Baton Rouge." The tune is in 5/4, so the "five reduction" worked perfectly. We start on beat 1 with five quarter notes, then five dotted 8th notes, then five 8th notes, and finally three sets of five 16th notes. In my shorthand notation, here is how we played the reduction for the intro to the tune. (See Example 5.)

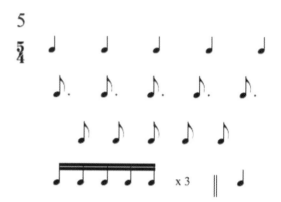

In Western notation, it looks like this. (the LLL's are ghosted 16th notes played in the left hand.)

Another way we can use this rhythm is in combination with an **expansion**, where a rhythm gets "longer" each time it's played. I'll illustrate this with a short piece that starts with an expansion and ends with a reduction. In order to understand the piece, you need to develop it one step at a time.
There is a group of reduction exercises that I will address later, but in order to explain how this piece is conceived I need to borrow from this future concept now. Part of these future exercises is to play a rhythm eight times in a row and have it resolve perfectly to 1. To play eight groups of five 16th notes that resolve to 1 without adding or subtracting any notes, you need to leave six quarter notes of space and then start playing the fives on beat 3 of the second bar. If you then continue to play the phrases of five "over the barlines," they will fill two and a half more bars of 4/4, completing four bars of 4/4 before ending on 1:

Those four bars will be the foundation of the piece. Now we fill the first six beats with rhythm. We could play six groups of four 16th notes, but it will be more interesting to play four groups of six 16th notes. In fact, instead of steady 16th notes, we'll play a six-note rhythm that looks like this in my shorthand notation. (See Example 8.)

8

Or in Western notation, like this. (See Example 9.)

9

Here is where the fun begins. Let's take those four rhythmic phrases and develop them into an expansion. To do this we need to "borrow" one group of six notes and divide and add them to the remaining phrases.

First, we play the original rhythm as is, then we play two of the borrowed 16th notes before the original phrase. Finally, we take the four 16th notes left and play those before the third time through the rhythm. Now we have three rhythmic phrases that gradually get longer, or "expand," as they go. In my shorthand, hopefully this will all start to make more sense, (See Example 10.)

10

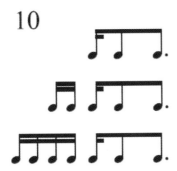

Indian Rhythms for *Western Drummers*

For those of you who prefer Western notation, it looks like the following. (See Example 11.) I've included two ways to perceive the phrasing.

To complete the piece, instead of playing eight groups of fives, we can play a "five reduction" in the same space. Here's the entire piece written in my shorthand. (See Example 12.)

Here it is in Western notation, with konokol and suggested stickings. (See Example 13.)

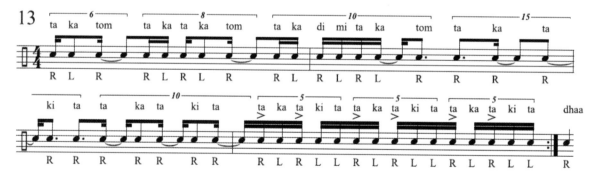

Notice it ends with a "tihai"—the three phrases of five, which take up the last fifteen beats of the fourth bar.

This is a standard Indian rhythmic "composition" that has been played by Indian drummers, singers, and instrumentalists alike. I've taken you through the theory behind its creation. But the bottom line is, it sounds good and is fun to play. The main rhythms are a "fixed" composition, but how you embellish them is open to interpretation. My suggested stickings are only a start.

Once you memorize the piece and play it on your snare drum, you can start to get creative with it on the kit. Try playing this in unison with other drummers, or use it as a theme in a solo. The applications are up to you.

During my career I've had the opportunity to perform with some true masters of Indian drumming, and I've learned new rhythms and different soloing ideas from each one. By being exposed to a drumming tradition that has evolved over centuries, I've tapped into a rich resource of rhythmic ideas, and I've been able to incorporate some of these ideas into my own drum soloing. Though the concepts are not new to Indian drummers, they are new and fresh to me as a Western drummer.

There are two basic "schools" of music in India. South Indian music, called **Carnatic** music, is the older form. North Indian music, or **Hindustani** music, has its roots in south Indian music, but it's been influenced by the music of the Middle East and Islamic culture, which is more prevalent in the northern region of India.

The Instruments

There are numerous drums used in Carnatic music, the most common being the mridangam, tavil, ghatam, and kanjira.

The **mridangam** is a doubleheaded barrel drum about 11 to 12 inches long, played with the hands. The "high" sounds are in the right hand, and the "low" sounds are in the left hand. The **tavil** is a double-headed barrel drum that is about 16" long and is played with a stick in the left hand and thimble-like hard caps on the fingertips of the right hand. This is an "outdoor" drum, and unlike the other Indian drums, can be *very* loud.

The **ghatam** is a clay pot that is tuned to a specific note. The **kanjira** is a small, single-headed frame drum played with one hand, similar to a tambourine with one jingle. Both of these drums started as simple folk drums, but in recent years have become part of the Carnatic classical tradition due to the virtuosic breakthroughs of a few amazing players like Vikku Vinayakram on the ghatam and Harishankar on the kanjira.

The vocal percussion called **konokol** is considered an art form in Carnatic music.

In North Indian classical (Hindustani) music, there is one main drum, which is the **tabla**. The tabla is actually two drums: the low drum, called the **bayan**, which is played by the left hand, and the **tabla**, the high drum, played by the right hand. The two drums are collectively known as **tabla**.

The **"drum solo"** is usually a major feature at an Indian music concert, in both the Hindustani and Carnatic styles. These solos take a long time to develop and can range from twenty minutes to a few hours in length. In Carnatic music there are usually at least two drummers accompanying the vocalists and instrumentalists—for example, a mridangam player and a ghatam player. Carnatic music has a long tradition of drum features that are actually "drum duets" that feature both drummers soloing, trading, and playing in unison.

Since the Carnatic style is very conducive to two or more drummers playing together, it is usually the Carnatic percussion concepts that are used as a fundamental common ground when I play with Indian drummers.

Indian Rhythms for *Western Drummers*

Most of the Indian drum features that I've been involved in take this form: a unison opening statement, followed by solos, then trading, and a final unison statement. Let's look at each section individually.

Unison Opening Statement

There is a repertoire of Carnatic drum compositions that most Indian drummers know. These are fixed rhythmic compositions that the drummers can use to begin and end their solos with. Because the Indian drummers have this shared repertoire, they can get together before a concert, work out a solo form in the dressing room, and go onstage and play, with no rehearsal. An analogy to the West is when jazz musicians get together for a concert, they can play without ever rehearsing by playing "standards." For instance, if they decide on "Autumn Leaves," "All The Things You Are," and "Green Dolphin Street," everyone will know the tunes. The Carnatic drum compositions are so well known that they are the Indian drummer's version of "standards." I've learned a number of these drum compositions.

When I have a concert with an Indian drummer, first we agree on a **"tala,"** which is the beat cycle—in Western terms the easiest way to explain tala is the time signature—and we determine the tempo. Then we decide on a unison opening statement. This can be one composition, or we might put together more than one composition for an extended beginning.

We will keep the entire solo in time. To help us do that there is usually a person onstage who "keeps the tala" by clapping their hands in a very specific pattern, or we clap for each other. This way it's easy for the musicians to keep their place and have their phrases end in the correct places. Once the tala is established, it doesn't change. There are no "free form" or "impressionistic" drum solos in Indian music.

Solos

Sometimes each drummer plays one long solo before the trading starts, or they may play a series of two or three shorter solos with the "secondary" drummer playing first and the "primary" drummer playing second. There is a very clear hierarchy of status and respect that the Indian drummers adhere to. The elder (and usually superior) drummer will follow the younger drummer. In the Indian world, I am always the secondary drummer, because the Indian drummers that I play with obviously know much more about their music than I do.

In the solo, I improvise on the tala using inspiration from the opening statement. As my solo builds I will finish my ideas with "tihais" (explained earlier) or play some Hindustani or Carnatic drum compositions in between improvisations. I'll finish the solo with an obvious tihai. The primary drummer catches the tihai, and then he solos.

His solo will build on my ideas, and he'll develop his own ideas. I try to incorporate some of these into my next solo. His solo will also be a combination of improvisation, memorized compositions, and tihais. During the soloing, if a player moves from subdivisions of four to subdivisions of five, the players will improvise strictly in the fives—without mixing subdivisions. The same rule applies if they move to sixes, sevens, or nines. It's not hip to mix subdivisions.

When the primary drummer has finished his last solo, he will start to lead the trading section.

Trading

The trading will start with the primary drummer determining the ideas and the length of the beginning trades. Most of the time the trades start with each drummer playing two cycles of the tala. If we're playing in adi tala, which is an eight-beat cycle, each cycle would be like two bars of 4/4 time. This makes the beginning trades four bars each.

After trading for a while, the primary drummer will cue to cut the trading length in half. Then the trades go on for a while with one cycle—or two bars each. During this part of the trading, it's common to trade in ascending subdivisions of the beat, starting with four-note groupings and moving up to groups of five, six, seven, nine, and then coming down to eights.

The trade lengths will be halved again and again until each player is playing only one beat each. Then we play 16th notes (or 32nd notes) together or play a groove together for a few cycles and end the trades with a tihai, which is usually not planned in advance but is cued by the lead player.

Ending

The ending is the most exciting part of the solo, and it's determined ahead of time. It's usually at least two compositions in length, called the "mora" and "korvai," which will further demonstrate the musical virtuosity and sophistication of the players. They also provide a spectacular and powerful unison ending.

Carnatic Compositions

The following are some Carnatic rhythmic compositions that you can use to play with another drummer or play on your own. The first is a rhythmic transcription of the Carnatic drum composition that kanjira virtuoso Ganesh Kumar and I used to begin our duet at PASIC 2005. I'll first write it in my "modified-Western-shorthand" notation so you can clearly see that it is a "reduction" (explained in Part 5) with a tihai at the end.

The konokol syllables in the tihai are a "stretched five." I'll explain: We've been using ta ka ta ki ta for groups of five, which implies a phrasing of 2+3. The konokol syllables for a group of five notes that is not 2+3 but is actually five even notes is: ta di ga na tom or ta di ki ta tom, which we will use for the tihai on Examples 1 and 3.

Example 1 ends with a tihai that is made up of phrases of six, but the second note is sustained, so there are in fact only five notes played. Typically, the konokol syllables for this are the same as a group of five, but you "stretch" the second note, ta diiii ki ta tom. In the following examples there are some other new konokol syllables that are self-explanatory.

Continues on the following page

Indian Rhythms for *Western Drummers*

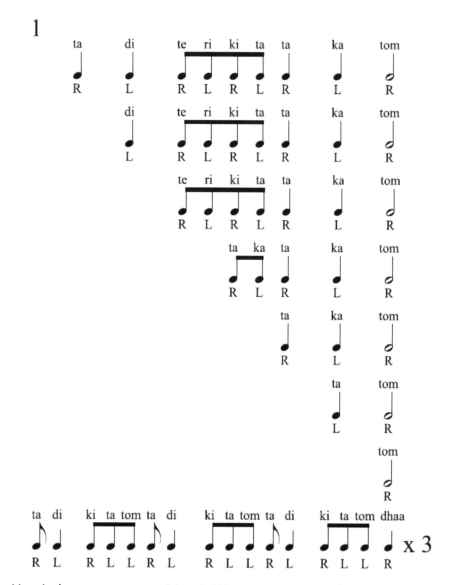

Here's the same composition in Western notation. These examples are written in "cut time" to avoid a lot of 16th and 32nd notes. The actual tempo for this piece is approximately quarter note = 100, which for the written examples makes the half note = 100. Even at that tempo the notes are moving quite fast. Of course, start very slowly and work your way up to tempo.

If you want an extended beginning, play this next composition in addition to the first one. This is a well-known drum composition that Zakir Hussain and I played as the main theme of the tune "Mad Tea Time," which is on the Magna Carta release *Modern Drummer Presents Drum Nation, Vol. 1*. The piece is played three times, and then you play the extended tihai. (Remember you can embellish the "five tihai" at the end of the piece.) After the extended tihai, your solo starts.

During your solo, try the many ideas that you've been learning in this column. If you're memorizing the examples from each month's column, you're building a vocabulary for playing with other musicians and soloing. Use the sequences of threes, fives, sevens, and nines from Part 2. End your improvised phrases with tihais, play the reductions you've learned, and try some of the rhythms from Part 4 that are repeated three times and resolve to 1. At first, you'll have to think quite a bit as you play. But the more you do it, the ideas will flow and it will get easier and more natural.

After soloing (and trading), here are two famous ending compositions. Again, these last two pieces are on *Drum Nation, Vol. 1* as well as other recordings like the tune "Get Down And Sruti" from the 1977 Shakti recording *Natural Elements*.

Continues on the following page

Indian Rhythms for *Western Drummers*

This final ending piece is an extended "five reduction." Go directly from Example 4 to Example 5.

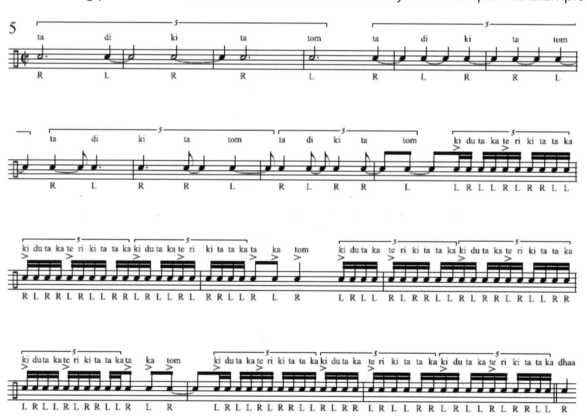

If I'm playing a solo in a Western situation, either unaccompanied or soloing over a vamp, I now use many of these concepts and compositions. These rhythms sound great in Western music, especially in fusion or rock/funk settings.

Learn the rhythms, memorize them, and take your time and play them over and over again until you get to the point where you have internalized them. Then you can start to get creative with them on the kit. Listen to Indian drummers to give you ideas of how to orchestrate the rhythms on the kit. The Web site www.abstractlogix.com has many Indian classical and Indian "fusion" recordings available.

For the Hindustani style, a fantastic recording is *The Soul of Tabla,* by Swapan Chaudhuri. Zakir Hussain has a number of outstanding solo recordings, such as *Selects* or the duo recording with his father entitled *Ustad Alla Rakha, Ustad Zakir Hussain and Ustad Sultan Khan—Shared Moments (Live— The Basle Concert).*

For the Carnatic style, listen to *Laya Vinyas* by mridangam master Trichy Sankaran (www. trichysankaran.com). Look for recordings that feature maestro A. K. Palanivel on tavil, Vikku Vinayakram on the ghatam, and his son Selvaganesh on kanjira.

Once you start doing some research, you'll find there are innumerable Indian drum solo recordings available, which can serve as pure listening pleasure and/or a plethora of ideas and inspiration for your drumset playing.

George Brooks Summit: Steve, Zakir Hussain, Fareed Haque, George Brooks, Kai Eckhardt

Steve on tour with Masters of Percussion in India 2014

The Fabric of Rhythm:
The Artwork of Steve Smith

On November 30, 2012, Steve Smith performed on a Sonor kit in a completely dark room at a Los Angeles rehearsal studio; the only source of light were the drumsticks he was using. Some of the sticks were the Vic Firth Lite Stix with LED lights in the tips. Others were plastic sticks where the entire stick lit up in a single color for a split-second upon impact. A photographer, using exposures from five to fifteen seconds, took hundreds of photos from various perspectives. Steve decided on thirteen outstanding photos and Ravi Dosaj, SceneFour's art director, worked on computer enhancements of the images. The result of this endeavor is Steve's SceneFour, Rhythm-on-Canvas, art collection entitled *The Fabric of Rhythm*.

In the beginning of 2016 Steve was approached by Cory Danziger, SceneFour's marketing director, to record spoken-word thoughts about each piece of art to be included on a vinyl LP as part of a book that would be based on the thirteen art images of *The Fabric of Rhythm* collection. Steve remembers, "When Cory said SceneFour would release a book of my artwork, plus a vinyl LP, I was hooked. But immediately, I declined the idea of spoken-word thoughts; this was the perfect opportunity to make a solo drumset album, something I had been wanting to do for many years. That was the same year that I committed to tour with Journey after not playing with

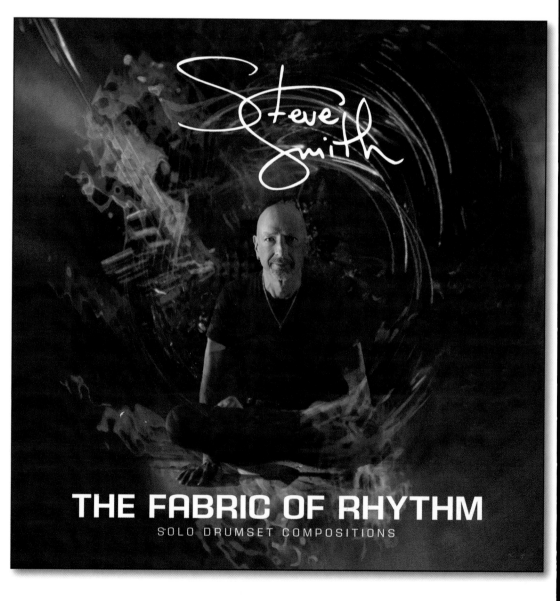

THE FABRIC OF RHYTHM
SOLO DRUMSET COMPOSITIONS

them for over 30 years. I knew it was going to be a very busy year, but I wanted to record an album of drum solos before the Journey tour started."

Steve recalls the process, "It was very inspiring to

come up with drum solo compositions that would relate to the pieces of art. That process gave me some structure to work with. I don't think I would have come up with all of the different solo ideas had it not been for the process of coming up with a solo that was something like a 'soundtrack' to the artwork, plus I knew it had to fit on a vinyl LP, approximately twenty minutes a side."

"I worked on the album the way I would work on a band recording. I wrote and conceived all of the solos, booked time in a studio, and recorded a couple of solos a day. I didn't want to do long days, because I wanted to stay fresh, so the sessions were about six hours each day. Some pieces were live performances from beginning to end and others required a basic track with overdubs. I had it all mapped out in a notebook before I went into the studio. After I finished all the recording I took a break, and went back and mixed."

"I've included solo drumset pieces on most albums that I've produced, so the idea of coming up with a stand-alone drumset solo was not new for me. But to make an entire album of solo pieces was a new experience. I would like to make another solo drumset recording whether or not there is visual art involved. On the next one I'll play a few different kits; in fact, I've already started to run with this concept. During lockdown, I started to conceive, and perform, different solo pieces that are documented on my *From the Practice Room* series on YouTube, so I have already started moving towards the next one. I really enjoy creating different drumset compositions, recording them and then playing them live, as I would play a jazz tune, with a different interpretation each time. I've been doing that for many years inspired by seeing Max Roach play solo drumset concerts. Max created great solo pieces like "The Drum Also Waltzes" and "For Big Sid" that have rhythmic and melodic hooks and he performed them live. I'll be carrying on in that tradition."

Since these solos have yet to be released in a digital format, we at Legends are proud to include these solos for you to enjoy. In the SceneFour book *The Fabric of Rhythm: The Art of Steve Smith*, Steve included detailed explanations and breakdowns of each solo piece. We recommend ordering Steve's SceneFour art book at www.stevesmithdrumart.com We asked Steve to share some thoughts on his thirteen solo pieces for *Modern Drummer* Legends.

"The Arc of The Groove."

I transcribed a few beats that I knew would work together as a piece. A compositional technique I used is: I extracted the rhythm of the bass drum from one of the grooves and used that as a rhythmic theme by itself. I orchestrated that bass drum rhythm around the toms, reinforcing the rhythms with my left hand on the Korg Wavedrum, that's the sound with the low frequencies. This solo is a series of grooves in a specific arrangement; in fact, the middle groove is the "Seven and a Half" groove played in four. Putting together grooves like this is how I come up with some Vital Information tunes. This solo was played live with no overdubs.

"Improvisation: Endless Variations."

The opening theme is an Alan Dawson "stick on stick" phrase that John Ramsey showed me. It's a hip way of playing a paradiddle-diddle figure that Alan would sometimes play as triplets and sometimes as 8th notes or 16th notes. Then I play a Max Roach melodic idea as thematic material to launch into an up-tempo jazz drumming improvisation. And what is improvisation other than "endless variations" on our own vocabulary?

"Banyan."

This is a very detailed Indian composition with konnakol and drumming, it's the most complex composition of all the solos. This was my feature when I toured with Zakir Hussain and Masters of Percussion in 2014. The themes are highly embellished but based on the simple rhythms of 3+4+5 with lots of mathematical theme and variation. There are only a few areas of improvisation, the first occurs when I settle into a groove, and scat some konnakol improvisation on top. For the compositional parts, the konnakol was overdubbed and doubled. When I stop the konnakol at 1:55 the drumset improvisation is all based on quintuplets. The improvisation at 2:53 is based on sextuplets and the improv at 3:50 is septuplets. This solo uses many individual South Indian rhythmic compositions organized into one piece.

"Zen Roll."

This is simply a press roll that starts at pianissimo, and it opens up to a fortissimo, and then closes again. You can get a smooth roll by utilizing lateral motions, like the classic Buddy Rich "whipped cream roll," I've worked

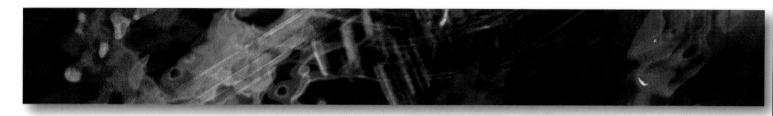

on that press roll approach quite a bit. When you look at the artwork, you can see the side-to-side, lateral motions, of the sticks on the snare head. Interestingly, this is the only solo on this set that was unable to be copywritten, because as the expert listener at ASCAP said, "it's *just* a roll."

"Condor."

This solo starts with the same basic roll as "Zen Roll," but my strokes are wider on "Condor," as you can see in the art; then it breaks into a slow 6/8 groove. This piece has a lot of parts and was planned out. I played a basic track and overdubbed two additional snare parts that I had written so I could double them exactly. Later there are metric modulations that go to a few places and eventually come back to the original tempo. It's an exercise in theme and variation, and what you can do within a specific tempo.

"Infinity Knot Part One."

Drummer/philosopher Efrain Toro introduced the idea to me, of playing the harmonic overtone series as rhythms on the drumset. This is my interpretation of that idea. Playing with mallets, with the snares off, I start with one note on the 18" floor tom, graduate to two notes and then three. Once I get to three, I play an ostinato in three on my pedals and keep that going throughout. After that you'll hear me ascend the rhythmic scale: four, five, six, seven, eight, nine, ten, eleven and finally twelve. After that I methodically descend in reverse order. Taking the time to learn to play this has helped me immensely in gaining rhythmic freedom on the kit.

"Infinity Knot Part Two."

After the structure of Infinity Knot Part One, I wanted to interpret the art with a loose improvisation using sticks.

Steve Smith Library

"Choreography of Sound."

Some people might recognize the first rhythmic theme; it's from Tony Williams'"Some Hip Drum Shit." He also played this on the Lifetime live clip from Montreux on YouTube (with Warren Smith and Don Alias playing percussion.) The opening idea is in 6/4 which led to the second theme, which is a 6/4 groove that I used on some of my more recent Journey drum solos. I keep the solo in 6/4 and you can really hear the drummer-perspective panning with my side-snare panned hard left.

"Fire and Ice."

Another extended Indian inspired piece that mixes composition and improvisation. The composed parts are the

left and right panned "snare drum with konnakol" parts, reminiscent of two konnakol artists having a duet. The two parts go back and forth, and then they eventually come together. The composed parts are broken up by different grooves with some improvisation. One of the grooves is a beat that I love from the Broadway musical *Hamilton*; I play it with a washy ride and a high-pitched side-snare. The main South Indian composition was taught to me by ghatam master Vikku Vinayakram. Vikku was booked to play some gigs with Summit, he flew into the USA

Steve Smith Library

and we picked him up at LAX. As soon as he got in the van, he began teaching me this composition, he didn't even say "hello." And then he said, "We will play this tonight!" I didn't get it *absolutely right* on that first night, but by the second night of the tour, I got it right. This piece took time to work out, and record, all the various elements.

"The Bat."

It sounds like there might be some overdubbing on this, but I assure you that this is one live performance, except that I doubled my konnakol part. I'm playing steady eighth notes on the Korg Wavedrum with my left hand as a bass part and playing the 2 & 4 on a 12" snare drum to the left of the Wavedrum. With my right hand I trigger the chords on the rim of the Wavedrum and play the hi-hat, cymbals and main snare. Using the double bass pedal, I play phrases that first "reduce," going sequentially 777, 666, 555, 444, 333, 222, then a tihai.

The next compositional part plays the same rhythms in reverse, they "expand," 222, 333, 444, 555, 666, 777, plus a tihai; then they "reduce" again with an extended tihai at the end. I've played this solo often live and I have a tutorial and demonstration of the solo on a Hudson Music video pack.

"Kinetic Dance."

The subtitle of this is "Tihai Training." It's an exercise in improvisation and ending phrases with tihai's. A tihai is a rhythm or a phrase that is repeated three times and then comes to beat "1." After eight bars of an introduction groove, I play the "theme," 7+9, 7+9, 7+9, 7+7, 9+9, 7+7+7, 9+9+9, which is 8 bars of 4/4; then we start the tihai training. I improvise for 8 bars and end with a 5+5+5 tihai, improvise for 8 bars and play a 6+6+6 tihai and so on, using the tihai's: 7+7+7, 8+8+8, 9+9+9 and 10+10+10. Then the opening theme, and onto 4 bars of improv and the same set of tihais, finally the 2-bar improv is so short I'm essentially playing the

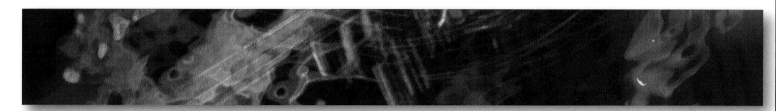

tihai's from 5+5+5 to 10+10+10. You have to make sure that you know where to start the tihai's in the improv so they come out right, that's why I call it, "Tihai Training." Having all of those tihai's in your back pocket is a pretty good rhythmic arsenal to have. I overdubbed the konnakol and the Korg Wavedrum, playing it very lightly with my hands.

"Quadraphonic."

This is a drum groove that I came up with for a Zildjian demonstration, which I filmed at the Zildjian factory. I thought the beat had a cool hook to it and incorporated the hi-hats creatively. Vinny Valentino heard it and wrote a tune around the beat, which became the title track of the Vital Information album "Heart of the City."

"Interdependence."

The melody of this piece I've used for many years. It first appeared on the 1996 Vital Information album *Ray of Hope* and the piece is called "Maxed Out," in an obvious reference to Max Roach. The AABA melody, played on five toms, is quite versatile and I've played it in many different ways over the years. On my 2002 Hudson video *Drumset Technique/History of the U.S. Beat* I played the melody over a left-hand snare drum ostinato and called it "Interdependence." For this recording I play the melody with three different interpretations. The first time is with mallets, and the double bass drum pedal, using the hand-foot pattern Right Hand, Left Foot, Left Hand, Right Foot. This was especially difficult because crossovers were needed to play parts of the melody plus, I played with a light touch at a low volume. For

Nick Kirby

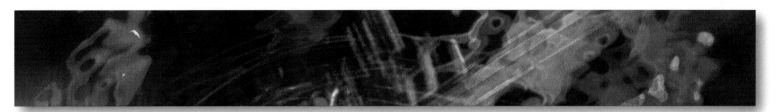

the second part of "Interdependence," I play the jazz swing rhythm on the hi-hat with my left hand, playing the melody and improvisation with my right hand. The third interpretation uses the same double bass/hi-hat ostinato as the Raga Bop Trio tune "Katyayini," keeping the jazz ride beat on a left-side ride cymbal, and again, playing the melody and improvising with my right hand.

"Cymbalic Alchemy."

The artwork for this looks like you are peering at a distant galaxy. This is all cymbals, sometimes played with sticks and sometimes mallets. I held a mic in my hand during the recording and at times, put the mic up to the edge of a cymbal to hear the overtones. Especially interesting was putting the mic between the two hi-hat cymbals as they vibrated. It felt like a nice way to end the album, with a spacious soundscape.

All the content of *The Fabric of Rhythm* is available as a digital download.

To listen to these recordings you can find the download code on page 1 of this issue of Legends.

Steve Smith Library

Album Credits:
The Arc Of The Groove
Improvisation: Endless Variations
Banyan
Zen Roll
Condor
Infinity Knot Pt. 1 (Harmonic Overtones)
Infinity Knot Pt. 2
Choreography Of Sound
Fire & Ice
The Bat
Kinetic Dance (Tihai Training)
Quadraphonic
Interdepence
Cymbalic Alchemy

Produced by Steve Smith
Recorded and Mixed by Nick Kirby
Recorded at Foundation Soundstage, Ashland, Oregon
Recorded January 27-29, February 1-4, 2016. Mixed February 5-9, 2016.
Mastered by George Horn and Anne-Marie Suenram
at Fantasy Studios, Berkeley, CA on February 12, 2016
All music by Steve Smith - Vital Information Publishing ASCAP
Administered by Wixen Music Publishing, Inc.
Drum Legacy Records
www.stevesmithdrumart.com

LOOKING

1981: Steve Smith

Journeyman

By Robyn Flans

Although Journey has been around for eight years, tremendous public acclaim has come for the band only recently, particularly gaining momentum within the last three years of existence. With the addition of lead singer and writer Steve Perry, five albums ago, Journey's music has encountered much more mass appeal. Perry's first album with Journey called *Infinity*, released in 1978, rose steadily in the charts, finally becoming top 20, while their following album, *Evolution*, attained a top 20 position much faster with the inclusion of their first top 20 single, "Lovin', Touchin', Squeezin'." *Departure* and their live album *Captured*, rose quickly as well, and their current record *Escape*, the first album sans keyboardist Gregg Rolie and with new member Jonathan Cain, begins the first in a new trilogy, displaying Journey's constant development and change.

Another change occurred four albums ago in 1978 when band members decided to replace drummer Aynsley Dunbar with their present drummer. Steve Smith. As Perry told the *Seattle Times*, "The reason we

BACK

changed is because we want to have the versatility to do anything we want. With Aynsley that was impossible. He definitely was one of those stylized drummers. He has a fantastic style, really strong, but I just feel the nature of the word 'journey' is a movement situation. We had to change because *Evolution* could not have been done with Aynsley."

With Smith, band members envision greater opportunity for variety, which confirms that the extensive training Smith has received since the age of nine, has certainly been worthwhile.

"I never really decided that this was going to be my profession," Smith said, seated in his hotel room close to L.A.'s Forum, where Journey would be performing that evening. "It is just what happened. I never thought about doing anything else. When I look at it now, it's like, I can't help but be a drummer. It's just a strong feeling to want to play the drums. I can't live without that."

Growing up in Whitman, Massachusetts, 25 miles south of Boston, Smith became interested in the drums while at a fourth-grade assembly. Soon, he began taking lessons in elementary school. His parents, who remained supportive of his musical aspirations, found him a local private teacher by the name of Bill Flanagan, and Smith started learning the technical aspects of reading and playing the rudiments, staying with Flanagan from the fourth grade through the twelfth grade. In the sixth grade, he got his first drum set, a Rogers Champagne-sparkle set, and in the eighth grade, he played in his first band, The Road Runners, a horn band that played a lot of Herb Alpert and Tijuana Brass material.

By high school, the music Smith was listening to was a cross between Count Basie to Oscar Peterson type trios, Jimi Hendrix, and Cream, and he began playing in a rock and roll band that played a lot of Grand Funk Railroad and Deep Purple tunes. At the same time, Bridgewater State College in the town next to Whitman, had a big band in desperate need of a drummer, and Smith managed to fill that position, while also working in a circus band to earn some money. Upon his graduation from high school in 1972, Smith decided

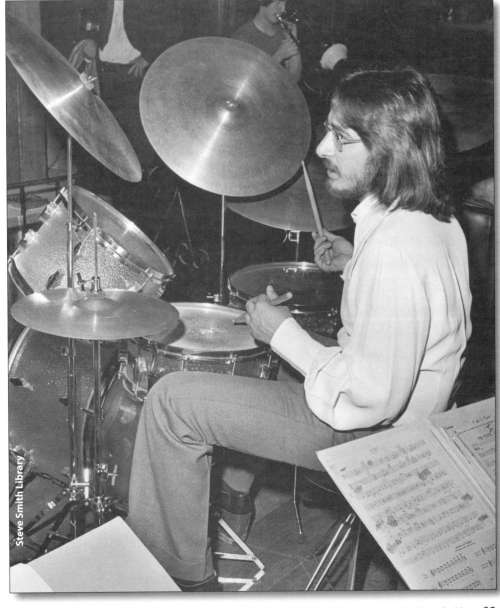

Steve Smith Library

to further his education and enrolled at the Berklee College of Music in Boston.

"My parents were always very supportive of my music, but the one thing my dad would always say was that he didn't know if I would be able to make a living at being a musician, so he felt that I should get a degree in music education. I didn't really want to do that, but it was a chance for me to go to Berklee. I wasn't really ready to go out and play anyway. I was just 18 and I didn't really feel that I was ready to make a living at it."

"All through high school, I had been doing a lot of different kinds of things, and the thing that helped me the most was my reading ability, but I didn't really have great time back then. The things my teacher had stressed the most were sight reading and chops, and while it was good background, he had never really stressed time and feeling. That was something that I didn't learn until after I was out of high school. It was when I got to Berklee that I really started to find

Lin Biviano Big Band

Steve Smith Library

out that reading was great, but I needed to develop a strong sense of time. After my first year at Berklee, I went to a Stan Kenton clinic. Peter Erskine was the drum teacher and he had a way of playing time and demonstrating time that I really tuned into and picked up on. He was probably my strongest help as far as time is concerned."

Smith's newly acquired focus altered his practice techniques radically. "Through the years I had always practiced from slow to fast, but then I found out that that's the worst possible thing any drummer can do for his time. If you practice like that, you end up playing like that. After that clinic, I started practicing everything in time and in meter. I started playing along with the metronome and records and being really conscious about it, and then I looked for bass players who were better than I was, who would work with me. That was the best thing about Berklee—there were so many musicians. Every night I could find people to play with. That's where I got a lot of practical playing experience, playing every night with somebody, whether it was a gig or just a jam session. To improve my time, I geared myself to

Trumpeter Lin Biviano with Steve on drums

Steve Smith Library

think in that way. I really set out in search of wanting to play with good feel and I think that was probably the most important thing I did. I know a lot of players who don't play with good feel but haphazardly think that you're either born with it or you're not. You must develop it, so I tried to do everything to do so. I talked to people about it and listened to a lot of records, like a lot of Aretha records with Bernard Purdie and a lot of old James Brown records and studied in- depth exactly what notes were being played. I would try to write it down and then try to play it and get the same feeling they had gotten. I guess I understood the importance. Most of the young people I know now, and those I have taught, don't realize the importance of working on their time and feeling. They think it's more important to work on their flash, chops, technique, and reading. If they would only understand that it's time and feeling that is going to get them the work, they would devote themselves to do that."

Because he has gotten so much out of the clinics he attended, Smith now conducts them whenever he has the chance. "I don't know that many drum shops where I really like to do them, though," he admitted. "I went to one where it was, 'Okay, go in there and sell some drum sets,' and that kind of feeling is not really conducive to doing a good clinic. I would rather just do a few of them but do them at places where the people are really sincere about them, like the Creative Drum Shop in Scottsdale, Arizona."

After returning from the Stan Kenton clinic, which Smith termed "the most valuable learning experience I ever had," he got his first professional gig with Lin Biviano, a trumpet player who had worked with Buddy Rich and Maynard Ferguson. While continuing his studies at Berklee, Smith spent two years touring weekends and summers with Biviano's 15-piece modern big band. For a brief period, he also played with

clarinetist Buddy DeFranco in a quintet.

One semester Smith was given a full scholarship to go to the University of Tulsa in Oklahoma because their stage band needed a drummer. Discontented with the lacking music scene in Oklahoma, Smith stayed only one semester, forfeited his scholarship, and returned to Berklee for his seventh semester.

It was shortly thereafter that bass player Jeff Berlin, with whom Smith had played many times, asked Smith to accompany him to New York for an audition for Jean-Luc Ponty's band. Both musicians got the gig, but only Smith accepted the position, and in October, 1976, close to his graduation, Smith left Berklee for his first important gig.

Ronnie Montrose and Steve

Steve Smith Library

"What I've done is followed my opportunities rather than setting out in a direction and following that direction. I was capable of playing almost any type of music, so I would just go with what came along, and really, it all felt good to me. I had really been into the ECM style, but I got away from that because that wasn't really happening for me. If I had gotten a gig doing that, I would have probably gone in that direction, but I got the gig with Jean-Luc, so I went into the heavier fusion style of drumming.

"It was a great experience to play with great players in Jean-Luc's group. I had to be real consistent and I was learning a lot because I had never played with such a consistent group of people. But from being in that group, the one thing I learned that I didn't want, was to work for somebody who was always telling me what to do and telling everyone what to play. I wanted to be more in control." After a year and three months, Ponty fired two guitar players along with Smith all at once "because he wanted to change his musical direction and wasn't happy with us anymore."

Smith moved to Los Angeles for a brief time, and after auditioning for Freddie Hubbard and Ronnie Montrose, he was chosen for both gigs. "I had the choice of staying *in jazz* and being a sideman and playing for a leader, or playing with Ronnie, who was into rock and roll. The biggest difference was that Ronnie's band was more group oriented and he would let me have a lot to say and let me play more. I really wanted to be more a part of a group, which is why I decided to go with Ronnie. I also wanted to learn how to play authentic rock because I still hadn't really played that. He let me play very free because the tour I did with them was an instrumental kind of fusion rock." Since Montrose spent half its tour opening for Journey, Smith became very friendly with its key members, and at the conclusion of his tour with Montrose in August 1978 Journey asked Smith if he would like to join their band. He did so the following month.

"I love playing in this band," Smith smiled. "The way I look at it is, if I weren't playing in this band, I probably wouldn't be playing rock and roll at all. The thing that this band had to offer that I like so much is the high caliber of musicianship. Steve Perry and Neal Schon (guitarist) are people that I really respect and are great to work with. I've probably learned more from Steve than from most people because Steve, himself, is a drummer. He started out as a drummer, so the concept I've learned from him is how to play drums behind a singer, and how to play really strong rock and roll drums. I had never played with a singer before. It had always been instrumental music, so I really needed his input to help me. I have to play much wider time. By wider time, I mean you have to be careful not to squeeze the measures so the end of the measure comes too soon. A lot of drummers can play good time, but sometimes their meter within the time is a little off. The notes get squeezed together and the spaces in between the

Steve Smith Library

notes aren't perfect. That's what I had to learn: to make my measures all fit exactly into place so nothing gets squeezed; so that the notes are evenly spaced; for every note to get its full value, and to be stronger and even more soulful—more feeling in my playing. I had to tune into what he was doing and think. 'What would I do if I were singing? How would the beat sit right so I could sing easily over this?' I've applied that to everything now. I'm pulling together all the background I have and everything I've learned musically, all kinds of odd groupings, time signatures and phrasings and I'm trying to put it all together into a style that I can use in this band. It's a whole new style within rock and roll.

It's really hard to say exactly what style Journey is. The way we approach it is as musicians that are playing definitely within a rock world with a rock public, but trying to come up with music that we are really proud of. Music that will still appeal to the masses. That's the direction I want my playing to go. To use everything that I've learned musically, and without obscuring myself, I want to try to put it into a new kind of package that is really interesting, which, at the same time, everyone can hear and appreciate." The fact that Journey is finally receiving mass recognition has created certain benefits for Smith that did not exist before, including an increasing seriousness about his position. "Something inside of me is giving me a constant inspiration to constantly practice and perform. Before, it was really hard work to go in and practice, without much to look forward to. It's really hard to inspire yourself, but getting as popular as we are getting is a constant inspiration to continue to practice. If many people like me and are buying our records and coming to see us, I've got to really play something for them. It keeps me working really hard and has made me even more intense about growing musically. Another couple of benefits of the success has been that I can afford to get a house so I can stay in the house and practice, pick and choose a little more of what I want to do, and afford to get the different drums I want."

Smith has gone through several drum sets, including a Rogers, a Fibes and a Slingerland. When he joined Ponty. He got a Sonor set, which he has played ever since. "When I first went out with Ponty I had my basic little Gretsch set with the 20" bass drum, two mounted toms and a floor tom. After I had done one tour with him, he asked me if I'd get a bigger set. I actually needed a stronger sounding drum set, which is why I got the Sonor set with two 24" bass drums. I'm mainly looking for a really big, fat sound, and that's what I get with those drums. Gretsch drums really have a good sound too, but the Sonor drums are even bigger sounding for what I need right now." His live and recording set-ups are identical, using almost all Sonor drums. For some time, he was using two 24" bass drums, but then decided to use one 24" and one 22". "The reason I went down in size was for a little different sound, and also so that the hi-hat is a little closer," Smith explained. His toms consist of 9 x 13 and 10 x 14 mounted toms, and 16 x 16 and 16 x 18 floor toms. Steve has two snare drums which he alternately plays, a regular Sonor metal, 6 1/2" deep snare and a Slingerland Spitfire. On his snare, he uses the Remo Fiberskyn 2 head.

"That's the best snare drum sound I've ever heard because it gives the drum a muffled sound. I don't like the snare sound to be real ringy and I don't like the sound if you put a muffler or tape on it either, because then it's too thuddy. This new head gives it the crack and more of a funky sound. The only thing is that they

Jean-Luc Ponty and Steve

Steve Smith Library

don't last too long. I go through two a night, although I was going through one a night anyway when I was using the other heads." On his other drums he uses Remo clear Ambassadors on both tops and bottoms. He cuts a hole in front of each bass drum to get a better mike sound and doesn't put any muffling on any of his drums. Steve uses Dean Markley Stix which are comparable to a 5B, and a DW 5000 chain foot pedal with a felt beater.

Smith's cymbal set-up is extremely practical. Last year, one of his roadies. Jim McCandless, invented a unit of two large bars on which all the boom stands are built.

"There are no cymbal stands going down to the floor. They're just coming off of this T-bar," Smith explained. "It's also easy for him to put up and take down. I wouldn't have been able to use as many cymbals as I do if it were not for this invention. If I were just using cymbal stands, I would have only been able to use four or five, but I really like having all the different sounds." He has recently switched to Zildjian because, "In the bigger places that we're playing now, the sound is a lot thicker." His cymbals include a 24" heavy ride, 16", 17", 18", 19", 20", 22" crashes, an 18" swish, a 22" swish, an 11" splash, and 14" hi-hats.

Smith takes an entire spare drum set on the road now, with which to practice. It is combination of some of the old drum sets he has, with a 20"Gretsch drum, an 18" Sonor bass drum

up for the evening's concert, if I go out there cold and start hitting hard right away, I'll lose my muscles and they'll either tense up or rubber up and I'll get out of control." He also has a drum machine that he uses for his practice and feels that it is a good way to work on time, and more interesting than a metronome.

For Journey's upcoming 1981 tour, Smith will be changing his equipment to include the new Sonor Signature set with longer drums. His red custom-made

Jean-Luc Ponty Band: Allan Zavod, JLP, Steve, Ralphe Armstrong, Daryl Stuermer

Steve Smith Library

and some Pearl concert toms. "The worst part about going on the road in the beginning was that I couldn't practice. I had to practice on a little practice pad and that was a drag. Now that we're playing in the type of places that we are, I can afford to have a guy who does nothing but take care of my drums and I can carry an extra set along. I practice a couple of hours every afternoon. I never run out of things. Every single day I have all kinds of new ideas and new things to work on and to play. The two-hour practice serves as my warm-

12-ply wood set will have an 8" deep wood snare, two 22" bass drums, and four mounted toms in sizes of 10", 12", 13" and 14" with 16 x 18 and 18 x 20 floor toms. "What's different about them is they have all brand-new super heavy-duty hardware and the drums are extra long with a really big sound and more tone. They're comparable to buying a Steinway Grand piano and they cost about $6,800. It's a new concept in drums.

Steve will also be returning to a smaller cymbal set-up with regular cymbal stands for a different feel and look. At home, he has some Synare equipment which has accompanied him on various tours, but he prefers just using his regular set. "When I'm at home. I use the Synare 2 a lot to set up odd time signatures and stuff, but I haven't used it live. One of the reasons goes back to the recording sound. What Journey is trying to do when we record an album, is record a timeless record that you can buy now, or you can buy later, and it will still sound good. If I put a Syndrum sound on it, which I believe is just a fad, it will date our records."

He has also participated in Journey's writing and hopes to do more of it. Smith is thrilled about the fact that when the tunes are being written, the band leaves it wide open for him to come up with his part. "What I like most is the freedom of improvisation. It's a certain level of communication between players. We have a certain level of communication where you can create spontaneously."

Another such situation for Smith is a trio with which he is involved in his spare time. The trio consists of Smith, Tom Coster, keyboardist and producer for Santana, and bassist Randy Jackson who used to play with Billy Cobham. In addition to performing live, they plan to record in the near future as well. "We're all coming from kind of the same place of playing in rock bands. The concept is that we're trying to play something that we don't have to compromise on or make saleable, because we don't have to earn money from it. We all have our other thing which we earn money from. So we just get together and play. We got together for a month off and on to rehearse, and we played a gig at the Keystone Corner in San Francisco. It went really well, so now. whenever we have the chance, we're going to keep it together and try

Journey

Steve Smith Library

to play a lot and record. The music itself is going to be in a different direction because it's coming from a different place. My background is in really authentic jazz and rock. Our backgrounds are really true, so we're going to come up with an interesting music. That's the perfect outlet for the direction that I've been developing. Journey is also, but it's more on a mass appeal level. I don't think I would be able to do this thing if I hadn't been in Journey." In his spare time, he has also been doing sessions at Fantasy Studios to keep his other musical playing capabilities vital and alive.

He has been involved with Sonor as much as possible and represented them at the Frankfurt trade show last February, as well as having done a clinic for Zildjian last November at the Percussive Arts Society, in which he was the first rock drummer to participate.

A project of which Smith is particularly proud is an album recorded with Journey in Japan at the close of their 1980 tour. Group members wrote and performed a score for a film called *Dream After Dream*. While it will not be released in the U.S., the band felt it would help build their Japanese following and present new musical challenges. Mostly instrumental with strings and horns, the effort bears little resemblance to the group's past albums, but Smith said. "I think my playing is some of the best playing I've ever done on any record."

At 26, Smith is pleased with the way things have gone. "There is no real ultimate goal," he concluded. "I just want to keep playing, keep developing like I have been, keep playing with good musicians, and come up with new music."

1986: Steve Smith
The Next Step

By Robyn Flans

When I met Steve Smith in 1980, I must admit that I knew little about him, as I was contacted about the interview only one day prior to our scheduled meeting. Of course, there wasn't that much to know either. The band he was in, Journey, had only had one top-20 hit two years earlier with "Lovin', Touchin', Squeezin'. " Yet, they were due to play one of L.A. 's largest venues, the Forum, that night. Soon after that, however, there was no mistaking the band's success. *Departure* sold 1.6 million records in 1980, *Captured*, Journey's live album, sold 1. 4 million, and in that same year, 1981, *Escape* sold 6 million, making it obvious that, for this group, the sky would be the limit. It was also obvious that the new chemistry accounted for this success. With the addition of vocalist Steve Perry in 1977, Smith in 1978, and Jonathan Cain in 1980, the elements were just right.

What I suspected, but didn't know during our first interview, was that Journey was the odd gig of Smith's career. I knew that his background included working with Jean-Luc Ponty, and that he was asked to play with Freddie Hubbard (although he chose to go with Montrose instead,) but he seemed tailor-made for Journey.

Steve Smith Library

I learned that Steve can play anything, but he is a jazz musician at heart.

In 1983, that was made clear when he regrouped some musicians with whom he had played during his days as a student at the Berklee College of Music. They released their first, self-titled LP, *Vital Information*, followed a year later by *Orion*. Currently in release is their finest effort to date, *Global Beat*, of which Steve is very proud. What he is most excited about, however, is that, now that he is no longer a member of Journey, he will be able to put all his energy into playing the music he most loves with his own band, as well as with Steps Ahead, of which he has recently become a member. It is obvious that, while the last several months have been a period of intense change and growth for Steve, he is finally enjoying the opportunity to blossom into the musician and artist he truly is.

RF: Tell me about the infamous practice sessions you are known for.

SS: There have been all different kinds. The first kind took place from the time I was in eighth grade through my high school years. My practice sessions then didn't take place on the drum set. I used to practice on a practice pad all the time-just practicing to records. Half of it would be trying to understand the different drum parts and copying them, and the other part would be improvising, using the record for tempo. I think that not practicing on a drum set then was a mistake. It would have been better if I had, because I would have developed faster as a drum set player. Practicing on the pad was very good for my hands, but I didn't really get much of a workout for my feet, or for being agile on the kit and developing a touch for the drums and cymbals. But the teacher I had back then, Billy Flanagan, really insisted that I practice on the pad. He was an old-school guy who grew up learning very rudimentally. He was a big band drummer who did get into drum set, but he was very insistent that I practice sight reading and that my hands get a lot of chops. That's what I concentrated on in those practice sessions, and they would be hours and hours long. When I had days off from school and during summer vacation, I would just practice all day.

Then through college, I didn't really practice a lot. When I was going to Berklee, I *played* a lot. I'd play for hours every day. Each day in school, we had sessions or ensembles, so I got a lot of chances to play. At night, if there wasn't a gig, it was a session that a bunch of people would put together so we could play. I really learned how to play music just through the experience of playing. That's different from learning how to play the drums. I just kind of relied on the chops I had developed before I got there. And I thought it was the cool thing not to practice, but just to play a lot. Again, in retrospect, a balance would have been the right thing to do.

RF: Why did you think it was cool?

SS: It was just what was going on there at the time. It seemed like the thing to do. Certain things become hip in your environment, and that was one of the things that was hip. It was like, "Well, I bet Elvin Jones doesn't practice." It was coming from there.

Then when I was on the road with Ponty and Montrose, again, there was not much practicing-just playing. There was just enough practicing to keep in shape and to keep from getting rusty. When I joined Journey, I had the time and a real need to practice, because I really needed to get a lot of new chops together. Those chops were not what I used to think chops were, which was playing fast and hard. At this

point, the chops I needed were playing very slow and steady. Those weren't things that I had a good background in.

RF: So they were chops primarily for the Journey gig?

SS: Right. I started practicing for the gig. That's a good point, because before, I used to practice just to play the drums, and it almost didn't relate to what I was doing every night. I would practice my weekly lesson, which would be this very complex thing, like all these polyrhythms. I would practice them enough to do my lesson each week, but it didn't relate at all to the gig I was playing at night or even the jam session I was doing in the evening. But the practice sessions when I joined Journey related very much to what I needed to learn to make it happen for that gig.

RF: How did you learn to play slow?

SS: By practicing with a drum machine. That was really the best thing for me. I just got a cheap Roland drum machine, and turned it up real loud through a guitar or bass amplifier. I would spend hours practicing to it.

I could play the things I wanted to play, and I could tell if they were coming out right by what they sounded like and how my playing felt if I taped it. I'd listen to the tape and say, "Okay, that sounds right. Now what did it feel like when I did that?" And I'd try to remember the feeling of what it was like for all the notes to land just in the right places. Even though it was real slow and there was a lot of room for error between those notes, it did have a certain feel. Then I would really try to tune into what it felt like, so I didn't have to rely on the drum machine. I could take it away, remember that same feeling, and try to recreate it every time I played. Eventually, it started sinking in. I developed a practice technique. I found that what really helped me to nail down those slow tempos was to play a samba pattern very slowly, to keep my feet going very steady, and not even play my hands. I was trained from the hands down, and found out that music is built the opposite way. It's really built from the bottom up, so I had to practice a lot with my feet and get them under control without them following my hands. I would practice with my feet and then add the hands, just playing very simple things, like quarter notes or 8th notes. At those slow tempos, it's very easy to put the beats in the wrong place, just a little bit ahead or a little bit behind, because there is so much space in between the notes. Finally, I started getting the feel of that, building it from the bottom up, and eventually, it started feeling more and more comfortable to the point where I could go in the studio, play live, and have it feel really great all the time. It took a long time. I would practice for four or five hours every day, and if I didn't practice that many hours in a day, at least I would practice something every day. I really noticed that, if I practiced every day, it made a difference.

RF: Were there other considerations for the Journey situation coming from your background?

SS: I practiced double bass drums, which I had never practiced before. I started working on that quite a bit.

RF: How did you work on that?

SS: At first, I just got the other bass drum, stuck it on there, and played it with the left foot leading, because that was what my hi-hat was used to doing. Eventually, I started thinking about it and working things out a little. I found out that I wanted to lead with my right foot. That way, when I did fills with my feet and with my hands, it would come out on the downbeat with the foot and the hands together. I got this book called *Bass Drum Control* by Colin Bailey. It's written for one bass drum, and it's a series of exercises using your hands and one bass drum. I just disregarded his concept of having it be for one bass drum and used it for two bass drums. I played everything with a right-left, right-left, right-left sticking, or hand-to-foot combination. Everything I worked on had that same right-left, right-left, right-left approach. I would just practice what was written in the book and try to get the dexterity, so I wasn't locked into a bunch of licks. I could have the freedom to hear something and be able to play it, which is basically how I've played all my life. I practice so that I can improvise, and not just to learn a series of licks to pull off. I try to get a command over a conception and develop the conception so I can improvise with it. So I did the same thing with the two bass drums.

Another thing I had to practice, believe it or not, was dynamics. In Journey, we played a lot softer than I had ever played with other bands-keeping the tempo really steady, but still playing soft and then playing very loud.

RF: Is there a way to learn that?

SS: It's the same thing. When you practice, practice with dynamics. Don't practice everything at the same volume level. It's very easy to do. Try to practice musically and not practice a separate thing from when you perform. You have to be thinking that it's very similar.

For my first three years in Journey, I did that intense practicing as much as I could. I practiced not only the slow tempos, but all different tempos. I practiced a lot with the drum machine to make myself very aware of my time, my tempo, and the spacing of the notes-the subdivision of the beats. Those were things that were brought to my attention especially by Steve Perry, who is a good drummer himself and has great time as a musician. He made me very aware of those things, because he needs them in order to do what he has to do. He really demanded that of me. Then he helped me find out how to develop that, too. After three years, I started feeling very secure and very comfortable with the Journey music and the drumming I had to do conceptually to play the music. So I started spending more of my practice time practicing jazz, applying those ideas to things I had learned in jazz, practicing my swing time with the drum machine again, and making it very accurate. I started practicing jazz, jazz-rock, and all of those things I had played before, but now I started seriously practicing them and trying to get them a lot more under control than they ever were before. I was finally learning how to practice as a complete thing, not just with the hands on a practice pad and not just practicing enough to get by. I learned how to make that practice session really mean something and come out with a good end result that I could apply. I started feeling, "Okay, this feels good. I can put this aside and deal with it on a day-to-day basis." I had the space in my mind and in my playing to be seriously interested in the jazz again. So I started practicing that with the same approach.

I found that it was really starting to develop to the point where the next step I needed was an outlet to actually play it. I was playing it a little bit, off and on, but I didn't get the chance to really do it until I met Tom Coster and started playing with him. That kept developing, and then I was playing with the White Boys, which has now become Vital Information. We've been together for a long time. That started happening more often until it got to the point where we decided that we'd go into the studio and record. We did a record, Columbia put it out, and we went on tour for two months. I didn't practice during that time, because I didn't really have time, but my playing really progressed to the best it's ever been, because I was getting a chance to play the music that really demanded the most of me. It demanded that I had the rock chops, the jazz chops, and the fusion chops.

Steve Smith Library

In two-and-a-half months, we played about 50 gigs, so I really played a lot every night. That brought it all together and made a complete circle.

RF: Like you said, you brought it all together-the rock chops and the jazz chops. Can you be specific about the difference between them?

SS: One thing about rock playing is that, first of all, it has to be very supportive. That's basically the role. In jazz music, the role is to be supportive too, but also to be very much of a participant in what's going on with the entire group and to interact, on the spur of the moment, with the improvisation that's going on. With rock 'n' roll drumming, there's very little of that interaction. It's mostly supportive in the sense that you're being a composer. The most creative part of the gig is when the song has been written, it's been brought to you, and you have to come up with a drum part. There's where you have to do the work to come up with the right thing to play to make the song come alive. Once that's done, it's basically part of the composition, so even when you play the song live, you have that as the center. You almost have to stick to what you did on the record, because people become so familiar with that. It's part of the song-even the drum fills. I don't play it exactly like the record all the time, but I really stick close to it.

In jazz music, there's the interaction, but most of the time, when I play on a jazz record-my own record or Tom Coster's record, and even when I played on Ponty's record-it doesn't really have to be exactly the same live.

It is close-the same kind of feel or something-but there is a lot more room to change it, and there's a demand to change it. If you played it the same every time, it would cease to be jazz.

There's a generalization that rock drumming is strong all the time, usually loud, very deliberate, holding the time down, and real solid. Jazz time, on the other hand-say swing time-is very light with a lot of forward motion, and the whole feel of swing is a completely different feel-that triplet feel of swing versus the 16th-note or 8th-note feel of rock 'n' roll. The time has to be strong. It can't be nebulous, but lots of times, it's implied as much as it is stated, so it's a very different approach.

RF: How do you fuse the two?

SS: I put them together just for my own music, which is a part of who I am as a person, and what personal experiences I've had as a rock musician and a jazz musician. I'll try to do exactly what I've described, but all in the course of maybe one record or one song sometimes, in order to have that kind of lightness and implied time together with something that's very strong and forceful. Another way of blending the two together is to improvise using jazz phrasing and jazz ideas, but playing them with a rock sound-very strong and powerful. 'So I'm actually playing what a jazz drummer would traditionally play very light and very sensitively, but playing it very strong with two bass drums and with the toms. Sometimes, I even change things I would play in a triplet context in the jazz playing into 16th note concepts and play them in the rock feel with the rock sound. That's why, if someone saw me playing a drum solo in a Journey concert, even though it was rock energy in intensity and it had the rock beat, the information I was playing was coming very much from a jazz school. It was the combination of the phrasing and the drums I used, and the way I was approaching the drum set was very much from a jazz approach. An approach I developed on the drums, which is a jazz idea, is to see the drum set without a road map, in order to avoid the typical high tom to low tom, one-way street type of approach. I spent a lot of time thinking about it, watching great jazz drummers like Eric Gravatt and Tony Williams-two people who really approach the drum set from that manner-and also studying with Gary Chaffee. You try to think of all the different motions that are available on the drum set,

and then you try them out. Some of them are just going to sound dumb, but some of them are going to sound great and very different.

RF: Were these the things you were practicing during the first three years of practice sessions with Journey?

SS: No. I wasn't really concentrating on that. I was just practicing the basics of being able to get the timing, the feel, and those things right. That's what I talked about a lot during the last interview, and that's what I was really consumed with then. Once I thought that I had a good command over the time and the feel, then I was open to explore the creativity part of it. I felt that I had been presented with the information backwards. First, I learned how to approach the drums in these different ways when I was at Berklee, but nobody had ever spent any time trying to help me develop my time. They were giving me other things before the basics, so I went back and re-learned everything with the right perspective knowing that I had to get the time together before the other thing could happen.

RF: Have you found that reading has been necessary?

SS: I'm really glad that I can read, and I've found it necessary to develop all the different chops I have and the different styles of playing, because I've relied heavily on reading the material out of a bunch of different books. A lot of times, it made the difference of getting a certain gig. For example, I needed to read on Jean-Luc Ponty's gig, because I only had four days to learn his music. There have been many other situations where reading has been necessary.

RF: We touched on where your education fell short a little bit. What did your education do for you? What did it prepare you for, and what didn't it prepare you for?

SS: There are some definite problems and disadvantages when it's all education and not a whole lot of practical learning. The first problem is that teachers are probably teachers because they are not very good players. That's something I ran up against. I had teachers who were great for expanding my mind and filling it with credible information, but when it came down to practical playing, they didn't have the right information. If they did, they probably wouldn't be teaching, or teaching as much. That's a real problem. You can pick up your teacher's bad habits, which I experienced, and I had to go through unlearning and relearning.

On the positive side, though, it helped me learn the

discipline of being a practicing musician, instead of a musician who just learned a particular song. This is very general, but I find it to be pretty true: The difference between a lot of jazz musicians and a lot of rock musicians is that the rock musicians basically learn to play their instruments good enough to play just certain songs, whether they are the songs they're learning off of a record to play in a rock band, or the ones they write themselves. There's nothing wrong with that, because that's all they're going to be required to play, but jazz musicians learn more about their instruments and understand the theory of music. I took that approach. It kept me from being limited just to playing my songs, but on the other side of that, I had to learn how to play songs. A lot of times, if drummers have Ringo Starr for a hero and they grow up listening to that and just playing songs, then they're tuned into what took me ten years to find out. Neither one is better than the other. They're just very different ways of doing it.

RF: Can you be specific about the art of improvisation? How do you learn that?

SS: First of all, I feel that you have to have a great command over your instrument. Then, you have to do a lot of homework. You have to do a lot of listening to the history of drummers who have been there before you. You have to listen to what they did and try to imitate it, so you can conceptually understand how they were approaching it and you can develop a vocabulary. You need to develop a vocabulary. The ultimate in improvisation is to be able to play differently every time. That's impossible, but how you express that each time has got to be different.

Steve Smith Library

Then, you have to develop your own style, which just comes from playing. Tape yourself as much as you can, listen to it, and analyze it. If you listen back and hear what you played, you have to think, "Did I really want to play that, or is that just what came out? Why did that actually come out that way?" If it isn't what you wanted, you're going to have to spend time learning how to hear in your head what you wanted to play, and then try to find that on your instrument. If you can hear in your head what it is you want to hear on the drums and get the chops to pull it off consistently, then you're on your way to developing your own vocabulary and your own individual voice, and to improvising.

RF: I think that people sometimes had trouble seeing you in both worlds-the Vital Information and the Journey worlds. How did you feel about that?

SS: I didn't spend a lot of time thinking about it.

RF: You weren't worried about the acceptance and didn't feel that you had to prove something when you first started Vital Information?

SS: My main concern was the direction of music. I

wanted it to be serious, and I wanted my participation as a drummer to be very musical. I took a very supportive role in what I played, and I felt as though that was the most musically mature role I could have taken. All I wanted to prove was that I could make a good musical record.

RF: Tell me about Global Beat.

SS: The band that tracked for the new album is Tim Landers, bass; Dean Brown, guitar; Tom Coster, keyboards, Dave Wilczewski, sax; and Mike Fisher, percussion. We also feature a lot of percussion with African percussionists Kwaku Dadey and Prince Joni Haastrup, Latin percussionist Armando Peraza, and steel drums with Andy Narell. We also have Mike Stern, Barry Finnerty, Ray Gomez, and Jeff Richman on guitars, and Brad Dutz on percussion. Tim, Dave, and I wrote the music, and it is influenced by many different types of music from all over the world-the jazz and blues from the U.S., the classical influence from Europe, and the rhythmic influence from South America, Trinidad, Jamaica, Cuba, and Africa. I'm very happy and excited with how the record turned out.

RF: What are some of the Journey tunes you've played on that you think are the best?

SS: I really like what I played on "After The Fall" from *Frontiers*. What I played on "Frontiers" is what actually started that tune. I came up with this drum feel, and we wrote the tune from that. That's about it. That's not to say I don't like the other tunes. I do, but I think those tunes are very special. On the *Escape* record, I like what I played on "Mother, Father," "Don't Stop Believin'," and "Dead Or Alive." Those are my favorite performances. I can't remember very much before then. "Walks Like a Lady" on *Departure* was something I really liked. I played brushes on that one tune, and that was pretty neat. I like a lot of the stuff on the live record *Captured*, and there's a Japanese album called *Dream After Dream*, on which there are some really great performances. It's an import, and they only made 50,000 for the States.

RF: What was the recording process like with Journey?

SS: First of all, we rehearsed a lot before we went into the studio, so we were really prepared before we actually started recording. Up until this last album, during the writing/rehearsal process, somebody had an idea for a song, and then that idea was presented to everyone. Everyone contributed ideas to that, and we created a song out of it. There was only one time

that a complete song had been brought to us, and that was "Faithfully." Jonathan Cain had really finished the whole thing with words and melody. Other than that, all the tunes were finished by the band. We spent hours every day practicing and taping, going home and listening to the cassettes, coming back in and changing things around, until finally we felt that we were ready to go in and record without spending a lot of time experimenting in the studio. We usually worked from 11:00 in the morning until about 7:00 at night-very sane hours. Those tunes that we worked out in rehearsal always ended up changing a lot. The process was that basic tracks were played by everybody-not just bass and drums, or just drums. Steve sang, and we usually saved everything. So if we didn't end up using a guitar solo or a lot of the lead vocal, it was left there as reference to do one with. Then, we went back and overdubbed for a couple of weeks-guitar parts, keyboard parts, lead vocals, and harmonies. Not everybody was there for that. Usually, the producer and the one person who was working were there. The rest of us came in and out, listened, and added a little bit. However, we noticed that, if somebody was working all day and another guy bopped in off the street and said, "Hey, that stinks," it was like, "If you want to say that, you should have been here all day." Everybody trusted the other person to have enough maturity to do what was going to be right. Then when it came to mixing, we let the producer or the engineer work all day to get a tune ready and make a mix of the tune at night when they were done. For *Frontiers*, Steve Perry and I went in a lot and listened to the mix. If we liked it, we left it. If we didn't, we'd suggest changes, they'd make them, and we'd finish the mix right there. We'd leave, and they'd go on to the next tune. We'd come in in the morning with a fresh perspective, and that's how we finished the mixes.

RF: Compare and contrast the equipment you used for both situations.

SS: With Journey, I was using the big Sonor drum set with two 24" bass drums and three rack toms. I used the standard drum sizes, and had three rack toms, two floor toms, and the A Zildjian cymbals. I used that same drum set when I did the first Vital Information record. The only difference was that I had a lot of K Zildjian cymbals-lighter cymbals-which really made a big difference in how I approached the drums. It had a much lighter, softer sound. I tuned the drums up a little higher. Then on the first side of *Orion*, I used the big set, and on a couple of the songs, I used some Simmons toms. On the second side, I used a real small drum set with a 20" bass drum, two rack toms, and one floor tom. I found that it worked even better. I used the same lighter cymbal setup and one bass drum. On the newest record, *Global Beat*, I just used the small set for the whole record and the K Zildjian cymbals. I'm getting an even more personal sound for Vital Information, because I'm finding that, even though I changed the cymbals, it made me play much lighter and more sensitively. Now that I've gotten rid of the two bass drums and five tom-toms, it also changes things. It changes the approach, and the tuning of the drums is very different. I also went back to using the white heads instead of the clear heads, and it gives the drums a warmer sound.

RF: When you were spending so much time with a set format with Journey, wasn't it difficult then to turn around and gear your head toward a more improvisational approach with Vital Information?

SS: It took a while to feel real comfortable at it and to start understanding it completely again. Most of the conceptual understanding was there already, and I could slip from one to the other pretty easily, but it did take a little while. What took time in the jazz thing was getting the facility and sensitivity back to do the subtler things, and getting that control back.

RF: What about tips for playing a power ballad, as you are known for having done in Journey?

SS: I think the arrangement is very important. We tried to develop a real nice arrangement of the song. Sometimes the arrangement was that the drums wouldn't play through half of it, or they came in and went out. You have to be very aware of when it's right *not* to play. That was everybody's contribution-not just my own ideas. First off, I like to look for a really nice feel. When you play those slow tempos, that's when you really have to dig into the beat. A lot of times, I pull it way back, not to the point where it's slowing down, but just enough so it really feels majestic. When you play the big tom fills, there has to be a lot of air in between the notes, so the drums have a chance to really ring out. You have to have a great sound first off, and let that sound ring out so you hear the toms, and you're not hurrying through the fills. A lot of times, I composed those drum fills. It wasn't that we would be in the studio, and all of a sudden, I would have a fill to

lead up to this thing. I'd try a lot of different ones and settle on one. So even if we did ten takes of the song, I'd usually play the same fills every time. Because I would have tried enough possibilities so that I would know it was right, the other guys in the band would know it was right, and we would have settled into it. Then it was just a matter of really pulling it off so it worked. Sometimes, I'd change them at the last minute, and that change

would be the magic that we were looking for, but most of the time, I would have already worked them out in that rehearsal time. Then they became part of the song, and I'd play the same ones in the live performance. I wasn't afraid to do that. Sometimes for a jazz musician, that's a bad thing to do. It's predictable or contrived. Maybe it is, but it also works best for the song, and it was the best way for me to do it.

RF: The ballads were really lush and dynamic.

SS: We had really become known for those, and in a way, I've become known for doing that. Bryan Adams had me play drums on some ballads, for just that reason. I played "Heaven" on *Reckless*, which was a number-one hit single. I like doing sessions. Since leaving Journey, I've played on some cuts of Glen Burtnick's album, and I've done an entire album with Tony MacAlpine. He's a young, black, rock guitar player and classical pianist who just recorded his debut album. Billy Sheehan plays bass, and it was produced by Mike Varney. The album is instrumental, and it's absolutely smoking. It has my best rock playing on it to date.

RF: In our last interview, we touched on the difference between playing in a vocal oriented situation and playing in an instrumental situation. In the first interview, you mentioned giving the notes their full value. Aren't there other considerations?

SS: That was when I was first experiencing being in a group with a singer, and that was what I was being presented with by Steve: "Don't hurry your fills and don't come out of the fill a little bit early, because I'm holding the note and I know when it's supposed to end. Don't get there before I do." I was very conscious of everything's proper length and time. That concept works with everything now. I've applied that to the jazz music as well, because good time is good time. He just made me aware of how to make it even better by being aware that sometimes, at the end of fills, I got there a little too soon. I got all excited about it and hurried my way through it.

I guess the main thing is that, before I played with Journey, I was always interacting with what was going on, and I stopped doing that. I don't do that when I play rock. I do it to a slight degree enough to add to the composition-but not enough to take away from the foundation. Never leave that foundation. I don't think of it so much in terms of a vocalist anymore. I guess I take it for granted that, when I'm playing in rock, I'm playing with a singer. That was a new thing for me back then.

RF: Yet, I would think that, in a rock context, it might be hard to be forceful and not overbearing.

SS: I focused all my energy through Steve when we were playing. It wasn't like I just listened to the bass player. When we played instrumentally, I could dish out a lot more stuff and it was okay. Neal could pick up on

it, and I could really cut loose. When Steve was singing, I was focusing everything through him to make him feel comfortable, to stay out of his way, and to support what he was doing. I was listening very closely to what he was singing and to his phrasing. I made sure that what I was giving him felt good for him. I could usually tell how he was singing and if the tempo was right. One of the most important things in working with a singer is that the tempo has to be right, so you can hear the words. With an instrumental thing, a lot of times you can play tunes a little faster than the record, and it will still be okay. But with lyrics, the words can get squashed together, and you have to make sure the tempos don't get too fast.

RF: So what happened with you and Journey?

SS: This is very hard to explain, because it's very emotional and I also have a lot of confusion about it. It's not very clear to me. I would have to say that it all started with Perry's solo record, and how that experience really changed his approach as a musician/songwriter. In my opinion, he became more interested in being a solo artist and enjoyed the feeling of writing songs with maybe one or two other people, rather than a whole group situation. He quit the band, and to get him to do another record, we agreed to his producing the record and that he could bring in anyone he wanted to play on it. Most of the material for this new record was written by Jonathan and Steve together or Neal, Jonathan, and Steve together. The band ceased being a band. They did very extensive demos of the songs at Jonathan's studio, complete with drum machine beats and bass parts that they specifically wanted. So I felt a lot less involved, and there was much less leeway in what I could contribute. They felt very specific about what they wanted in the drums and the bass. They also felt that the parts they had come up with were integral to the tunes. First they said, "Let's record the whole album with the drum machine and have you maybe put some parts on later." They felt that the drum machine itself was part of the compositions. I started feeling that it wasn't a band, and it certainly didn't have the same band approach as when we wrote collectively.

RF: How did you feel about their wanting to put a drum machine on the album?

SS: I felt terrible about that.

RF: Was that because you honestly, in your heart, believed that the tunes could have been great with you on them?

SS: I really felt that they could have been better with me playing, rather than the drum machine playing. To me, it goes back to the feeling of a band. I feel like each member of a band is an important contributor. If I were a fan of a band's sound, I'd feel bad if I bought an album by that band, and the bass player and the drummer didn't play on it. It really bothered me that those decisions were being made, and I didn't really have a lot to say about it. As much as I tried to change that, I wasn't effective. There was a lot of friction to start with, simply because of my resentment of their using a drum machine. I have a whole set of feelings about drum machines, which I really sorted out through this whole thing.

I believe that there are four parts to making an experience complete: a physical part, an emotional part, an intellectual part, and a spiritual part. The engineer and the guys in the band would ask me to make the drum machine parts a little more believable by changing the programming a bit. They said that, if I was thinking of the stuff, why couldn't I let the machine play it for me? They couldn't understand why that didn't satisfy me. So I had to think about it. I realized that it took away the physical pleasure of playing the drums, it took away the spiritual pleasure of playing music, and it took away the emotional feeling. The only thing that was left was the intellectual part of programming the machine. That's not enough for a complete experience for me. I've had too many years invested in actually *playing* the instrument to feel good about being a programmer.

RF: And yet, on the last couple of Journey albums, the drum sound was explosive. Why would they do away with that?

SS: I think it comes from a paranoia of thinking that we have to keep up with the trends and the times, and that what we've done in the past is lousy. On a scale from one to ten, maybe what we did on the last record was an eight in comparison to our potential, but I think that some people in the band looked at it as if it had been a zero. It was totally irrational and unrealistic.

RF: So what happened after you rehearsed?

SS: We went into the studio to record those tunes. The whole time, I had a very pessimistic attitude that it wouldn't work out. We started the first week with the whole band. By the second week, Ross wasn't playing, and Bob Glaub was playing bass. I felt very bad that Ross wasn't going to play. I also felt very threatened by it, because I thought that a can of worms was being opened. I felt very insecure about my position, so I expressed my fears and I was assured that it would all

Steve Smith Library

be okay. We tracked for about two weeks, and then Randy Jackson came in on bass. We tracked for another couple of weeks, doing some of the same songs over again. We spent two months tracking. At that point, it was decided that they would bring in another drummer to re-do four of the songs. Steve just felt that what had been recorded didn't live up to the demos. On one hand, I wasn't completely surprised, because it wasn't fun going to work every day. There was so much tension. I felt a bit relieved to be out of that pressured situation. But they had no intention of just doing four songs. When they got Larrie [Londin], they wanted him to play everything again. When I heard that Larrie was there for two weeks tracking, it was a terrible time for me. Nobody called me to talk to me about what was going on. It became very impersonal. I ended up calling the other members.

RF: People don't know how to deal with hurting other people.

SS: That's what happened. It got so uncomfortable that my attorney was informed that they wanted me to retire from the band. I felt like I didn't know how I could work with them again because I felt so bad about the situation, and I'm sure they felt the same way. That's one aspect of the split up. Another aspect is that you taste what it feels like to hire different people for different tracks. There are definitely specialists, and Larrie can do certain things better than I can do them. But I can play other things better than somebody else, and in a band, you have to be everything. But when you taste what it's like when you don't have to accept what another band member offers, I'm sure that's an intoxicating feeling. In addition, you figure that you only have to pay someone for a day's work and not share the royalties with that person. All that added up to my being asked to leave the band.

RF: How did you feel, Steve?

SS: I felt really hurt, personally betrayed, and really unappreciated. During the whole thing, it was, "You're not happening." I was constantly made to feel that I wasn't a good musician, and that hit me where I live. That is something that is so important in my life. It's left an impact on me and made me a little insecure, but only a little, because I felt there were so many other reasons besides musical ones.

RF: How did you build up your confidence after you had been shot down?

SS: At first, I really withdrew a lot and stayed at home. I was very upset and went to therapy. Susan and I had a new baby, Elizabeth Ann, on July 1, 1985. That was very uplifting. Then I made a 100% commitment to my solo career, and I made a lot of creative decisions about what I want to do with myself as a musician in the future. I started finishing a solo record that I had recorded the basic tracks for in July of 1984. I had put it on the shelf because every time I had planned to work on it, management would call me up and say, "We're going to start Journey rehearsals next week," but they would inevitably get postponed. I started working on

Global Beat full time, finishing the overdubs, starting to think about album covers, and all these things that I had put on the back burner. The positive effect was that I was happy not to be in a situation where I was not appreciated.

RF: How long did it take you to get to that point?

SS: Some of it was there from the beginning. Along with the grief, there's also relief that happens simultaneously. That didn't start to become a bigger part of it for maybe a month or more. Then I started looking at it differently, because I started seeing it as: Now is the time to be a captain of my own ship, rather than a passenger on somebody else's. Now is the time for me to really develop as an artist, rather than just a good musician.

RF: Although, you're also doing some varied work as a player.

SS: Yes, and I've really enjoyed it. I did a European tour with a guitarist by the name of Torsten de Winkle. That was with Tom Coster and Ernie Watts. The bass player was Kai Ekhart-Karpeh, and he was great. That was more in the vein of Vital Information or Steps Ahead. I also did records with T Lavitz, Jeff Richman, and Jeff Berlin, and a live recording with Players, which is a group with T Lavitz, Jeff Berlin, and Scott Henderson.

RF: How did the gig with Steps Ahead come about?

SS: I was doing a Sonor drum clinic tour and one of the clinics was with Lenny White. After the clinic, Lenny and I started talking about what we were both doing, and I told him that I was looking to do some jazz gigs. That's when he told me that Steps Ahead had just called him, but he couldn't do it because he had his own band together with Marcus Miller. So he was going to call and recommend me, which he did. That led to my being asked to join Steps Ahead. It was more than I ever dreamed of, as far as playing with good players goes. The band is Michael Brecker, Mike Mainieri, Mike Stern, and Victor Bailey, although Victor is going to be playing with Weather Update, so Daryl Jones will be the bass player for the summer. I went to New York, rehearsed for three days, and then went out and did four gigs. It feels great, and it's opening up all kinds of doors for me as far as my growing as a player is concerned. It's giving me the opportunity to develop to the highest degree of my potential. To play with musicians who are *that* good makes it an open ended situation. I don't feel any restrictions; what is required of me is to play as much as I can possibly play. There is a rock influence in their music and, at the same time, the requirements of the gig are to be really strong, real sensitive, and to be able to improvise with the band. I've done all of those things before in jazz, but the level of musicianship is the highest I've ever experienced.

RF: How will this affect your work with Vital Information?

SS: I think it will give Vital Information more credibility, because I was fighting against the stigma of being the Journey drummer. It will also give me a lot more input as far as writing and direction, and also develop my musicality to a higher degree.

RF: Since practicing has always been important in your gigs, what things did you start practicing when you got this gig?

SS: I'm practicing just to develop an incredible amount of facility, because I need a lot more facility and vocabulary to deal with the gig.

RF: How does one practice facility?

SS: The same way I've always practiced: focusing on

time, I'm meeting a lot of the local jazz musicians in San Francisco, and I'm getting involved in the local jazz scene. I have the opportunity to get out and play now. It feels good to me not to be cloistered in a band and to be an active, working musician again.

RF: Being in a band of that nature can almost become a star syndrome, and it sets you apart from people.

SS: Yes, it does. It removed me from the musical community. Just the other day, I did a Charlie Brown TV show soundtrack. I was called at the last minute, and it felt great to do something like that. I met all these studio players in San Francisco. I didn't even know there was a studio scene here. I had a great time. I had never done anything like that-watching the screen and playing along.

RF: Were you nervous?

SS: Yes, I was. I didn't know what to expect. The whole thing was jazz brushes. There are a lot of things I'm thinking of doing now. I want to write a book, do a video, and develop the educational aspect more.

"I've always pushed myself to get into situations that are challenging, but Steps Ahead is more than I ever imagined"

what the gig requires, and then practicing jazz chops, funk, fusion, and all that stuff. The level of musicianship is so high that I'm just going to have to keep pushing myself. For example, I have a couple of places in the set where I just play with Brecker. One of them is a real fast jazz tempo, and the other one is a real fast rock fusion tempo. I can deal out everything I'm capable of playing, and he just eats it up like it's nothing. So I have to work on surpassing everything I've ever done before in order to play with a musician of that caliber. Everyone in the group is at that level. It's challenging for me to push myself beyond my limits. I've always pushed myself to get into situations that are challenging, but this one is more than I ever imagined.

RF: What are your immediate plans for the future?

SS: Of course the Steps Ahead gig, and then to promote the *Global Beat* album, first with clinics and then with band touring. I'm studying piano so I can write more, and I'm spending a lot of time practicing. For the first

RF: Is it hard when you've been cloistered in a band to become "one of the people"?

SS: I experienced the feeling of being a "so-called" rock star for maybe the height of the success of Journey. Some of it probably came from me, but I think most of it came from how people treated me, more than how I treated other people. I was on the road for most of ten years, but for the last two years, I've been home. I have a wife and two kids now. I started feeling very grounded and normal. Plus, living in a neighborhood where I see the neighbors every day made me feel very normal. Taking Ian to school and being one of the parents at school was good, and I lost that whole feeling of the rock 'n' roll world. I don't miss that kind of touring and the intense life-style. I'm looking forward to touring with my own band and Steps Ahead, and doing as many other creative projects as I can fit into my schedule. Music feels very fresh to me right now, and the future seems very exciting.

1993: Steve Smith
Vital Transformation

By Robyn Flans

It was really a blessing in disguise when Steve Smith's gig with Journey came to a halt in 1985. Of course, it hurt at the time, but as the dust settled, Steve began to focus his life in a long-overdue fashion. He started to realize that, while he learned a great deal from Journey, the music that truly made his heart beat was jazz. Steve and the other members of Journey have actually reconciled their differences lately. In fact, since the breakup, Smith has worked on both guitarist Neil Schon's and keyboardist Jonathan Cain's solo albums. But jazz-in both its pure form and fused with other styles-remains Steve's passion.

Since the age of nine, Steve Smith has been interested in learning drums, not just playing them. From the fourth grade through the twelfth, Steve studied with Bill Flanagan in Massachusetts. His love of many types of music, from Count Basie and Oscar Peterson to Jimi Hendrix and Deep Purple, helped prepare him for his next musical quest, at the Berklee College of Music. After a year with Lin Biviano, a trumpet player who had worked with Buddy Rich and Maynard Ferguson, Smith left Berklee just before he was to graduate, for a gig with Jean-Luc Ponty. After a little over a year, Smith won gigs with both Freddie Hubbard and Montrose, but chose Montrose because the direction was more rock 'n' roll. Montrose opened for Journey on quite a few occasions, and in '78 Steve was offered their drum chair.

Looking back, Journey has definitely been the odd gig in Smith's career, though Steve has previously explained that if it hadn't been that band, he probably would never have played that type of music. The high caliber of musicianship appealed to him, though, and it was a situation in which his playing could-and would-grow immensely. You need only listen to the recent Journey compilation to appreciate how right Smith was for the gamut of their material-from the raucus rockers to the lush ballads.

But in 1983, Smith began to pine for his roots. Luckily, he was given the opportunity to record with his then new band, Vital Information. Ten years later, it is his primary focus, though he alternates between gigs as Vital's leader and as a group member in Steps Ahead. Smith admits it hasn't always been an easy road to travel, but now, with the release of his sixth album, *Easier Done Than Said*, his perseverance finally seems to be paying off.

RF: I'd like to examine your role in Vital Information, including how much input you have in the songs, what the musicians play, and the shape the band takes-since you're at the helm.

SS: The concept has been pretty much the same from the beginning: to surround myself with musicians I really enjoy, both in their playing and writing. When I put a group together, I try to let the group find the natural place where we all come together. Each record is different because the combination of musicians meets in a different place. What I find with the current line-up is that the players are more oriented to be artists themselves.

RF: Why is that good?

SS: For me it's good because I'm much better in a collaborative situation. I can write some music, but as far as I'm concerned, I'm really not capable of writing a whole record. I'll contribute my share, but then I look to the other members to contribute. In this band, it's real nice for me because each musician is at a stage in their careers where they're not quite ready to have their own band full time. This is kind of a stepping stone for them because they can perform the music that they compose for this band as well as music from their solo records. They enjoy the band experience, and they also know that they're exposing themselves individually to an audience who will see their talent in a much clearer light, as opposed to their other situations-for example, Frank Gambale with Chick Corea, or Jeff Andrews with Steps Ahead and Michael Brecker.

I enjoy playing with the strongest players I can find because it brings out the best in me. That requires giving them a lot, but I like that because, like I said, I can't write all the songs. What I will do is set up an environment that is attractive and comfortable for great players to want to spend some time in. And that's what's happened now.

RF: What do you mean by "it requires giving them a lot?"

SS: It requires really listening to their input and not just dominating the situation. That's the contract of a sideman-just show up and play. You can offer some ideas, but the leader doesn't have to listen. You might get upset, but that's the contract. This contract is different from that.

Live, we don't have any problems because everyone has enough room to do what they want. When we play music from the other members' records, they have the final say in their own tunes. There is also a lot of solo space now, especially now that there are only four members, since we've dropped the saxophone. In the studio, I'm the producer, so if there's a dispute, I'll settle it. They give me that space, and it doesn't seem to be a problem. Tom Coster and Frank Gambale each make their own records, and it's only a matter of time before Jeff does, so it's not so important to fight over something. They have another outlet, so this isn't the all-important thing to them. The chemistry is very good, which is why the guys have committed to this band. We're really looking forward to turning it into a full-time group. It's taken a long time-ten years. It's been a slow building process.

RF: Has it been frustrating at times?

SS: Absolutely, in that it's taken so long.

RF: What obstacles have made it take so long?

SS: I can point to a number of things. First of all, I didn't have the right image. It has to make sense to the club owners and the audiences.

RF: So having been in Journey was a stumbling block?

SS: It gave me name recognition and an "in" with clubs and the press, but the audience I was aiming at wasn't aware of me, so I spent years up against a "Steve Smith of Journey" tag, which says "rock drummer." The jazz fusion audience either didn't know me or didn't care. Besides that, I didn't have the right personnel. Also, my playing was good, but it wasn't to the level it's at now. I have to give a lot of credit to Mike Mainieri for hiring me in Steps Ahead.

RF: Why did that help, just for your credibility?

SS: It helped in credibility, audience recognition, and

• DRUMMING IN LAS VEGAS • MICKEY CURRY ROCK CHART •

MODERN DRUMMER®

Now Incorporating Drums & Drumming Magazine

FEBRUARY '93

STEVE SMITH

FREE!
BUDDY RICH
Sound Supplement

PLUS:
○ ED THIGPEN
○ UFIP CYMBALS ON REVIEW
○ WHEN CALFSKIN WAS KING
○ WIN A GREAT MEINL PACKAGE!

U.S. $3.95
U.K. £2.50
Canada $4.95

playing experience. Steps Ahead is a band that a lot of people in the U.S. have heard of, but not a lot of people have seen. For the past three and a half years, we toured Europe and Japan almost non-stop, but very little in the U.S. It has exposed me to the very audience I am trying to penetrate. Now it makes a lot of sense for a member of Steps Ahead to go out with his own group.

The other thing that made a difference was the personnel. Frank Gambale has been touring with Chick Corea for the last six years, Tom Coster toured with Santana, and Jeff Andrews had been touring with Mike Brecker, Mike Stern, Bob Berg, and Steps Ahead. So as a quartet, we have a lot of name recognition.

RF: You said your playing has improved. How so?

SS: In every way imaginable. My time has gotten a lot better, my understanding of what each type of music needs in order to work, and how to play behind a soloist.

RF: That's an interesting topic. Can you give us some pointers?

SS: There are general rules for playing behind a soloist, and then there are specific ones that depend on each individual that I'm playing with. Basically, it's important to make the time feel as silky smooth as possible, to outline the form, and to listen. The level of interaction and contribution differs from person to person. Some people just like a smooth time feel without a lot of interplay. There are other people who like a lot of back-and-forth action. That knowledge has to come from playing experience with that person, from finding out where they're at.

RF: Could you get specific about the musicians you are currently working with?

SS: Jeff, for example, enjoys my laying down a good, solid groove. In certain tunes, he likes to have the snares off so the bass doesn't resonate the snares while he's soloing. As the solo builds, he likes more interaction. Tom, for the straight-ahead swing, likes a very loose rhythm section at the beginning-not a lot of stated time, more of a loose, implied time-and as the solo builds, then you come in with straight-ahead time locking in. He really enjoys a lot of interaction as it develops. With Frank, I notice that my role is a little more supportive throughout. There is some interaction, but I think he sounds best when I'm playing real solid time behind him. It lets his playing flow over the top. A lot of what he does flows all over the bar line, so I need to be pretty solid.

In Steps, saxophonist Bendik [Hofseth] likes lots of space behind his soloing. I can actually sometimes lay out at the beginning of his solos or play just a spacious cymbal thing. All of the players like some interaction, obviously, but some more than others. Rachel Z likes a lot of interaction from beginning to end. Mike Mainieri really likes a nice cushion. In fact, Mike got me to change ride cymbals. I had been using a K Custom, and he found it to be too dry for his taste. One day, we were rehearsing in New York, and Colin Schofield from Zildjian happened to be in town. He brought me several ride cymbals and I tried all of them. Mike picked the 20" Pre-Aged K.

The concept of the Pre-Aged is that Zildjian tried to make it sound like an old cymbal. As a cymbal gets older, it mellows and has less overtones. The Pre-Aged is already like that because it goes through extra hammering. It has a very loose kind of washy sound without lots of definition, but enough where people can hear the beat. It has a lot of sustain between the notes.

And Mike really likes that sound. Mike also likes the flat ride with rivets in it, which has the same kind of effect. He likes that seamless, straight- ahead swinging feel. The interaction is there, but it's understated. It's more of just a pulse, which I find is very common with the players from his generation. Most of the great players of that time were less of the highly interactive players, which developed later with Tony Williams, Elvin Jones, Jack DeJohnette, and Billy Cobham. But before that, with Buddy Rich and Philly Joe Jones and Papa Jo Jones, the tradition was more solid undertone. I especially enjoy Mike's input, because he is the player with the most experience. Now I use that PreAged K cymbal in most of what I do, and I've developed the touch to play it.

RF: You have to develop a touch to play it?

SS: Yes. What I've noticed is, over the years, the ride cymbal became thicker and less sustained as a reaction to people playing with less touch. They try to find a cymbal with that clarity built into it, so they don't necessarily have to develop the finesse to get a nice pingy sound. But to get a nice sound like that on a cymbal that has a lot of wash, you have to play it with a lot of touch. So that's been developing in my playing. Zildjian has also come out with the A Custom line, which has much lighter cymbals that sound a lot like the A cymbals that were made twenty or thirty years ago. I've been using them lately, and most people in the studio comment on how great they sound because they're so light and have so much tone to them. It's different from a lot of the heavier cymbals today.

RF: Back to improving yourself. I know you attribute some of it to playing with Steps, but some of it must be because of your own personal woodshedding.

SS: In everything I get involved in, whether it's a recording session or a tour, I find that there are things I need to work on. I'll spend my practice time working on those ideas. Another way is opening myself up to ideas from mentor type people. I have noticed that through-out my development as a musician, from the time I was nine years old, I've always had people who were mentors, people who really gave me a lot of inspiration, and also people who really believed in my talent. I find that to be a really important aspect in the development of a player, especially regarding confidence. I notice that people who don't grow up with a mentor-type person sometimes struggle with a level of confidence. I was very lucky that my first drum teacher, Bill Flanagan-an older guy maybe in his 60's-gave me the feeling that I was a good drummer and that I had a lot of potential. It was a very fortunate gift that, at nine years old, I had somebody giving me that kind of feedback. It really gave me the inspiration to move forward. So I've noticed that I've been open to that kind of input throughout my life.

One person who has helped me a lot is Jim Chapin. He shows up at a lot of NAMM shows, and every time I see him, we spend hours together talking about technique.

in certain areas of my playing, I would run into a stone wall. I could only go so far and then I would stop, because physically I would get in my own way. There are ways that the body moves that are very natural, circular- type motions. If you understand the way the body moves and go with it, rather than resisting it, you'll have a much higher potential of what you can do technically. Fred calls it "universal principles of motion." There are ways that the body moves very efficiently that have been harnessed through the years in different art

Steve Smith Library

He shows me what he does, and I'll learn that and try to incorporate it into what I'm doing.

Another guy is someone I began studying with two years ago is Fred Gruber. Fred has such an amazing insight into what happens physically and emotionally to a person when they're playing the drums, and how to get the most out of your body-your hands, your arms, your feet-the whole thing. He showed me where, if I continue to use the same technique that I was using

forms like dancing, tennis, baseball, and martial arts. The connection is using your body in a way where the motions are very smooth and natural. He applies that to drumming as well, which makes total sense, though it seems to have been overlooked through the years.

My wife, Susan, is involved in martial arts and body building. Both of those areas are very codified; they have a lot of organization when it comes to body motion. There are ways of doing things so you don't hurt yourself. You have to understand the way your body moves most efficiently and naturally, and then align with it; you don't want to fight it. I've been reading some of the books she's been reading. She's been studying Kenpo karate at Marin Kenpo, and the father of Kenpo, Ed Parker, has written volumes about that; One of them is called *Infinite Insights*. It could easily be about drumming instead of karate. I found another great book called *The Warrior Athlete*, by Dan Millman. He's written it to apply to everything physical. It's really improved my drumming to study it and think along these lines.

Another thing about Freddie is, while a lot of teachers have one technique that they've developed to a very high degree, he has the insight to understand that there are so many drum techniques available-more than I know. First, he helped me develop and make more efficient the particular principles I was using. After being with him for a while with that coming together, he opened me up to different techniques that I wasn't

more enjoyable. And I can play more interesting things. I like that feeling, and I enjoy the process of getting there.
RF: I know so many people who have trouble practicing.
SS: It's not for everybody. It's my way of doing it. And I don't want it to look like all I do is practice. I do the other stuff too, which is play the music. But off stage, I do a lot of work on it as well, just because I like it. It feels good.
RF: Do you ever get practice burnout?
SS: Sometimes, but not very often, because it's not like I practice every single day. There are days where I can't fit it in. I try to do it for a few hours every day, but I have so many ideas in my head that I can't seem to get to them all. But I am aware of practicing past the point of getting any result, too. Just like with weightlifting, you can only do so many reps before lactic acid builds up and you can't lift a thing anymore. You're not going to get anything out of it after that. It's not that drastic or noticeable with drumming, but there is a point where my control is really diminished and I feel like I'm playing

"You have to understand the way your body moves most efficiently and naturally, and then align with it; you don't want to fight it"

using. I've developed a more encyclopedic knowledge of techniques that I can choose from. And it's not that you have to give up one to do another; I just keep adding them all up. Here's a really basic version of that: Some people play matched grip, others play traditional, and other people play both. If you watch Tony Williams play, he'll switch between the two techniques.
RF: Every time we talk, I am hit with an overwhelming observation. What is it inside of you that makes you constantly motivated to go further?
SS: For one thing, I love the process. One of the things I enjoy about being a drummer is just the process of improving and practicing. I really enjoy practicing.
RF: You're good at what you do. You could just go on doing what you do.
SS: I don't look at it that way. It doesn't feel like that to me. I feel like something could definitely be done to make it easier to do what I'm doing. The more that I work on these ideas, the easier it will get, which makes it

incorrectly. I'm pushing too much, hitting too hard-or I'm just totally fatigued. I'm really just practicing mistakes and it's actually going to keep me from improving. There is a point where the number of hours isn't always the point. It's how efficiently you use your time and how disciplined your practice is so that you get the most out of it.
RF: How can you efficiently use your time to practice?
SS: You have to be organized and know what you're going to do, so you're actually building, day to day, on similar ideas. Things don't happen in one-day intervals. They happen over months and years, so there has to be some kind of consistency in your practicing concept so things can develop logically and slowly, and you're giving them the space to do that. One of the things I like to do is practice in front of a mirror so I can always examine the motions and make sure they're efficient. I've been doing that forever.

As far as staying motivated, I've found it very

important to find a good teacher. That's what really worked for me. I've always had good teachers, from my original teacher, Bill Flanagan, to Gary Chaffee, Alan Dawson, and now Fred Gruber. And someone who recently reinspired me was Ed Thigpen. He helped me quite a few years ago, and then recently I spent a week with him over in Germany when I did a one-week artist-in-residence teaching situation with Ed, Terry Bozzio, and Joey Heredia. It was really great and very inspiring. Ed is a master. Terry and I hung out with him quite a bit, and he gave us a lot of insight into the history of drumming, especially about Jo Jones, who was Ed's mentor. That was really educational. And Ed himself is so open. He was asking the three of us all kinds of questions about what we do.

RF: Who were the people you came up emulating?

SS: There wasn't really any one person, which is something I feel good about. I think that's one of the reasons I don't sound like anybody else in particular. I've always been a combination of people, but that list would take up the whole magazine. I've gotten something from everybody I've ever heard. Of course, in particular there was Buddy Rich, and the rock drummers of the time-Mitch Mitchell, Ginger Baker, and John Bonham. Later I discovered Tony Williams, Elvin Jones, Roy Haynes, and Jack DeJohnette. But there are hundreds of drummers I've heard who have had an impact on me. Even if I learned what not to do from them, it still had an impact on me. I'll pick up little things from someone, and it'll spark something in me that I can develop and make my own.

RF: Why do you think that this is the music that makes your heart beat?

SS: The type of music I've been involved with in the last few years-Vital Information and Steps Ahead-allows me to express a very complete picture of myself. It has elements of rock, funk, electric jazz, and straight-ahead jazz in it, so it is made up of all the things that I enjoy playing.

RF: What do you think your own strengths are?

Steve Smith Library

SS: I'm very consistent from night to night. When I was with Ponty, I was fresh out of Berklee, and I had a very young jazz-student attitude. Ponty was somewhere between rock, jazz, and classical, but I was trying to play the tunes completely different every night. I didn't have the vocabulary or experience to successfully do that, and it wasn't the best thing for the music. I realized that the other guys who were consistent from night to night didn't necessarily play completely different solos each night. In a particular tune, certain licks, certain concepts would work, so they would keep that. I realized that was something I needed to work on, and it was actually with Journey-where the music was so part-oriented-that I developed the ability to play a part, lock into it, and make it happen night after night. As I got in other groups like Steps Ahead and my own band, that music was in-between again, similar to the Ponty material. The jazz part of the music was the looser, freer part, and the rock part was the more composed part. By really locking in on the composed parts, and by being aware of how far I could go on the loose parts before I lost it, I developed the ability to be consistent from night to night, which I realized when Mike Mainieri commented on it.

Another strength is my time. That's something I'm always working on, and now it's at the point where it's very comfortable live, without a click. And with a click or sequencers it also feels very comfortable. It's taken a lot of work, and I've gotten a lot of input from different people, but I can really say it's a strength now.

RF: Does that just come from doing it?

SS: Yes, and I got a lot of help from producer/composer/engineer/keyboard player Jay Oliver. He produced one of my Vital Information records, and he really helped me become aware of how to use dynamics and make the drumming flow easier when playing with a sequencer.

RF: How did he help you?

SS: Jay has such a keen awareness of the technical makeup of a good drum performance. He's aware of the relationship dynamically of each limb. He was able to point out to me what I was doing wrong in a very technical sense, which I appreciated, because I worked with so many producers who would say, "It just doesn't feel right," "It's not rockin enough," "It isn't swampy enough." But what does that mean? Jay is able to articulate it in technical terms: "You played that ghost note a little too loud before the backbeat, so the backbeat was just a hair late. Then when you came down on the cymbal, it was a little bit in front of your kick drum, so I heard a little flam there, and it made it sound loose next to the machine."

RF: We never finished your strengths.

SS: I learn music quickly. I think that developed through years of being a music reader, for one. That really helps because it allows me to get a mental picture of what the tune is about. And having experience at different types of music, I can learn something quickly. A lot of times I'll write out my own chart so I don't have to spend a lot of time trying to memorize. I'm also good at coming up with parts. That probably was also helped by Journey and working so much on songs. I was always trying to be as creative as I could be in that environment, so I'd always try to come up with signature parts if it would work. I've learned to use that concept with whatever I'm called on to do.

RF: What would you say are your weaknesses?

SS: The things that I have worked on lately feel more like subtleties than weaknesses, things I'm interested in developing. My inspiration for doing it isn't because I feel inadequate, it's because I have an interest in developing something to a higher degree. It sounds like I'm saying I don't have any weaknesses, which I don't think is true, but there isn't anything staring me in the face.

There are things that I'm developing, and one of the things I'm doing is reading books like Mickey Hart's *Drumming On The Edge Of Magic,* which gives a great history of drumming. I also read the Mel Torme biography of Buddy Rich, which was very inspiring. Both of those have lead me to spend time in used record stores and to talk to people who have videos of a lot of the older drummers who were the predecessors, people I never got to see live. I'm trying to get a picture of what their contributions were. I'm sort of going back to move forward. I don't want to sound like I'm just a product of the last twenty years. I want my playing to sound like I'm rooted in the entire history of drumming in the United States. The concept of what I am doing is something I call-for lack of a better name-"U.S. ethnic drumming." A couple of things inspired my thinking about that. One was noticing how many American musicians are interested in studying Brazilian and Cuban music. As great as a lot of these players are, I think the ones who are really the best at that are the people who are from Brazil or Cuba. It's not just about studying the music, it's an entire cultural thing. You have to live in the environment. I live in the United States, so I really understand this music.

Another thing that brought it on was talking with the

sax player in Steps, Bendik. There is sometimes a dispute about the music we do. Bendik, being from Norway, has roots in classical music and Norwegian folk music. He really doesn't have jazz roots. It becomes obvious when we play American jazz. But instead of it being a problem, he's just strong in where he's coming from. He's a Norwegian. He sounds like a Norwegian. And that makes a lot of sense. He uses that background in his compositions and in his playing, and it sounds great. He has a unique approach. And that got me to start looking at what I do. Yes, I play some Latin and Brazilian stuff, but really what I do is the Latin, Brazilian things that have filtered into the United States.

As a drummer, I belong to a family that spans every country in the world, which dates back in history to the origins of civilization. In time, I might be able to shed some boundaries that I feel now and be a true world-beat drummer. But I'm overwhelmed by the richness of the American tradition, let alone Indian, Afro-Cuban, Brazilian, Middle Eastern .... My background is more in the history of drums as it has evolved here in this country-the marching drums, dix-

Timothy Charles Ellis

ieland, swing, big band, bebop, rock, blues, R&B, avant-garde, heavy metal, and fusion. One of the reasons I feel comfortable playing a lot of different styles is because I don't quite see it as a lot of different styles. It's all part of the U.S. style to me.

RF: You actually get to explore many facets of that "U.S." style with Vital Information. Can we briefly talk about each album?

SS: I like each of them for different reasons. They are all a personal documentation of where I was at that moment. On the first one, *Vital Information*, I used the same drum set-although I had different cymbals-as I had been using in Journey, and I was still in the band at the time. It had kind of the same big Journey sound, so I had yet to develop a different sound drum-wise. We did everything as a group live in the studio, with first and second takes. I was really craving that experience.

The second record, *Orion*, was kind of a transition, where half the record was with the rock drum set-even incorporating some Simmons drums with it-and the other half was on a little jazz set. I still hadn't come up with a new drum configuration to incorporate both worlds. It was like black and white. Most of it was also done with live tracking.

On the third record, *Global Beat*, I really started developing a new sound and identity for myself. I used a new configuration drum-wise, with smaller bass drums and generally a smaller drum set. It focused on the world beat rhythm thing I was really into at the time.

The *Fiafiaga (Celebration)* record was the one co-produced by Jay Oliver, and it has a lot of computer technology and more funk- and jazz-oriented music with some world-beat music. It's more of a produced record.

The *Vitalive!* record was purely to document the live performance. We were constantly hearing, "We like your records, but it's nothing like the live experience."

RF: Let's talk about this current album, *Easier Done Than Said*. There's one song that knocks me out every time I hear it. It's the one where you just play brushes.

SS: That's "I Remember." It's the only tune on the record that I completely wrote. I'm playing what I feel is the right thing for that tune, which has a kind of Brazilian feeling. To me, the writing style has a lot of Tom Coster's personality on it. It was a great vehicle for him to play

and there are improvised sections as well. That's one of the drum solos in the piece. I extracted it because I really liked how it worked as a segue between two of the tunes. The Gary Chaffee thing is available from CPP Belwin. The package has two copies of the sheet music and a cassette of our performance.

The only other drum solo is on the tune "Step Aside." That's a great tune that Tim Landers wrote, and the ending has a drum solo. I was sort of thinking a bit in terms of a Tony Williams concept on that. That's another great tune to play live.

The second and third tunes, "Necessary Autumn" and "Chimes," were a little more highly produced, mellower tunes that are aimed at getting some airplay. "Mr. Man" was something that Jeff Andrews wrote, which is a great showcase for him. Then "Catch 22" was very much a collaborative effort between Jeff Andrews, Frank Gambale, Kit Walker, and myself. There are great guitar and bass solos on that tune. 'W.B.J." ("We Be Jammin'") is

"There are some realy great concepts, techniques, and approaches that are being lost. One of my goals is to integrate them in to my playing so they will live on."

and improvise.

RF: Tell us more about the tracks.

SS: The idea behind the first one, "Snap Out Of It," was from the very first Billy Cobham record, *Spectrum*, which I always loved. He had a tune called "Quadrant 4" that had that kind of real fast double bass drum shuffle. I always wanted to play that, and I had never actually recorded anything with that feel. I sat down with Tim Landers and Bob Marlette, and we came up with that tune in about an hour. That's a great opening tune live. It's really exciting.

RF: You do a couple of solos on the record.

SS: There's one unaccompanied solo on the second side, on the title track. That's an excerpt of a piece of music Gary Chaffee and I recorded called "Seventh Heaven," which Gary wrote for two drumsets. It was very challenging music. It's rhythmically very difficult, with a lot of odd groupings and metric modulations. He wrote out each drum part tom-tom, snare drum, bass drum-

Tom Coster's tune, which was basically written for the Korg booth at the NAMM show. "New Boots" is a tune from Frank Gambale, which is a real up-tempo swing tune that we've been playing live. "Night Dive" is one that I wrote with a friend of mine named Marco Zonka, who was my tabla teacher years ago. That one features Andy Narell on steel drums. The last piece, "Church of Milan," was written by Tom Coster, Jr., Tom's son, and it's a great showcase for Frank. It's something very different for him.

On this album, as producer, I was trying to showcase my own drumming in a way that would excite me to hear. Hopefully in doing that, it will also be exciting and interesting for others to hear. I didn't want to overdo it, though. I wanted to leave the space so the other musicians could shine as well. I was also using that concept on the other players so that they're satisfied with their performances and their fans are also excited.

RF: What about the new Steps record?

SS: We recently recorded a new one called *Yin Yang*. Mike Mainieri called it that because it goes in so many directions. It's a great representation of the current band, which has been touring for the last few years. Bendik does a lot of the writing, and his style is what I would call the "Norwegian-folk-ECM style." Mike's writing is all over the place. He writes New York street-hip-hop sounding things and great straight-ahead jazz tunes, and ballads as well. Rachel did some writing, a straight-ahead bebop tune, a little more of a radio commercial-sounding tune .... The record really goes in a lot of different directions, but to me, it all makes sense. It has some really nice playing on it and a great documentation of my straight-ahead playing.

RF: For fans looking at you from the outside, sometimes it seems that things always come easy to someone of your stature. Have there ever been gigs that you couldn't cut? Did anything ever happen to you that was a trauma?

SS: I've been fired from a lot of gigs. And I learned a lot from those situations. My first one was when I played with Lin Biviano. It was a big band, and I worked with him for about a year when I was nineteen. I didn't have a lot of experience, but I did have a good concept of big band. After a year, I wasn't doing the job he wanted to hear. It really devastated me. I thought I was doing a good job. He thought my time could be better, and I was crushed. That was my first one. Then I got fired from Jean-Luc Ponty. I was guilty of being a bad sideman at that point. I had a bad attitude. I was in cahoots with the two guitar players Jamie Glaser and Daryl Stuermer-and we developed our own little clique. We would talk about how we didn't like this and that about the gig. We got off into our little trip, which is a real typical sideman thing to do. And we'd complain how the money wasn't good enough, how he was making all the money. Now

Steve Smith Library

when I look back on it, I realize I didn't understand the sideman contract. We all got the axe simultaneously. He ended up calling all three of us back to work at some point, though. It was a good lesson.

Then there was the Journey one, which we all know about. One of the last ones that happened was with Bryan Adams' *Reckless* record. It was the one I played the track "Heaven" on. Initially he had me playing on the whole record, but I just could not play with the click track. So I ended up getting fired off the record. I just hadn't played with many click tracks before that. I grew up in a time when the click track wasn't what time was judged by. That has been a relatively new development for the drumming world to be judged by. I grew up developing what I call "internal relative time," developing a good feel and a good pulse-but it moves around. None of the Journey records were ever done with a click track, and nothing I had ever done before Journey was done with a click track. So I had never had any experience with it. Bryan wanted to do everything with a click track, so I was virtually trying to learn how to do it and do his record at the same time. I was disappointed, but I got to work on it. All those situations were hard for me to deal with, but I've gotten very focused because of them.

RF: What are your goals these days?

SS: You asked me why I practice and work so hard. What I hope to do in my lifetime is assimilate as much as I possibly can of this whole U.S. drumming concept. As a lot of the drum masters are getting old and passing on, they're taking a lot of secrets with them. There are some really great concepts, techniques, and approaches that are being lost. One of my goals is to integrate them into my playing so they will live on. Then I'll be able to pass that on when *I'm* an old guy.

1997: Steve Smith
Journey Revisited

By Robyn Flans

For Journey lovers, 1997 is a landmark year, as one of the best-selling rock bands in history reunites to please audiences with their classic material-as well as songs from their first studio record in ten years, *Trial By Fire*. Reprising his role as Journey drummer is Steve Smith, who joined the band in 1978 and was "let go" in 1985, largely because of musical differences regarding the making of the band's last studio album, *Raised On Radio*. It was no secret that musical and personal dissension had infiltrated the group. Journey disbanded two years later.

The past ten years have been well spent by Steve. He's been incredibly productive, taking part in many outstanding projects: seven albums and road work with Vital Information; a seven-year relationship with Steps Ahead; albums with the Storm, Shaw/Blades, Y&T, and Italian artists Zucchero and Franchesca de Gregori; a couple of tracks on Mariah Carey's *Emotion*; Jonathan Cain's and Neal Schon's solo albums; the *Burning For Buddy* project; and tours with Stanley Clarke, Allan Holdsworth, and Randy Brecker. When he's at home in Northern California, Steve enjoys working with local bands, covering a variety of styles such as fusion with Marc Russo, straight-ahead jazz with Mel Graves and Mike Zilber, hip-hop with Alphabet Soup, and blues with a trio called the Russell Brothers.

Despite the fact that all of the members of Journey were busy with projects early in 1995, when Sony proposed that the band reunite, it seemed to make sense to everyone involved. To date, Journey has sold more than forty-five million albums, with *Escape* and *Frontiers* remaining on Sony's Top-10 list of best-selling albums to this day. Journey's multi-platinum *Greatest Hits*, released in 1989, continues to sell more than 500,000 copies per year, making it obvious to group members that there is still an enthusiastic audience out there ready for more.

To Steve, whose larger body of work has been in the jazz field, the reunion is an opportunity to make a good wage replaying a role that he can now infuse with ten more years' worth of musical experience and wisdom. "I do some things that make a lot of money," he candidly explains. "I do some things that make a fair amount of money. I do some things that make me very little money, and I do some things that lose money. But all in all, it's a balanced portfolio ... and it feels good."

RF: Are you still practicing like a madman?

SS: Yes. I really enjoy the practicing process, so part of my day is allocated for that. It's one of the first things I do every morning after I get up and have breakfast. I'm more focused if I do it, say, around 9: 00 in the morning.

RF: Until?

SS: Maybe noon. I have a lot of great rational reasons for doing it, but the overriding reason is that it feels great; I enjoy it. I see it as part of my job, just like an athlete must stay in training. I don't understand why it's so surprising that I do this. I'm fascinated by the instrument and the music and want to make it easier to play and access more ideas. Also, I feel it is a way for me to help respect, enhance, and develop the potential of the musical gift I was born with.

RF: Can you elaborate on how you are doing that?

SS: I'm constantly readdressing the foundations of what I do.

RF: Can you define "foundations"?

SS: The basic grip I'm using, the motion that my hands are making, and the path that the stick is making as it's moving through space ... the basic physics of holding the sticks, sitting at the drumset with the feet on the pedals and a sense of balance and centering.

If I'm developing something to a specific degree of proficiency, a lot of times I'll hit some kind of wall. The way to break through that wall is to readdress the foundation. It really gets down to, what does it feel like when I play? The less I break the laws, the easier it gets. I am becoming more and more aware of the physical laws and trying to align with them rather than resist them.

RF: Let's get specific: What does being grounded require?

SS: It requires that we don't get in the way of gravity, that I let the sticks and the pedal fall, and allow them to naturally reach the bottom of the beat. I allow the sticks to touch the surface and play off the surface of the drum, but without going below the surface of the drum.

A tap dancer will use his toes and heels to float on top of the floor; he's not trying to drive his feet through the floor. You don't get anywhere doing that, and you can hurt yourself. That's a common way people play the drums. They don't dance off the top of the drum, they play as if what they're striking is inches below the head. It's really important to find out where the surface lies and play off of it.

It's also about being very aware of the motion that happens once the stick hits the drum. How does it travel between one strike to the next strike? That motion in between is important. To draw an analogy to a percussion instrument, let's use the tambourine. As we drop the tambourine and it hits our hand, we hear that as an impact, like the drumstick coming down and hitting the head of the drum. But as we move the tambourine away from the hand, we hear the other side of the beat; we hear the release. With the drumstick we don't hear the release, so we're not often conscious of what the stick is doing in the release. With a tambourine, the release also has to be in time. Both motions must be in time to work. The motion of time and space being equal is the result of respecting the laws.

It's difficult and meticulous work addressing this. And this is just breaking down one piece of the puzzle. When I strike the drum, the stick will naturally bounce as long as I don't inhibit that bounce. So I have to move my hand out of the way of the stick to allow it to move through space, and then I have to guide it back down, to start the trip back down and allow gravity to take it

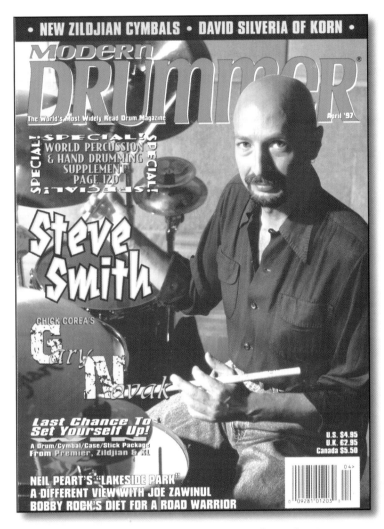

back down. I don't want to force any of it. I don't want to lift it up or push it down. I want to facilitate its bounce, and then its rebound, by letting gravity take hold. How my hand moves is really dependent on what dynamic level I'm playing at, and what instrument I'm playing-a cymbal, the snare, a tom-tom, whether I'm moving from the snare to the tom to the cymbal; there are so many variables.

It takes an amazing amount of concentration to slow down the process to the point where it's meditative. I just have to work with microscopic pieces and watch and adjust my body to the point where I'm just breathing and relaxing. Eventually, when the motions are developed and I get out of the way, it starts to play itself.

Every time I go to Fred Gruber to take a lesson-every four to six months-I'll get a piece and develop it. After I've developed that, there will be even more detail to take it a step further: How can I make it easier and lighter? What I mean by lighter is, when you have less and less resistance, there is actually a physical sensation of the stick being lighter, almost weightless-though the sound that comes out can be bigger and stronger-sounding, yet without the effort that I expended, say, ten years ago. That's the analytical practice stage, but when I play the drums in performance, I pay less attention to the mechanics of it because I've spent the time in practice, so it's easier for me to play and it's more of a creative experience.

I feel a new sense of balance and grounding-sensing the bottom of the beat, sensing my body movement on the drumset with increased ease. I've discovered that I don't often break sticks or cymbals. I occasionally dent drumheads, and they wear out, but not quickly. I changed the upper tom heads once during the whole tracking sessions for the Journey record. It's because of touch. The sticks wear out eventually, but I notice that without forcing things, I'm not breaking them, which brings up the subject of common injuries. When you're using tension, something has to give. Hopefully your arm will not break; the stick will break first, the cymbal will break first. But usually, your body has already taken quite a beating.

RF: Certainly this is applicable to the Vital Information situation, but what about the dynamics and power in the Journey situation?

SS: There may be a misconception that what I'm talking about can only work in a soft context, but that's not the case. Buddy Rich is such a great example of somebody who embodied all of this. That was one of the reasons he was such a technically accomplished player. Buddy didn't break the laws; he was aligned with them, which explains a lot of his facility. But he was capable of playing incredibly loud. You can utilize all of these principles with a full range of dynamics.

I'm finding the Journey situation very comfortable in fact, it's easier than it used to be. I have just as big a sound as I used to have, but I would have had to play with a lot more force to fill up the same space with sound.

RF: There was a ten-year absence of playing in that group. You're ten years older, more musically mature, more studied, more experienced, and now you're going back in a situation from your past. Did you need to redevelop certain techniques you used back then because that's what worked, or can you truly apply your maturity to a situation you were in ten years ago?

SS: When I realized this reunion was inevitable, I decided to really do my homework on rock 'n' roll. When I first joined the band in '78, I was coming from more of a jazz background, with pretty limited rock 'n' roll knowledge. I knew of the groups of the '60s, like Hendrix, Cream, and Led Zeppelin, but I had never done any major research on rock 'n' roll history. I had done that with jazz.

In the last few years, I really traced the rock roots of the instrument, the music, and all the different players. When I first joined Journey, I played the music intuitively. I was sort of a toned-down fusion drummer at the time. But for this reunion, I decided to approach the music from a completely different perspective, more from the roots of rock 'n' roll.

In my researching the history of the drumset I decided to go back and try to find the point where the music began to diverge from jazz. The instrument itself was basically designed to play jazz. If you were a drummer before a certain time, you were pretty much a jazz drummer. Eventually they used the drumset to play the blues. I tried to find the point where the blues started to evolve into the early rock 'n' roll feels. I read books, bought videos and a lot of biographies and histories of rock 'n' roll, and then went out and tried to find the recordings to accompany all of that. I enjoyed it. This is my work. If you talk to somebody who writes a book, they do research before they start writing, so this was no different.

I really dug into the whole blues thing and found as many of the earliest recordings as I could. Most of them have no drums, and some of them have a washboard. Then eventually, there are drums.

Louis Jordan & the Tympany Five were called jump blues, but they're credited for creating some of the early rock 'n' roll. Jordan had a drummer named Shadow Wilson, who was a great jazz drummer. Some of the other early breakthrough guys were Little Richard, Fats Domino, Jerry Lee Lewis, and Elvis Presley, and I listened to original recordings and checked out what their drummers were playing, and then found the common threads.

Earl Palmer was somebody who really came up as a strong influence as far as all this goes, because most of the early rock stuff came from New Orleans. He was the session player on many of the records coming from there. There's a DCI collection called *New Orleans*

Drumming, and I thought his part was fantastic. I learned a lot about the earliest rock 'n' roll feels from listening and watching him play.

What struck me was that nearly all of the early rock drummers were basically jazz drummers who, while doing the studio work, had to come up with parts to fit the new music being played. Thus, rock drumming was born. The one thread I heard with most of the first generation rockers was that they swung like crazy.

It was coming out of swing, it was coming out of a shuffle. If you listen to Little Richard or Fats Domino, it's not an even 8th-note feel for the most part. It's a shuffle type of feel, a swinging, swampy feel, which Jim Keltner so embodies and has kept alive through the years. The whole British Invasion had to base their music on something, and this is pretty much what they based it on. Rather than going to John Bonham and Ringo, which is legitimate-and I did readdress all that-I wanted to hear where they got their stuff from. From what it sounds like to me, they got their influences mostly from jazz drummers like Max Roach, Art Blakey, Elvin Jones, Philly Joe Jones, Buddy Rich, and Gene Krupa, and then the work of Earl Palmer and his contemporaries. When I listen to those early English drummers, they have this great swing as well.

The further we get from the source, the further drummers move away from their orientation of the instrument being based in the 4/4 swing pulse, or at least the shuffle. Consequently, we're further removed from the essence of a grooving, swinging, downhome funky rock feel.

I did personal examinations of the different musicians I knew who were influential to Steve Perry, Neal Schon, and Jonathan Cain. I know Steve's major influence is Sam Cooke, so I read his biography and I had a sense of where he came from with his gospel roots. I bought many of his recordings, which encompassed all of his different periods. Jackie Wilson is also a big influence on Steve, as well as many of the great soul singers of the '60s. I bought Motown collections-Wilson Pickett, Marvin Gaye, and Otis Redding, to name a few.

I wanted it to be that when I walked into the rehearsal hall with Journey, it would be different from before. Like when Steve would talk about this Sam Cooke tune or the feel of this Motown hit-back then, if he gave me a hint of what it was about, I could fake it; I could come up with a good approximation and something intuitively that worked. But now I was coming at it more from having firsthand knowledge of what it was he was listening to. It was easier for us to connect musically.

It was always easier for me to connect with Neal, with his heavy background in blues and then Eric Clapton and Hendrix and the whole '60s guitar thing, because I was pretty familiar with it. But I went back even further to check out Neal's blues roots. It was an interesting period of months where I was listening and reading. I'd then try to play along with the records and try to cop the feel, getting right back to how I practiced

Steve Smith Library

when I was a kid. I also went out and played gigs with some of the local San Francisco players. This way I could embody it, feel it, and develop it, so I could play it whenever it was appropriate. It gave me the feeling that I could enjoy this Journey reunion and get something out of it in a musical way.

RF: How do you see your evolution of the last ten years, and what do you see that you're bringing to the music, aside from the studying?

SS: I've had a lot of studio experience in the last ten

for me to bring to the situation.

Something new I brought to the reunion was a sense of detachment from the "band experience." Before, the band was incredibly important to me and the outlet was really crucial in that I wanted to demonstrate everything I knew, my ability and knowledge, and I was trying to squeeze everything in, which can cause a lot of tension. In some ways it can create some great music, and there's something to be said for that. But behind that, there was also somewhat of a lack of awareness of

Steve Perry playing Steve Smith's drums at the Trial By Fire session

Steve Smith Library

years, so I have a lot of newly developed skills in "song drumming." I have a lot of technical awareness of the studio environment and playing with click tracks, sequencers, loops, and all of the modern technology, which I didn't have any knowledge of when I had originally joined the band. That was a lot of experience

what might be the most appropriate thing to play. Now I just cut to the chase without taking some unnecessary, circuitous route. Having a lot of experience as a hired hand now, I do what the people who hire me want, and there are boundaries to be creative within, which is the challenge. So I take the challenge and if they like it, great, and if they don't, I'm not attached to it; I'm just there to do my job. I've learned something through the experience, but I'm not attached to it. I approached this situation with that sense of professionalism and objectivity.

RF: Having done a lot of session projects, you probably came back to this situation with more confidence.

SS: Yes. I had the confidence to know I could do a good job and to know I have worked with very demanding people who have been very satisfied with my work. I

working day would be 11: 00 to 5:00, five days a week, like a regular day gig. We would jam and come up with song ideas and nurture them to completion. We pretty consistently created one song a day for a couple of months. That would result in a pretty good song form- verse, chorus, bridge, with an arrangement and some melody, although no lyrics. Then we would make a rough demo with a couple of mic's in the room.

The other approach taken was that Jon, Neal, and Steve, or just a couple of them, would go to Jon's

Ross Valory and Steve's drums at the Trial By Fire session

went into this situation with that attitude.

RF: In the early days the creation of the music was a band process. When Journey recorded *Raised On Radio* in 1985 it was much less that way. How was the new material put together?

SS: It was a combination of approaches. A normal

house and sketch out some song ideas. What they did differently from the *Raised On Radio* project, except for two tunes, was they didn't use a drum computer or synth bass, which was really nice. They just left it open, so when Ross [Valory] and I came in, we could take their ideas and put ourselves into it. They had the knowledge that there was something of value in that spark of chemistry and creativity that happens with the five of us in the room. That felt great.

After a few months of this, we had around thirty songs in various stages of completion. Then we tried to hone down the best of those because the lyric and final melody writing was rather painstaking for Jon and Steve, and they didn't want to do it if it was unnecessary. We got it down to eighteen songs, and they completed them. We ended up choosing sixteen to record.

By the time producer Kevin Shirley showed up, we were ready to record-or so we thought. He took a different approach and wanted us to rehearse. All of us had done a lot of studio work while we were apart, and everyone was comfortable with the idea of going into the studio with a pretty good idea of what the song was and focusing on that one song and cutting it. If we had to play through the sixteen songs, we really didn't know them. We knew them that one day, but without listening to the demo, we had completely forgotten them. I would write out a sketch of a chart as it went by, so I had my music to refer to, but I didn't

have it memorized. He wanted us to rehearse the stuff like we were a young band and get the music to the point where we had it just about memorized and could perform all the songs like a set. That is something we used to do way back when, but we didn't want to do it this time. So there was a lot of grumbling, but we did it. We spent three weeks rehearsing the songs that had already been written.

RF: Was there value in that?

SS: Yes, it turned out to be good. We got to the point where we honed the songs even more than they were, and we got very comfortable with them. So by the time we went into the studio, we were going for magical takes, rather than trying to learn the song and then trying to get the magical take. We only had to do maybe three takes per song, so there was a lot of energy and spontaneity in the performance.

We did play everything as a band. We used a click track on everything, which was almost more at my insistence than anybody else's. I feel very comfortable with a click track, and it makes it easier for me; I think of it as a ruler with which I'm trying to draw a straight line across a page. We cut everything live with vocals

Legend to Legend 1997: Peter Erskine & Steve Smith

"I have a long association with Peter," Steve Smith said in an MD Reflections article last September. "I first saw him when he was with Stan Kenton when he was eighteen years old; I was the same age. I was completely knocked out with his playing. I attended a Stan Kenton summer camp back then and learned so much from Peter. He was a major influence on me."
Knowing that Smith and Erskine were old friends, we asked Peter if he had any thoughts, comments, or questions he'd like to pose to Steve. He happily volunteered: "Steve, you have made all of us who have known you or followed your career quite proud by your drumming achievements. Your work in the

Steve Smith Library

musical, popular, and educational idioms has inspired many drummers. I salute you, old friend, and offer these questions, not only as the 'devil's advocate,' but also as a curious colleague."

Peter: You successfully traverse playing many different styles; how

important is it to be able to play more than one type of music?
Steve: In the big picture, it seems to me that I only play one type of music, U. S. music. The more familiar I am with the roots of U.S. music-the blues, New Orleans music, swing, big band, bebop, etc.-the easier it is for me to move around between today's different styles, since they all grew from those roots. We need to understand the past in order to play the music of today with depth. To follow that thread, we need to be versed in the styles of today in order to create a music of tomorrow that incorporates and reflects today's world.

Peter: How did your jazz experience help you with the Journey gig?

Marco Soccoli

and guitar solos, and I'd say a lot of the guitar solos ended up being live. We kept almost everything. Occasionally we would splice a verse from one take or a chorus from another take, but that felt better to us than doing it with a computer. Kevin Shirley was trying to capture what he felt was the essence of the band-sometimes against what we wanted to do. But he got his way, and he did a great job producing us.

RF: What things did you resist?

SS: The title track, "Trial By Fire," was written to a drum loop, and the guys were saying, "Let's just cut it to the drum loop, and then Steve can overdub the drums to it." I was fine with that because

---

Steve: My jazz playing is the foundation of my musicianship. When I play the Journey music, I aspire to the same degree of musical integrity necessary to play with great jazz musicians. So the jazz experience has helped by orienting me to think with a jazz musician's mind.

Peter: Conversely, how have you been able to draw upon your Journey experiences when doing other types of music?

Steve: The Journey experience has helped me to not always think with the jazz musician's mind! It freed me from some of the limitations of jazz-think. The guys in Journey will sometimes do something or ask me to do something that may not make musical "sense" to me, but it ends up sounding good. I've learned to be able to keep my playing minimal

and to the point and that can be universally applied.

Peter: It is difficult for many players to switch from a loud/hard-hitting playing environment to a quiet/small-group (i.e. jazz) setting. For example, if the complaint or observation is made that the drums are "too loud," the drummer responds, "Well, I've been playing a rock gig for the last couple of months ...." How important is it to always have all levels of dynamics available in your playing?

Steve: It is important to always have all dynamic levels available, and I have to be constantly vigilant that I don't lose my ability to play soft and with finesse while playing a rock gig. I try to work in a lot of soft-touch, ghost notes in the rock playing. You don't hear most of it, but it gives the drumming more flow, and it can

keep my touch relatively intact. I'll also do a fair amount of "damage control" practice to keep my finesse developing.

Conversely, when I know I have a hard hitting gig coming up, and I haven't been doing that, I'll get ready for it by building up my "big sound" chops.

Peter: I've noticed how excellent your posture at the kit has become in recent years. Why is that, and what purpose does it serve?

Steve: The posture is a result of developing better foot technique. If I do that properly, I sit more centered and stay grounded, which helps the groove. As far as the upper body goes, I had a "drum lesson" from one of your old bosses-Joe Zawinul. He told me I had my right shoulder higher than my left, and that wasn't going to work; I had to be balanced

I've done that hundreds of times. Kevin said no, so we learned the song, rehearsed it, and I imitated the drum loop, but did my thing to it, and it came out better. He really pushed the band toward the live performance thing.

Kevin is a very strong personality, and we needed that. Also, he's a musician, and it's the first time we had a producer who wasn't just an engineer/producer. He has musical knowledge, and he's a great engineer, so he got into suggesting different chords and different arrangements, but from a more musical perspective than in the past.

RF: It was probably good to have one ringleader to whom you had to defer.

SS: Right. It took the pressure off of us to always have to fight it out amongst the five of us. He earned his money. One of the things he did that I was really happy about was insist on there not being fadeouts on the record. Most of the songs really didn't have endings, and we were just going to fade. When it came time to cut the track, we'd goof around a little at the end and have some fun. Thankfully, we created some endings very spontaneously. Some of the endings were kinda wild and nuts, and he ended up leaving everything.

RF: Let's talk about some of the specific tracks that might have been more creative or challenging.

SS: "Message Of Love" reminded me somewhat of the drumming I did on "Separate Ways." I came up with what fit for that particular song, but it has a breakdown in the middle and drum fills. That one had a particularly exciting fade-out on it, which Kevin kept. That was an exciting tune to play.

On "One More," I really got into the sound of this new Zildjian cymbal combination called Trash Hats. There's a little 14" China cymbal on the bottom and a 12" top cymbal. It has a really nasty, trashy hi-hat type of sound. I put them up and played hip-hop feels, which really works well. I also used that sound on "Colors Of The Spirit," which has a sort of slowed-down hip-hop type of groove with a slight swing to it. I used the Trash Hats in the chorus, and it has a nice feel to it.

"Castles Burning" was a fun track because it's reminiscent of Hendrix and a Band Of Gypsys kind of feel, a sort of Buddy Miles or Greg Errico [Sly & the Family Stone] type of feel to it. It's got a little hip-hop breakdown in the middle. That one was really fun and exciting to play. At the fade of that one, there's a funky double bass groove I play. You can't hear it too well in

---

Legend to Legend: Peter Erskine & Steve Smith continued

and centered like a boxer. I took his advice and it has improved my feel and my movement around the kit.

Peter: What do you listen to while you're playing?

Steve: My listening focus will first be on the rhythm section, connecting with the bass and then the keyboards and/or guitar. Then my focus will go to the soloist so I'm supportive and responsive to where he is going. Basically, I want to hear everyone. In most live situations I try to either use no monitor or as little monitor as possible. Usually I have no drums in the monitors, but occasionally I'll have a little bass drum so I can feel it.

Peter: What about hearing protection?

Steve: I got into hearing protection

too late, and I have lost some of my high end and have tinnitus. I always use the molded earplugs when practicing, playing with Journey, or doing any loud gig. Gordy Knudtson has some great headphones [GK Ultraphones] for practicing that really cut down the volume of the drums so you don't need to turn up the level of the music in the phones. I also use them in the studio all the time now.

Peter: Which outside activities have contributed to your drumming (exercise, meditation, going for walks, reading, kids, etc.)?

Steve: Raising children, experiencing the vicissitudes of marriage and divorce, developing a relationship with my partner Diane, all contribute to my personal growth, which is

reflected in my musicianship. I do keep limber with some yoga stretches and massage. I do some moderate exercise, which keeps my body in shape. I try to stay inspired and fresh by listening to or reading Thich Nhat Hanh, Marianne Williamson, Deepak Chopra, and many others. Therapy, journalizing, and meditating are also important to keep me processing life's input.

Peter: How important is it to be able to read music?

Steve: Reading music has helped me in many ways, so I think it is important. I probably learn and play at least one hundred new pieces of music each year. I couldn't do it if I had to rely only on my memory. Reading music makes that work so much easier. I can relax and focus the mix, but it was a little groove that Tim Alexander showed me when we hung out one day. He's got some really nice double bass stuff.

Then there are a few of the typical Journey ballad tunes on the record, which I just did my treatment to, that ballad thing. Something different I used on this record from any of the other records was my Zildjian flat cymbal. I have a nice 20" K Flat Top ride with four rivets in it. I'd bring different things to rehearsal, not knowing what the reaction would be. Who would have guessed? Everyone loved the sound, so instead of playing the hi-hat for the verse on some of those ballads, I played that flat sizzle cymbal.

RF: Listening to the album, I was hearing a little more of a jazz approach. That may account for it.

SS: Yes, that might have been the jazz sort of sound. It's mellow, it has a flow; it's not jagged, it's smooth. I used that on quite a few of the tunes. I also used an LP tambourine mounted to my left on some of the songs for a backbeat. I did that on "When You Love A Woman" and "Forever In Blue."

RF: What about the double bass?

SS: I used the double pedal in the studio, although I'll probably use the two bass drums on the tour. The double pedal records well, so I used that on "One More," "Can't Tame The Lion," "Castles Burning," and "I Can See It In Your Eyes," which is only on the Japanese and European release.

One other one I'd like to mention is "It's Just The Rain," which I love the mood on. That one was written to a drum loop, and the part I'm playing is almost identical to what the drum loop played. "Trial By Fire" was also a drum loop song. It's sort of a reggae tune that's hidden at the end of the record. It was a tune that we demoed early on in the process, and it had a blues shuffle feeling. We were fooling around with it one day and played it as a reggae tune, and Kevin really loved it, so we ended up recording it as a reggae tune.

RF: You've become very proficient with traditional grip. Did you ever feel you wanted to use matched grip on the new Journey record, and what will you do live?

SS: On this record I played most of the tunes with traditional grip, but I played a few of the tunes matched grip as well. With me it depends on what feels right for the song.

RF: It's not about power for you?

SS: No, it's a feel thing. "I Can See It In Your Eyes," which is not on the U.S. record, was a matched-grip tune. The

on the playing. For the musicians who speak that language, it's an important form of communication. I'm glad I can participate in that dialog.

Peter: Who have been some of the more interesting people you've worked with? Best boss? Worst?

Steve: Ahmad Jamal was very interesting. He had a few hand signals I had to learn, and he would spontaneously create different arrangements night after night. I had to watch him like a hawk so I wouldn't miss one of these subtle cues-go to the bridge, to the top, solo section, lay out.... The music was loose and a lot of fun.

Mariah Carey was interesting because she is such a total babe! I was a total fan.

I always enjoy working with another one of your old bosses, Mike Mainieri. I think he's a great boss. He has a concept, but he remains open and allows the band to take on its own life.

Worst boss? Producer Beau Hill. I had a good experience with him on a Dweezil Zappa record, but on the Storm record I did, despite my numerous protests, he triggered samples on all of my drums, which destroyed the sound. It removed any trace of nuance, dynamics, and feel, not to mention the misfirings that occurred, or the complete omission of some fills or beats I played. A very unrewarding experience.

A producer I really enjoy working with is Corrado Rustici. He produces artists like Zucchero and Franchesca de Gregori in Italy, and the work is very musical and interesting. I love the way he combines loops and my live drums to create a complex hybrid of sound and groove.

Peter: What kind of drumstick do you use?

Steve: Great question! I use my custom designed, signature-model Vic Firth slicks most of the time. On some of the songs on Trial By Fire, I used the Steve Gadd or Harvey Mason models. I also like the Vic Firth 7 A for some lighter playing.

Peter: And, finally: Now that a great many others have adopted the shaved head/goatee look, whaddya gonna do?

Steve: I'm going to kidnap you and send you to my barber!

drum part was reminiscent of the Led Zeppelin song "Rock And Roll." I could just get more of the feeling I wanted with matched grip. "It's Just The Rain," which is more of a ballad, for some reason felt better matched grip. On "Trial By Fire" I used Hot Rods and matched grip. In "Still She Cries," I used a stick in my right hand and an Ed Thigpen brush in my left hand. "If He Should Break Your Heart" was half and half. The first half of the tune was all matched grip, and then as we reached the fade-out I went to traditional grip.

It's technically easier for me to play traditional grip; I feel more at home. But there is something to be said for the matched grip for a feel. One of the points of all the facility is to have choices. Each angle and each approach has a particular feel, so therein lies the decision. If you think of it in terms of different periods of the development of music, there were particular approaches to the drumset, technically, that worked. So in some ways to get a more authentic feel to certain roots of a musical sound, even physically approaching it in relation to the grip will help access that feel.

If I'm playing a backbeat on a particular song, I'll play traditional grip differently from the way I do when I'm playing straight-ahead swing. For swing, I'll have my hand up a bit higher on the stick. With more of an angle, you can get a lighter sound. For more of a rock sound with the traditional grip, the stick will be more parallel to the head so you get the rim and the full bead of the stick on the head.

RF: How did the group get back together, and what was it like playing together for the first time?
SS: As far as I can tell, how we got back together started with Columbia first working towards reuniting Steve with Jonathan and Neal, and then including Ross and me in the mix. It was difficult to get it off the ground initially. Steve was happy doing a solo project, as were the other guys.

Eventually Steve got interested, and he really was the crucial piece. The rest of us had had some dialog about whether we'd be interested in doing something like this if the opportunity arose. The other members were into it. When he consented to get together with everybody, we went into a rehearsal hall in L.A. and just played.

Actually, the story there was that we were supposed to play on a particular day in September [of '95], though we were going to get into town the night before and set up the instruments on the rehearsal stage. But you can't get people to just set up their stuff and not start playing. So it ended up that the four of us set up and started jamming right away. We had a list of some of the old Journey tunes we were going to play, which none of us had played for all those years. We were having a lot of fun, and then Steve Perry called to find out what was going on, and we said, "Come on over." So it actually started a day early. He came over, we ran through a bunch of the songs, and it felt really good. The next day we got together again and played, and the chemistry was instantaneous.

It was interesting to me that it still felt good after all those years; it didn't feel like we had been apart for so long. During the next few months, we worked out the legal matters, and then we worked on some of the personal issues that had been unresolved in the ten years.
RF: It's no secret that when Journey ended there were some problems. Ten years later you came back into this feeling ...
SS: ... a bit apprehensive about getting involved again. As far as having moved on from the pain I went through when I first left the band in '85, I felt resolved about that. I didn't harbor any resentment about being kicked out of the band, because dealing with those pains turned out to be a blessing in disguise for me. It helped me to move on as far as being a musician and developing as a person, and having to make my way in life without the protective cocoon of a successful rock band.

From the point of view of needing a resolution, it didn't matter to me if this reunion happened. What I was apprehensive about was getting involved in this type of lifestyle again, and opening the whole can of worms that goes with it. I enjoyed my life and really liked what was going on with Vital Information, the clinics, the sessions, and family life. But with the success of all the other reunion bands, it seemed like a great opportunity to further heal some of the wounds that happened when the band broke up.
RF: So let's talk about where you stand with Vital Information and your last release, *Ray Of Hope*. One of the reviews had applauded the playing, but was not overwhelmed with the material, which raises the question about instrumental music right now-who it gets written for and what impact it's supposed to make.
SS: That is a very big question. I'd have to start by saying it was written for the musicians and listeners alike-to

entertain, excite, and inspire them. When the music was first being developed in the late '60s and early '70s, there was a great musical openness and creative spirit that doesn't exist today in the same way. Rock was still fairly innocent and not formularized, soul music was very creative, jazz was experimenting with modal forms, and the climate was ripe for cross-pollination. We had a burst of creativity from Miles Davis, the Tony Williams Lifetime, Mahavishnu Orchestra, Return To Forever, Weather Report, and others that was socially supported as an expression of the times.

There is still some great music being played, and there are musicians coming up with some fresh approaches. But on the whole, I think the fusion era has come to an end as far as its being a vital movement.

It seems that it was assumed that listeners became less adventurous, and the music reflected that. I think there will always be an audience for it if it's played with integrity and high musicianship. The "young lions" are proving that there is still an audience for well-played bebop.

Vital Information: Frank Gambale, Jeff Andrews, Tom Coster, Steve Smith

Steve Smith Library

As for *Ray Of Hope*, we did a lot of group writing, which is the first time we ever did that. We got in a room and jammed on some grooves, and then completed the compositions based on those grooves, which is more or less the rock 'n' roll writing style I had experienced with Journey. The music we came up with for this record was, in some ways, surprisingly mellow. On the whole, it's not a hard-core fusion record. For whatever reason, that's where the group was at, and we went with it.

We hope to have a new Vital Information recording completed before I go on tour with Journey. We're going to go for a much looser, more improvisational approach. The writing will be blues-based, with Tom Coster playing the instruments he grew up on-Hammond B3 and Fender Rhodes. Jeff Andrews will be playing a lot of acoustic bass, and Frank Gambale will be using his hollow-body guitar. I'll be going for a more organic jazz drum sound. We're really looking forward to reinventing ourselves and taking on the challenge of making a statement that is personal and interesting to

us, as well as entertaining and inspiring to our listeners.
RF: When the journey with Journey is completed, what will you do?
SS: I think I'll just continue to do what I was doing before Journey came along, which is record and tour with Vital Information, do session recordings, clinics, solo performances-be a working musician, and spend time with my family and loved ones.

2003: Steve Smith
Confessions of a
U.S. Ethnic Drummer

By Bill Milkowski

There was a defining moment at the Drummers Collective 25th Anniversary Celebration last November in New York City in which Steve Smith revealed himself to be hipper than the room. Following an awesome display of mondo-technique from a succession of heavyweight chopsmeisters like Kim Plainfield, Dave Weckl, and Horacio "El Negro" Hernandez (all of whom the packed house of aspiring drummers ate up with delight,) Smith took the stage and proceeded to hold court with simply a snare and a pair of brushes. No imposing double bass barrage, no acrobatic fills or traversing the kit with pumped up attack, no heroic cross-sticking or clave action on a wood block triggered by a foot pedal. No chops grandstanding, no flailing, no sweating. Just snare and brushes, a totally relaxed approach, and a deep desire to make music. It was the perfect Zen-like response to the parade of whirlwind sticking that had preceded him, the ultimate example of "less is more."

If Smith hadn't won the crowd over by that point-playing Ed Thigpen in the wake of Billy Cobham's thunder-he certainly did with his next savvy maneuver. Taking his hi-hat and a single stick to the front of the stage, he proceeded to wow the crowd with a demonstration of stick balancing points that was part Papa Jo Jones, part Harlem Globetrotters. By the time he had the stick balancing and rebounding in seamless sequence off his shin, his ankle, his arm, rolling it between fingers without dropping a beat, the crowd offered up ecstatic applause. It's an old-school move that never fails to entertain. Papa Jo did it himself before an awed crowd at the 1957 Newport Jazz

Festival, and living legend Roy Haynes continues to do it to this day. But no one expected a bona fide fusionhead, Mr. Vital Information, to pull off such a slick, old-school trick with such smooth aplomb. Everyone in the house knew that Steve Smith was a killer drummer. But who knew he was so hip? As Roy used to say to himself, "There might be a better drummer than me, but there's no one hipper."

It might be because Smith had been spending a lot of time in the past, so to speak, that he channeled such old-school shtick. Or perhaps he is precisely what drum elder and bop guru Freddie Gruber called him, "An old soul in a young body." As the writer, narrator, and demonstrator of *Drumset Technique/History Of The US Beat*, a two-disc DVD set from Hudson Music that thoroughly examines the evolution of the drumset in US music while offering examples of how the kit was used in all the major styles, Smith immersed himself in studying the origins of this uniquely American instrument, going all the way back to Africa to find clues on how the drumset came to be.

Using a comprehensive and scholarly approach, Smith traced the evolution of the drumset from hand drums and talking drums to "patting juba" to the incorporation of cymbals and the development of the first practical bass drum pedal. This enlightening musical travelogue progresses from early New Orleans jazz at the turn of the twentieth century, to big band jazz in the '30s, to bop in the '40s, through rhythm & blues, blues, country, gospel, rock 'n' roll, funk, and '70s fusion. Steve provides detailed examples along the way of how the drummers implemented the kit into the style of the times. In addition, his group, Vital Information, performs seven complete tunes that feature applications of the techniques and complex rhythms that Steve broke down in complete detail in Disc One.

A massive undertaking, this comprehensive two-DVD set runs over four and a half hours, along the way providing enlightenment and entertainment for drummers and non-drummers alike.

MD: Did you consciously put yourself into a scholarly frame of mind to do this project, *Drumset Technique/History Of The US Beat?*

Steve: That mindset of exploring the history of US music is just something that I've been living for a long time, so I've been in that headspace for quite a few years.

MD: Then this project was merely formalizing something that you've been thinking about anyway?

Steve: Yeah, exactly. I guess the place to start is the Vital Information album *Where We Come From.* Before we did that album back in 1997 I had spent some time investigating Afro-Cuban music. I realized I could learn the patterns of that style of drumming, and I could play it to a degree.

But I didn't really play it well, in my opinion, because I didn't grow up in the culture. I realized that the best musicians of the genre are literally all from Cuba or Puerto Rico or somewhere else in the Caribbean, and most of them know the history of their music and culture. This inspired me to focus on the music of my own culture and use that same approach. I had to admit that as a US drummer I didn't know a lot about the origins of my own music. I knew some jazz history, and I had lived through '60s rock and the fusion era. But I didn't know a lot about early jazz, rhythm & blues, blues, country, and gospel. And at a point I really started seeing myself as part of a lineage, a US ethnic drummer playing the percussion instrument of the United States-the drumset.

MD: And that triggered your whole investigation of the past?

Steve: Definitely. I wanted to be informed about my own past and what I was connected to. I became engrossed in learning about the whole US music scene in general and the development of the drumset in particular. So now I really do see myself as a US ethnic drummer who plays all the different styles of US music. Not that I'm unique doing this-I think there's a

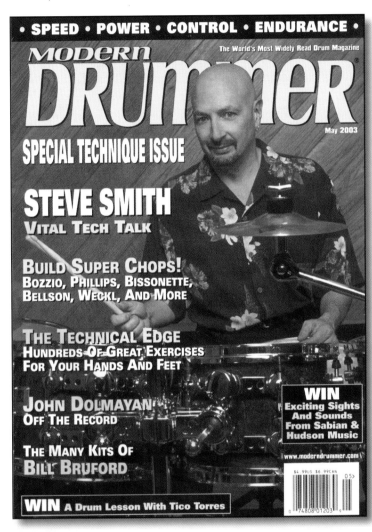

lot of guys doing it, but they may not have identified themselves as that. It's been helpful for me to think of myself as a US ethnic drummer. It's a bigger perspective than a "jazz drummer" or "studio drummer" or "fusion drummer."

MD: How did this project come to fruition? How did you research it and what areas in particular did you have to study that you weren't well acquainted with?

Steve: I started from the perspective of a jazz drummer, because that's essentially how I first learned to play the drums. As a kid I took lessons from a teacher named Billy Flanagan, who lived in Brockton, Massachusetts. In the 1960s he was already in his sixties, so he had played in the '30s and the '40s. He was a swing drummer like Louie Bellson or Buddy Rich, and that's the concept that I learned from him. But growing up in the '60s, I just sort of intuited rock 'n' roll, because it was in the culture. I find that you don't so much have to study the music that is of the culture that you're growing up in, you just seem to "get" it. I just got Led Zeppelin and Jimi Hendrix, so I didn't have to really study that music, just like a kid today wouldn't have to study Blink-182, Tool, or whatever bands they're listening to. And with fusion, I saw the first generation of it happen. When I got out of high school in '72 and went to Berklee, I got to see Return To Forever, Billy Cobham's band, Tony Williams' Lifetime, The Headhunters, and all of that. That music, because it was in the air, was part of the culture of my time.

MD: So what styles did you have to study in order to prepare for this DVD project?

Steve: Initially I had done research on older styles without ever thinking about doing a DVD. It was just something I was doing, following my own interests because I was curious and wanted to expand my knowledge and playing ability. But in preparing the DVD, I had to go back and study those styles that didn't come naturally to me. For example, I had to study the early New Orleans drumming. I didn't grow up in New Orleans, and obviously I didn't grow up in the '20s or the '30s, so that was definitely something I had to investigate.

So I studied the early New Orleans thing and just followed it sequentially through the swing bands and bebop and rhythm & blues and all of that. And then I eventually branched out and started to learn more about all the different styles of US music that at first didn't have drums but were still a big part of the culture. I looked for the earliest blues, gospel, and country recordings that I could find. So it started with jazz drumming, and then I followed it back as far as I could go through listening to recordings, reading about it, and talking to people-whatever I could do to get educated.

MD: I understand that you're currently involved in another musicology undertaking.

Steve: Yes, another project we're doing with Hudson Music is a history of rock 'n' roll drumming. And through that I've gotten to meet some of the early rock 'n' roll drummers, like Buddy Harman, who was probably the first Nashville country drummer, and D.J. Fontana, who toured and recorded with Elvis Presley. I've also met Jerry Allison from Buddy Holly's band, The Crickets, and J.M. Van Eaton, who was the house drummer at Sun Records. So I've gotten a chance to talk to and interview these guys-Earl Palmer, Hal Blaine, Sandy Nelson. I'm

getting a lot of input for this next project and learning about these other styles of music.

MD: Any revelations from that project?

Steve: I found it somewhat of a revelation that there was no such thing as country drummers, blues drummers, gospel drummers, or rock drummers in the very first generation of adding drums to those styles of music. It turns out that most of the guys who played on the early country, blues, gospel, and rock 'n' roll sessions considered themselves jazz drummers.

For example, in 1935, when Bob Wills wanted to add a drummer to his western swing group The Texas Playboys, he got Smokey Dakus, who was a jazz drummer, because there was no such thing as a country drummer at the time. Drums weren't added to Nashville country music until the '50s. And the guy who did most of those early country sessions, Buddy Harman, was a jazz drummer as well. If a country musician wanted a drummer on his record at that time, he hired a jazz drummer. So the real revelation is that for about the first fifty years of US music history, the only kind of drumming going on was jazz drumming, whether it was New Orleans style, swing style, bebop, or early rhythm & blues drumming, which is really more of a big band concept applied to a small group with a singer or sax player out front.

MD: And even into the '60s with Motown, those session guys were all working jazz musicians before Motown hired them as the house band.

Steve: Exactly. And the same with the blues guys. When Chess Records added drums to Muddy Waters' and other blues players' recordings in the early '50s, there were no blues drummers yet, so they added jazz drummers like Fred Below. Same with gospel recordings; they'd hire Panama Francis or some other New York or Memphis drummer who had a jazz background. It was interesting for me to see that the jazz drummers were really the original drummers in every genre in American music.

MD: That's the common ground that makes it such quintessentially American music.

Steve: Yeah! And it was even the same thing with early rock 'n' roll. Earl Palmer, who is essentially a bebop drummer from New Orleans, played on all of those early Fats Domino and Little Richard sessions recorded in New Orleans during the '50s.

Shortly thereafter, young drummers began identifying

themselves as something other than a jazz drummer. When I did these interviews with the early rock drummers, I asked them how they saw themselves. D.J. Fontana said he clearly saw himself as a jazz drummer. He grew up in the northern part of Louisiana listening to Gene Krupa and wanting to play jazz, but ended up getting the gig with Elvis. It was a great gig, so he did it. But he still saw himself as a jazz drummer. Jerry Allison, when he was a kid, saw Elvis with D.J. But Jerry was fourteen then and thought, "I wanna be a rock 'n'

You could extend that to today, where maybe an R&B drummer was playing on the first rap record in the late '70s and not considering himself a rap drummer, because there was no such thing at the time. But then quickly, probably within a year or so, there would be a young drummer growing up with the attitude of "I'm a hip-hop drummer," and that's his concept. So it doesn't take long for the thing to catch on where you identify yourself as a particular kind of drummer. But personally, I guess I see myself as this overall US drummer.

From left; Steve Smith, Paul Siegel, Jerry Allison, and Rob Wallis

roll drummer." He grew up with and played with Buddy Holly and perceived himself as a rock drummer. But if you listen to what D.J. and Jerry play on the records, their playing is not that far apart. They're both swinging and playing some real nice parts. The main difference is how they perceived themselves, one as a jazz drummer playing rock and the other as a rock drummer.

MD: And now you're a scholar too.
Steve: I guess so. But I want to address the common ground that you mentioned earlier, the rhythmic common denominator of US music that connects all of these drumming styles. Just like the clave is the rhythmic common denominator of Afro-Cuban music, the swing pulse is the rhythmic common denominator

of all US music. And if you listen to the early recordings of jazz, rhythm & blues, country, gospel, blues, or rock 'n' roll, it's all swing. All of those early guys were swinging, from Louis Jordan and Cab Calloway right up to Elvis and Jerry Lee Lewis. It all swung. It's a later development where things started to get straight-8th-note oriented, which comes out of the boogie-woogie piano influence. And that's a long transition.

You can hear records where Little Richard is playing more even 8th notes on piano while Earl Palmer is still playing with a shuffle swing feel underneath. But eventually the drummers started to play more and more with the piano players. Then the guitar players also began to imitate the piano with a more straight-8th feel. Listen to Chuck Berry's "Johnny B. Goode." Fred Below is the drummer on that and he's playing swing

strong swing pulse, you can adapt yourself to whatever the music needs. And you figure out what the music needs by hanging with the cats, by just hanging with the guys who do it, and listening.

MD: Will your investigation of US drumming eventually lead you to more current styles like hip-hop or drum 'n' bass?

Steve: I'm going to do a book that will accompany this DVD and go a little further with it in terms of '60s jazz drumming and present-day styles. But as far as doing several volumes of DVDs, I don't really see the point of it because, to me, all the essential ingredients to playing just about any kind of music that you're presented with today were developed in the '70s.

MD: There aren't any major innovations on the drums after that?

Marco Soccoli

Steve: After the '70s, drumming-wise, the next most influential thing that came on the scene was the drum machine. So things really changed in the '80s with that influence. Throughout time there were key players who had innovated playing concepts on the drums. On the DVD, I talk about how the hi-hat comes into play on the kit-that's like Papa Jo playing with Count Basie. The floor toms is Gene Krupa with Benny Goodman. The bebop style is Kenny Clarke. The rhythm & blues style ... that's really no one particular drummer but rather a lot of guys who played with people like Louis Jordan or Louis Prima. And then with the fusion stuff, of course, there's Billy Cobham, Lenny White, and Mike

with a backbeat against the straight-8th guitar. So the point is, if you develop a strong swing pulse in your playing, it opens the door to then being able to play all the different styles, because that is the rhythmic common denominator of all US music. After you have a

Clark.

The next drummer who really turned everyone's head around with a new concept was Steve Gadd. Steve was probably the first drum star who embodied a heavy studio consciousness. All the other drum stars before that, from Gene Krupa and Buddy Rich to Tony Williams to Billy Cobham, were guys who played live. They

perfection. Different music's have developed since then, but a whole lot of new vocabulary isn't necessary to play it. You can pretty much recycle everything that developed up until the '70s to play the music. For example, drum 'n' bass is basically funk drumming sped up, and hip-hop is funk slowed down. And both come directly from James Brown. It's still essentially the

From left; Paul Siegel, Rob Wallis, D.J. Fontana, Buddy Harman, and Steve Smith

recorded, but you wouldn't think of them as studio drummers, per se, and the studio players weren't stars. With Gadd, things really started to shift. You got the studio sound and deep feel and the very, very accurate time.

After Gadd, the next major innovation in drumming was really the drum machine. The Linn Drum became hugely influential. It was used on so many of the pop tunes of the '80s that it triggered a conceptual change, where drummers had to play like that in order to be a pop drummer. You had to play like a machine in order to get work.

MD: It's like the machine was emulating Gadd, and then the next generation emulated the machine.

Steve: Yeah, it's a real twist and a real shift. And so, to me, there's not a lot of new drum vocabulary since the '70s, because the emphasis became execution-

same rhythms and beats that the James Brown bands developed in the '60s and '70s. So even though some things have evolved and changed, it remains the same. Hopefully some new things will evolve, but for the most part the lion's share of the vocabulary is already there for drummers.

MD: What were some of the surprises that you had in researching the early years, even the African connection? Were there any revelations about how this music developed as you found out about it in your research?

Steve: I think what was significant to me is that in the United States there's no hand drum tradition, which in fact led to the drumset becoming the rhythmic voice of the African American community. If history had played itself out differently and, let's say, we had a hand drum tradition in the United States, the drumset may never have been a necessary invention, because we would've had a whole percussive orchestra just with hand drumming.

But because of the no-drumming laws that were enforced during the time of slavery, the hand drum tradition that developed directly out of African drumming was squelched in this country. It's true that slaves in New Orleans were allowed to play hand drums once a week at Congo Square. But when you look at that in the scope of how long slavery existed in the United States, which is from the 1500s until the mid-1800s, Congo Square only represents about forty years in the scheme of things. It began in 1817 and lasted until the mid-1850s.

I think in some ways the significance of Congo Square has been a bit overemphasized. In Congo Square drumming was legal, but there were other places in Louisiana and all over the South that had the African polyrhythmic percussive concepts still being practiced illegally or underground during the entire history of slavery in the US.

J.M. Van Eaton and Steve Smith

There's a great book by Dena Epstein called *Sinful Tunes And Spirituals*, which is a documentation of everything she could find on the African polyrhythmic concept surviving in the United States throughout the years of slavery. She found that people kept the African pulse alive in many ways, such as playing washboards and jawbones, beating sticks on the floor, or stomping their feet on the floor. Even some African hand drums or African-styled drums that were made in secret here in the US have been found.

MD: And you make an interesting point in the DVD about the polyrhythmic style of "patting juba" leading to the development of the drumset.

Steve: That's another percussion instrument, so to speak, that was developed in the US, where the person is playing with feet and hands, incorporating all the limbs just like the drumset. It's an African polyrhythmic concept, and it was eventually applied to the drumset, which is the only percussion instrument in the world that uses all four limbs.

So in effect, the slaves being deprived of hand drums set the stage for the African American community to embrace the drumset. Without hand drums they were forced to adapt to the European percussion instruments that were available in the 1800s, the snare drum and the bass drum.

I find it very interesting that the invention of the drumset is basically the invention of the bass drum pedal. After that happened in the late 1800s, the drumset wasn't really used for any purpose other than playing jazz, which was a creation of the African American community. So when people first played the drumset, they wanted to play with that concept one person playing a snare drum and a bass drum with that African American swing rhythmic concept. The drumset could just as easily have been used in a symphony orchestra, but it wasn't. It had some applications in, say, vaudeville and maybe a few situations here and there other than jazz, but they never took off as playing concepts. The playing concept that we now take for granted is essentially an African American concept of how to use the instrument.

This concept has been so thoroughly assimilated into the culture that most people don't even think about it or question how it came to be. Today the drumset is an instrument that's been accepted all over the world. But it is quintessentially an American instrument that developed from our unique history and culture.

MD: Has the drumset continued to develop as a vital expression in recent years?

Steve: Yes, there are some drummers who are developing new ideas and abilities on the instrument, and there are some players who are simply great musicians playing great music on the drumset. But in general, during the last decade or so, it's being used in such a limited and basic way, especially in pop music, that I find it uninspiring.

For example, they hit the snare drum and get one sound, hit the bass drum and get one sound, and play at one dynamic level rather than really getting into the nuance of everything you can do on the drumset as an instrument. There are so many sounds in just the

MD: It's so homogenized to the point that the tones themselves are homogenized?

Steve: Yeah, in pop music at least. Machines are playing almost everything. People sample a sound, and that one sound suffices as a backbeat. And that's what's used rather than getting into the nuance of actually playing the instrument. Meanwhile, I'm getting more and more into the instrument myself. Just the art of playing the snare drum itself-there's so

Marco Soccoli

snare drum alone, from a soft press roll to a rimshot or moving the stick from the middle of the head to the edge, where you get a higher pitch and more ring.

MD: And why is that being phased out?

Steve: Well, since the music industry is so driven by fashion and pop culture, there's really not much "music" left in what passes for music these days.

much to it as far as getting a nice sound out of it and exploring all the tones that are available. Or getting into the nuances of playing a ride cymbal-there's so much there.

MD: Well, there's still room for that in jazz.

Steve: There is. And that's encouraging.

2017: Steve Smith

Vital Journey Into
The Fabric Of Rhythm

By Ilya Stemkovshy

A long-overdue induction into the Rock and Roll Hall of Fame might be a big deal to most drummers, but Steve Smith is more excited to win not one but three categories in the 2017 *Modern Drummer* Readers Poll: MVP, Rock, and Educational Product. "I'm a longtime *Modern Drummer* reader, from the very first issue in 1977 with Buddy Rich on the cover, which coincides with when I began with Sonor drums—forty years," Smith says. "And I put a lot of meaning into *Modern Drummer*'s perspectives and the readers' perspectives. I've always been very excited to be in the Readers Poll, so this year has been way over the top. It's acknowledgement from my peers in many ways, my fellow drummers. That means a lot to me."

Well-deserved honors, of course—and *then* there's that whole Journey thing. After replacing drummer Aynsley Dunbar in the late 1970s, it was Smith who appeared on the band's classic albums and golden-era tours through the mid-'80s, and who was part of the lineup that fans remember with the greatest fondness. Those fans were treated to remarkable news in 2016 when it was announced that Smith would rejoin the group for his first live Journey dates in over thirty years. And he's still going. So now if you get the chance to see Journey on a stage, you'll hear classic anthems like "Don't Stop Believin'," "Separate Ways (Worlds Apart)," and "Open Arms" performed by the man who wrote the original drum parts to those songs, but with a little something different this time around, as Smith elaborates on below. And if re-learning intricate patterns from a lifetime ago wasn't enough, Smith still found time recently to release a new Steps Ahead disc, *Steppin' Out*; record and perform with his own jazz fusion group, Vital Information; occasionally fill in for Simon Phillips with the brilliant keyboardist Hiromi; and find new ways to practice and apply Konnakol, the South Indian vocal percussion vocabulary.

And it hardly ends there. Recently Smith released *The Fabric of Rhythm*, a deluxe package containing a vinyl solo album of drum pieces related to his own lighted-sticks canvas art, photos of those art pieces, his written descriptions of the music and art, and cool historical pictures. And during his downtime, Smith studied different examples of matched grip, which culminated with the informative DVD/book release *Pathways of Motion*.

Modern Drummer caught up with Smith in a recording studio just a couple days after the Rock and Roll Hall of Fame ceremony. The drummer was there with Vital Information guitarist Vinny Valentino, tracking drum parts for Drum Fantasy Camp, a yearly instructional and performance event that in the past has featured world-class players like Dave Weckl, Chris Coleman, and Todd Sucherman. Steve was relaxed and confident when asked to blow over the drum solo section of the Steely Dan classic "Aja." Though he hadn't heard the brilliant Steve Gadd–ified album cut in a while, he refrained from listening to it for reference and proceeded with take after take of beautiful phrasing, perfect control, chops galore, and his trademark musicality. When we sat down, we began with (finally!) that little award he'd just received.

MD: How does it feel to be a Rock Hall inductee?

Steve: There's no intrinsic meaning to anything other than what you give it. And with the Rock and Roll Hall of Fame, it's a self-appointed body of people that got together and decided to be tastemakers and induct people or leave people out. So as a musician oriented to playing jazz and rock, I didn't think about it very much. It wasn't important to me whether I was in or not. And I think that's the same with any person working in any kind of field, whether you're a writer and some people win a Pulitzer Prize or you're some kind of activist and you win a Noble Peace Prize: It's not going to change your work or work ethic. With the hall, it's a wonderful accolade, but what got me thinking about it was that the Journey fans were so excited and it means a lot to them. There was a long voting process, and in a nice way Journey won the popular vote. Then we knew we were going to get in and there was this stressful buildup. What are you going to wear? And then you have to write a speech. And what are we going to play?

But once I got there, I hung out backstage with Bill Bruford and we had a nice long talk. Once the show started, it was interesting to see the Electric Light Orchestra and Joan Baez, and it was a really wonderful event. I was able to get on stage and in two and a half minutes speak about my story and acknowledge some of my influences and how the path led to me playing rock. One of the things I walked away with was that I could see how helpful it is to bring new fans in. I never really listened to Joan Baez or Tupac Shakur, but after seeing their presentations, I want to check them out. So maybe it'll help Journey's popularity even more. I'm happy to be inducted, and I just hope it doesn't ruin my jazz career. [laughs]

The Long Journey Home

MD: What's it like to revisit the Journey material after so long?

Steve: When I started playing with Journey again in 2016, it had been thirty-two years since I played live with the band. We did the album *Trial by Fire* [in 1996], but that was a studio project and we didn't revisit any of the old songs. We didn't do "Don't Stop Believin'" or "Who's Crying Now," so I didn't remember any of those songs, because I hadn't listened to them in a long time. [laughs] And that was okay, because I approached the gig like any other gig that I get called for. I transcribed a big list of songs that the band wanted me to learn, note-for-note what I played on the albums.

MD: Were you surprised while transcribing?

Steve: I was. It was looser than I remembered it being. Looser, as in the parts were not completely etched in stone. I noticed that I had a verse groove but I wasn't super-strict with it. And then the chorus, it was a groove, but it wasn't an exact part, for most of the music. As long as it felt right, it was pretty loose. Then there were certain fills that are part of the song. In "Separate Ways" I play the exact same fills every night. "Faithfully," the same fills from the record, every night,

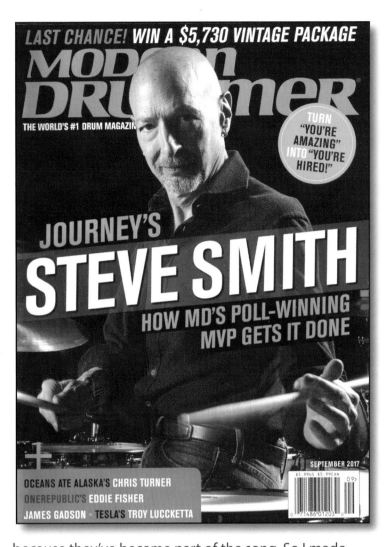

because they've become part of the song. So I made decisions about where to be loose with the fills and where to play verbatim what was on the record. Then I started to update the grooves a little bit, update the orchestration. Some of that came from seeing Andrés Forero with *Hamilton*, watching him in the pit with five snare drums and all the orchestrational ideas you can come up with. Sometimes you play with no hi-hat and sometimes with the hi-hat. And I started copping some of those R&B grooves from *Hamilton* and sticking them in the Journey music to make it a little funkier. It became a creative project for me. Then I decided to go back to a double bass drumset, add a third floor tom, and have three snares for fills. You're hearing a snare fill, but the pitch goes up and down. And now I'm using three snares on the newest Vital Information record. The process became a lot of fun, relearning the songs, and in some ways I left well enough alone.

MD: Sounds like you really applied yourself.

Steve: The process of memorizing all that music did take a while. It was like starting over. Then I had to condition myself to play that big rock sound for a ninety-minute show. There's a lot of dynamic shifts on the gigs with my own band, where I'll play brushes and then play some tunes that are real big. But Journey music is essentially a big sound most of the night, with some dynamics.

To get ready I did a lot of yoga, a lot of practicing and

that, because I'm not overdoing it and I'm playing just what they need to hear. And what they tell me is that all the parts are falling into place again.

MD: And the band is encouraging of these little tweaks you're making?

Steve: Oh, yes.

MD: They notice?

Steve: No, I don't think so. [laughs]

MD: So they're not tied to the album versions either, because you're also different from Omar Hakim and Deen Castronovo. [Castronovo played drums with Journey between 1998 and 2015; Hakim did the band's 2015 summer tour.]

Steve: Omar and Deen are fantastic drummers, but they didn't come up with those parts to begin with. They learned the parts, but there were specific things that I was thinking about when I played particular parts for something Ross

Steve Smith Library

blowing through the songs and improvising, just to get my chops up and have some fun. When I'm on the gig, though, I'm real disciplined and I play very clearly for the music. There's a feeling now that's different from when I did Journey in the '70s and '80s, when I felt like I was trying to prove myself, and maybe filling this up and that up a little too much. Now I don't need to do that at all. The guys in the band are really happy with

[Valory, bass] or Neal [Schon, guitar] or Jonathan [Cain, keyboards] did. In addition, I was trained by Steve Perry to play in a certain way that gave him support and freedom and brought a certain R&B element to the rock. And of course, no one else has been trained by him other than me. [laughs] But also, I went back to the well, the records—though not the live versions, because back in those days we played things too fast live.

MD: And you don't look like you're breaking a sweat. Letting the mics do the work?

Steve: During one of the lessons I got from Freddie Gruber, I was sitting in his drum room and I hit the drum really hard, and he said, "Why are you playing it like that? What, are you angry at that drum?" [laughs] And I told him I was trying to get some power here. And he said to me, "Power is for dictators. What you want is a big sound." And that stayed with me. It's about being able to draw the tone out of the drum or cymbal and then adjusting the touch. One of the first things he worked on with me was not hitting the drum, but rather just allowing the stick to drop and getting used to that sensation. So you can play without any stroke at all. If you start with letting the stick drop, that gives you a very quiet basis for your dynamic range that then can go up from there.

I've learned to play quieter and get a good sound on all of the instruments, and then make the correct balance internally. Like, make the bass drum and snare drum balance to themselves, acoustically, before even thinking about what the mic is going to do. That comes from years of playing on stage in acoustic environments where I'm two feet away from a saxophone player or an acoustic bass player and five feet away from an acoustic piano player. So I really have to control my volume. In a lot of those cases, there's either no miking on the drums or just an overhead and a bass drum mic. So I've trained myself. I don't play any differently from that on the Journey gig. I play the same way, so I don't hurt myself. And I don't play any differently in a studio from the way I do on stage. But that's taken years of study, practicing, and considering all this stuff.

MD: I saw live footage of Journey from this year where you weren't using a drum riser. Was that by choice?

Steve: I'm just used to not being on a riser, from all the jazz gigs. And it sounds better to the other musicians. They can walk right up to the drums. There's a vibe that happens when we're all on the floor. They can feel the vibration. With a riser, they feel less connected to the drums. But we need the riser to slide the drums off the stage when there's an opening band.

Staying Vital

MD: The new Vital Information record, *Heart of the City*, is a mix of standards and originals. You've been playing some of these standards for many years. How do you keep it fresh with the arrangements?

Steve: There are two ways we do the standards. Some are very thought-out arrangements, and then there are tunes where we play the beginning kind of funk and then go to a swing, and then we do some duets. It's a lot looser. It's not hard to keep standards fresh, because every time I play with whoever I play them with, those personalities make it new. So it's a lot of fun for us, and we don't have a lot of time to get together to rehearse and write original music, so we can fill up the set with standards that really work. People want to see us play our instruments and improvise and create a vibe and energy, and it can be done with all those elements.

MD: You've been doing the South Indian percussive

Vital Information: Baron Browne, Mark Soskin, Steve, Vinny Valentino

Alberto Terrile

vocalizing called Konnakol for a while now too. What's your relationship with the art?

Steve: I started that in 2002. I've learned enough to be fluent with it, to the degree that I *am* fluent with it. [laughs] First, I had some lessons with a South Indian teacher, and shortly after that I started to play Indian fusion music with the group Summit, with Zakir Hussain and George Brooks. That was on-the-job training, so it wasn't just studying and being at home practicing. Within one year of investigating Konnakol rhythms, I was working a lot more with Indian musicians, because when they heard there was a Western drummer that

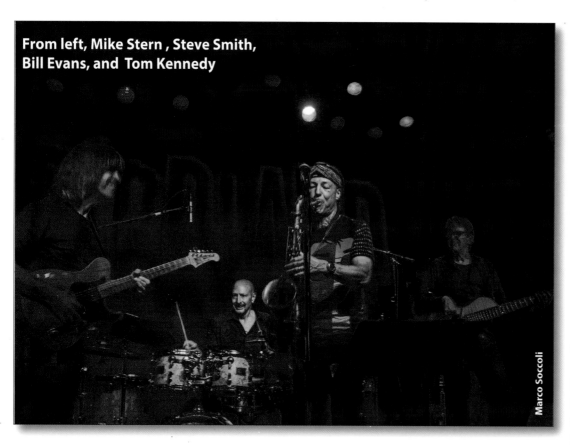

From left, Mike Stern , Steve Smith, Bill Evans, and Tom Kennedy

Marco Soccoli

could understand their music, I was getting hired a lot. And the more I got hired, the more I had to learn different compositions quickly and perform them.

Then I started to mess around at home with Konnakol and drumming at the same time. Traditionally, Konnakol is unaccompanied. So that was a big decision, in a way. Could I play the drums and do Konnakol at the same time? It took a while to get that coordination, but then I started to bring that into the Vital Information music.

MD: Like "Open Dialogue" on the new record, where you lay the Konnakol and drums over a little funk

groove?

Steve: Yes. I've been doing that kind of thing with a lot of the groups I've been touring with. I'll do it with Mike Stern, and Randy Brecker, and a little bit with Steps Ahead. For "Open Dialogue," I also doubled the vocal in the studio.

There are two ways I do Konnakol and drumming. One is that I play a groove and do the Konnakol over it. The other is that I do the Konnakol and exactly double it with the drums. So that was an exercise in how to be able to do that, to first learn and memorize the composition and then voice it on the drumset. That was a long time in the making, and I'm pretty comfortable with it now. It feels very natural.

MD: And Zakir is not a bad on-the-job trainer.

Steve: He's unbelievable. It's inspiring and humbling to play with Zakir. As much as I consider myself a good Western drumset player, when I play with him, he can go so far with his rhythmic understanding, repertoire, and abilities… it's really incredible to be in the presence of that. So no matter how far I go, he can always go further. And he loves to challenge me. It's been a big part of my musical growth over the last fifteen years.

MD: "Eight + Five" also has some interesting stuff going on with the Konnakol.

Steve: That was a tune in thirteen that we wrote together. I came up with the entire tune as a rhythmic structure. It was exploring a lot of different ways to play in thirteen, combining eight and five. [Bassist] Baron Browne brought the final pieces to the puzzle in the studio, with a melody and some harmony. I'm happy with that one. I notice the Vital Information fans like it when we do the odd-time tunes. On the album before, we did one in fifteen, and it's our most-requested tune.

Multimedia Man

MD: What was the idea behind your book and audio package *The Fabric of Rhythm*?

Steve: The people from SceneFour came up with the idea of doing a book. They had made two books with Carl Palmer and one with Dave Lombardo already. So I thought it was a great idea for a book to feature all thirteen pieces of art [photographs where Smith uses lighted sticks]. But I had the idea of making a solo record to go with it. I've had a lot of solos on records and have come up with many ideas for solo pieces for clinics and live gigs, but the idea to record a piece of music for a piece of art made a lot of sense to me. And they wanted to make a vinyl LP out of it. I took it seriously, like I was going in to make a record. So I booked studio time and organized all my ideas. It was really fun and very creative, and I could draw the connection between the art and the drumming in every piece. Then I went through the process of writing about each piece of art, how it came about and what my thoughts were, and then I wrote about the solo drumming. That was interesting to get into the rhythms and the technical concepts that I'm using. I thought if people are going to check out this book, they're going to want these details. The way it's intended to be used is you put on the record, you look at the art, you read about the art, and then you read about the solo and then listen to the solo.

MD: "Condor" and "Interdependence" are really creative.

Steve: "Condor" is a slower piece composed for three snare drums to play in unison. Then I just improvised to see what I can do with some metric modulation.

I've recorded the idea for "Interdependence" before, playing the left-hand ostinato on my side snare and then playing the melodies with my right hand. I did that on the DVD set *Drumset Technique/History of the U.S Beat*. So here I'm taking that melody and performing it in a different way. And that ties in to the fact that I learned how to play all the Journey songs open-handed. Right-hand lead, or left-hand lead. One of the reasons I wanted that option is because I didn't want to play backbeats with my left hand all night. It gives my left hand a break so it could play 8th notes on the ride cymbal or hi-hat. And it gives me more orchestrational ideas. I started to play more open-handed when I played with Hiromi, out of the necessity of learning Simon Phillips' drum parts. So on "Interdependence" I play the left-hand jazz beat on the hi-hat and the cymbal and play all the melodies with my right hand and right foot. And one of the ways I developed the open-handed playing was going back to the basics, the Jim Chapin book or *Syncopation*, and playing the ride cymbal beat and playing the figures with my right hand. I'm not completely ambidextrous at this point for jazz, but for the Journey music I can do it.

Going Through the Motions

MD: Your DVD/book package *Pathways of Motion* looks at four different matched-grip styles. Was the impetus your left-thumb injury or musical curiosity?

Steve: It did start because I was having some problems with the CMC joint, at the base of the thumb on my left hand. So I decided to do a few things to remedy that, including altering my traditional-grip technique, which Jojo Mayer helped me with. He told me to open

Marco Soccoli

up my fingers more. I was playing more with the first [pointer] finger over the stick most of the time. He said if you release that finger and grip more with the thumb, then you won't have that tension. But that takes some reeducating to be open and not afraid you're going to drop the stick, which I do sometimes. [laughs] But the other thing is just that I wanted to play more matched grip, and I realized how limited my left hand was in the matched-grip position. In front of a mirror, I started to examine the motions of my right hand, because my right hand feels very fluid, and I could start to see that I was using a lot of different grips with the right hand. It was one way on the cymbal, another way on the tom,

a different way on the snare drum. So I mirror-imaged that with the left hand. And the easiest way to do that is to play something in unison and really examine the motions and the pathways that the sticks are going through space. I realized I was using essentially four grips. And that led me to spending time with each grip.

MD: Describe each one, please.

Steve: Grip 1 is the basic, German grip, with the palm down and the hand over the stick. Grip 2 is the idea of the resonating chamber, where the stick is down more in the first joint of the fingers. Grip 3 is the French grip with the thumbs up. And Grip 4 is the "Tony Williams" grip, which I've been using for a long time. That's almost

like if you played a taiko drum and you're just holding the stick with the back two fingers, like the way I saw Tony Williams play matched grip. With that, it's very easy to get a big sound because of the range of motion.

MD: But that one's hairy in terms of dropping the stick, right?

Steve: It's more the transition between grips. As much time as I spend with the grips, the key to using all four is the transition from one to the other. I'll go from 1 to 4, or 2 to 3, and in making that transition is somewhere where I'll lose the stick. The French grip is the one that's the least secure for me, not the Tony one. So focusing on those, I was getting more control and more technique with my left hand. It's still not as good as my left-hand traditional grip, so when I really need to play something that's challenging, I'll go back to traditional grip.

MD: Well, it's been fifty years of that one for you.

Steve: Exactly. And when I started to talk to Rob Wallis about doing some demos, he said, "This is great—why don't we document it?" And the more I thought about it, most of the technique videos are by traditional-grip players, whether it's Dave Weckl or Jojo Mayer or Tommy Igoe. So there are a lot of matched-grip players, but no one is addressing the details of what matched grip is. And my observations felt like they could be helpful. We got into it and made it into a DVD and a book. A lot of drummers make these changes naturally but are not conscious of it. They'll have what I call the "nonsymmetrical" grip. They're playing French on the ride cymbal and German on the snare.

MD: What about someone like, say, Jon Fishman from

Phish? I see him playing French on the outside to the right of the bell on his ride, but he'll play German when bringing his right hand to the hi-hat. Isn't that weird?

Steve: No, not weird at all. Playing traditional grip is playing a nonsymmetrical grip. And that's a very natural grip to do. If you want a lighter sound on the cymbal, you can use the French grip. German grip for a heavier sound.

Leading and Following

MD: Dave Weckl told *MD* how difficult it is to keep a working group on the road, and how he had to take on more sideman work. Is there a bright future for leading jazz groups like Vital Information?

Steve: I'm in a similar position that Dave's in, where it is hard to keep a band working. And one reason is because we're drummers, and drummer-bandleaders have a smaller piece of the market. One of the classic examples is that of Buddy Rich and Frank Sinatra. They were roommates when they played with Tommy Dorsey. One of them ended up playing gigs and probably dying broke, and the other became a superstar. One was a singer and one was a drummer. They were equally talented. That's the life of a drummer.

I do the touring when I can and as much as I can, but it's not enough to make a living from. And it is expensive, so sometimes I break even or even lose money. The goal is that we all get paid decently enough to do the gig, and have fun and bring the music to people. So I'll continue to do it. But I'll still go out and play with Mike Stern, and Zakir called me for a gig but I'll be out with Journey. But those calls will keep happening, I hope, especially once I get back full time into my jazz and sideman career.

MD: Speaking of sideman jazz, talk about the Hiromi gig. That's complicated music.

Steve: Learning her music is intimidating and very difficult and takes a long time. I subbed for Simon Phillips for about three years. I learned her first three Trio Project albums. It's some of the hardest music I've ever played but some of the most fun I've ever had on stage. The music is incredibly rewarding and pushed my musicianship to a new level. The drum chair in Hiromi's trio is a chair of support, but also you're the second soloist. There was a drum solo in almost every song, and most of them in some odd time. And learning Simon's parts was a pleasure, because he did a really fantastic job orchestrating her music. She writes her music very clearly by hand. They're not computer charts. Some of the charts are literally ten pages long. And she and Anthony [Jackson, bass] are great to be on tour with. So it was peak experience for me. And now Simon isn't with Toto, so he plays all of the gigs.

The Live Experience

MD: Anything you do to keep your chops up while on the road?

Steve: I pulled out the Wilcoxon book that I had when I was a kid. I've been going through that, first of all just to read music and to work on some of those versions of how to use the rudiments in swinging ways. And I still practice Konnakol on a daily basis. I also recently brought my brushes out, which I practice backstage. I'd missed it. It felt good. It was therapeutic just to play brushes. I needed it for balance.

MD: Do you have a perspective on the technological advances today and how they've shaped the drumming landscape?

Steve: It does seem as though people are using YouTube a lot to get information, inspiration, ideas, drumming concepts. But nothing will substitute being in the room with a drummer. And I see videos that are impressive when the drummers are playing by themselves or playing with a track. Can they play with live musicians? And young drummers are playing very loud, in general. With headphones or to tracks. But if you adjust their playing to a room with a piano player over there and a bass player over here, they can't do it, because they can't control their dynamics, and without the click their time is not really there. So the idea of playing for the room is a foreign concept. As much as many young drummers are becoming technically good,

going. So we're talking about it, and it's possible that I'll do the third year. And in some ways, I feel like I have a shelf life as a rock drummer. And one of the reasons I decided to play with Journey now is that I'd better do it while I'm physically able to do it. It's hard work and I have to do a lot of pre-show warm-up and after-show

Steve Smith Library

without the experience of playing with live musicians, it's going to be difficult to bridge that gap of becoming musicians who have a lot of options available.

MD: Does Journey have a finite end time for you?

Steve: The original agreement was for two years, 2016 and 2017. And we're talking about me doing a third year.

MD: Well, they're not going to stop. We know this.

Steve: [laughs] No, it looks like they're going to keep

yoga and stretching and warm down.

I'm using good technique and I'm not denting heads or breaking sticks or cymbals, but it's still hard work to play ninety minutes or even two hours sometimes. And I don't want to go on so long that I hurt myself. I want to be viable for the rest of my career. Like Roy Haynes and some of my heroes, I want to play up until the end. There are a lot of great players still out there doing it into their sixties, seventies, and eighties.

The Amazing Journeys of Steve Smith

Over the past thirty years, it's no exaggeration to say that Steve Smith has had an incredible career-from the heights of pop-rock success with Journey, to becoming an acknowledged master of the instrument, to performing with his own group, Vital Information, as well as many other jazz greats. That said, in 2005 Steve experienced one of the most interesting three-week stretches any musician has ever had. What follows is Steve's travel diary during that time, in his own words.

In my life as a musician, I've had many unique and interesting experiences. But I'd have to say, the events of the past couple of weeks have been unprecedented in their diversity and intensity.

Friday, January 21 At 12:00 noon, Journey was presented with a star on Hollywood boulevard in Hollywood, California. It was great to see all of the members of Journey again and to catch up with them. Neal Schon, Ross Valory, Jonathan Cain, and Steve Perry were all there, as well as past and present members George Tickner, Aynsley Dunbar, Robert Fleishman, Deen Castronovo, and Steve Augeri.

I was amazed at the turnout. Over one thousand fans attended the event and cheered as the mayor of Hollywood gave a speech and unveiled the star. Journey had a gig at the Hollywood House Of Blues that night, and I was invited to sit in with the band. After lunch we all went to the HOB for a soundcheck/rehearsal.

I haven't listened to or played any Journey tunes in about nine years, so I couldn't remember the ones they asked me to play. Deen reminded me of some of the parts, and then they came back to me. I played "Walks Like a Lady" and "Chain Reaction," and then we really stretched out on the Jimi Hendrix tunes "Voodoo Child" and "Third Stone From The Sun." Aynsley Dunbar also sat in on a couple of

Steve and his wife Diane

tunes and played great. Deen Castronovo, who played most of the night, sounded amazing—playing drums and singing many of the lead vocals! I enjoyed jamming with the band and hanging with everyone.

Saturday, January 22 was an extremely busy day at the Anaheim NAMM show [National Association of Music Merchants.] I had commitments to sign autographs at the Sonor and Vic Firth booths. I then went to an afternoon soundcheck at the Coast Anaheim Hotel to prepare for that evening's Vital Information concert sponsored by Gallien-Krueger, the amplifier company that our bass player, Baron Browne, endorses.

One of the highlights of the day was speaking at the party Zildjian gave in honor of the eightieth birthdays of Louie Bellson, Roy Haynes, and Earl Palmer. I was in heavy company when, first, Steve Gadd got up and spoke, I went next, then Peter Erskine, and finally Freddie Gruber. It was a great honor for me to thank Louie, Roy, and Earl for their years of inspiration as great musicians, innovators, bandleaders, and examples of drummers with long and influential careers. I wanted to hang, but I had to run to another hotel for my gig with Vital Information. I just made the 10:00 P.M. downbeat! Playing at NAMM is always inspiring. The band tends to play a little harder, knowing that the audience is 99% musicians!

Sunday, January 23 was an easier day at NAMM. I had an autograph session at Sonor again, this time with fellow endorser Thomas Lang. At a later autograph session at the Remo booth, I met the great Scottish rudimental drummer Jim Kilpatrick, who gave me a jaw dropping display of his chops. Of course, I had him show me some of his stickings and cool moves.

I visited a lot of the booths and said hi to some friends I hadn't seen in a while. The evening ended with Diane, my partner, and I joining Rob Wallis and Paul Seigel from Hudson Music, along with Thomas Lang, for a relaxed dinner.

Monday, January 24 was a travel day for the members of Vital Information. Tom Coster [keyboards,] Frank Gambale [guitar,] Baron Browne [bass,] and I took a short drive from Anaheim to Hollywood to check into our hotel prior to our engagement at the beautiful Catalina's Bar & Grill jazz club.

Tuesday, January 25 through Sunday, January 30. Vital Information played for a week at Catalina's. Playing in one club for a series of nights usually leads to enhanced creativity, because we're well-rested each night. It's the opposite of what life on the road is usually like, where you're doing a series of one-nighters. Normally, each day features an early wakeup, long travel, hotel check-in, unloading of the van, set up, soundcheck, playing the gig, and then tearing the gear down and packing the van—only to do it all again the next day.

During the week at Catalina's, I had the pleasure of playing for some of the top drummers in the world. On Tuesday, January 25, Jeff Hamilton, Richie Garcia, Danny Carey, and Sonor artist relations manager Milan Goltz came down for our opening night. On Thursday, January 27, the vibe was electric, as Vic Firth artist relations director Marco Soccoli came to the club with an amazing group, including Gregg Bissonette, Myron Grombacher and his son Dylan, Todd Lane, Slim Jim Phantom [Stray

Cats], Danny Carey, Ricky Lawson, Ndugu Leon Chancler, Steve Sidelnyk [Madonna], Tommy Igoe [The Lion King], Zoro, Brenden Buckley [Shakira], Alicia Warrington [Kelly Osbourne], Jen Lowe [Jason Mraz], Nick Barker [Dimmu Borgir], Dino Cavares [Fear Factory], Chris Antonopoulos [Opiate For The Masses], Bobby Jarzombek [Iced Earth, Halford], Mike Fasano [Dad's Porno Mag], Bruce Jacoby, Chris Delisa, Chris Stankee, Walter Earl, and Carmine Appice, who brought guitarist Pat Travers with him. My friend Richie Garcia was also there with his son.

Playing for fellow drummers can sometimes be intimidating. But the vibe that everyone put out was very positive and open. It helped me get into a special zone where I wanted to play my best. Then the entire band just took off, playing with a freedom that was effortless.

Sunday, January 30 completed the week. My friend and drum guru, Freddie Gruber, came down for the final set, stayed late, and had us all roaring with laughter at his stories.

Monday, January 31 I had an afternoon flight out of LAX that landed in Frankfurt, Germany in the early hours of Tuesday, February 1. After a three-hour layover, I left for Mumbai [Bombay,] India, where I arrived on Wednesday, February 2 at 1:30 A.M. The day was spent preparing my drums for a concert the next day.

Ranjit Barot is one of the top drumset players in India, and last year I helped hook him up with a new Sonor Jungle Set, which I ended up borrowing for this concert. I spent a few hours at Ranjit's state-of-the-art recording studio, putting new heads on the kit and setting it up to my specs. I was ably assisted by Ranjit's student, Darshan Doshi, who became my assistant, driver, and student during my stay in India.

Let me back up for a minute and let you know why I traveled to India. At the end of December, Zakir Hussain called and invited me to perform at an event that he holds in Mumbai every February 3. The event is called An Homage to Abbaji, Abbaji being the great tabla maestro Ustad Allarakha, Zakir's father.

Most people are familiar with the tabla, a set of two drums—one high pitched (called the "tabla") and one low ("bayan.") It's the main drum of North India. Ustad Allarakha was one of the greatest tabla players who ever lived. He toured and recorded for years with Ravi Shankar. (Some drummers may recall the 1968 recording

Rich Alla Rakha, where Buddy Rich and Allarakha went head-to-head in the studio.) Allarakha's son, Zakir Hussain, is not only the greatest tabla player of all time, but I believe him to be the greatest living drummer of our time.

Many of the great drummers of India have performed at the Homage to Abbaji event over the five years it's been held, since the untimely death of Allarakha. For me, a Western drumset player, to be asked to perform was a great honor. Giovanni Hidalgo and Pete Lockett are two other Westerners who have performed at the event in past years.

I've been studying Indian rhythms for the past four years. During this time, I've had the chance to play concerts with many fantastic Indian musicians. In fact, Zakir and I have been playing together in an Indian/jazz fusion group called Summit, which you can hear on the Magna Carta CD *Modern Drummer Presents Drum Nation Vol. 1*. The more I learn about Indian music, the more respect I have for it and for Indian musicians' extreme knowledge and treatment of rhythm.

Thursday, February 3 got off to an early start with the morning session taking place from 6:30 A.M. to 9:00 A.M. Zakir's younger brother, Taufiq Qureshi, had the students of the Allarakha Institute of Music performing together on a piece that he composed. Then there was a beautiful set with Ustad Rashid Khan on vocals, accompanied by Yogesh Samsi on tabla.

The second session started at 10:30 A.M. with a performance by Zakir Hussain himself, with Ustad Sultan Khan accompanying him on the sarangi, a stringed instrument that's played with a bow. I've seen Zakir play many times in our fusion concerts around the world, but I'd never seen him in a classical setting. Nothing could have prepared me for it. Also, he was playing in India to an audience of 3,000 fans—and a front row that included many of the top musicians of India. Zakir and Sultan Khan played for ninety minutes without a break, and it was the best I've ever heard Zakir play.

In the classical setting, Ustad Sultan Khan played a repeating figure that Zakir soloed over. Tabla soloing is a combination of composition and improvisation, in a way similar to jazz. The improvisation would build to a peak and then Zakir would finish a section with a beautifully composed tihai—a rhythmic figure that repeats three times and then resolves to beat 1.

Another device Zakir used is called a chakradar, which is a composition that is a tihai within a tihai.

The entire composition is played three times before it resolves to 1. The elaborate tihais and chakradars that Zakir played were intricate and unpredictable, but were always perfectly composed and executed, resolving at beat 1 in a way that would make the entire audience gasp with disbelief.

After a long section of tabla solo, Ustad Sultan Kahn would make a short improvisation and Zakir would accompany him. Then Zakir would take over for another long solo excursion. The tabla masters in the front row were all keeping track of the tala, which is the beat cycle, or what we in the Western world call the time signature. They were amazed at the complexity, symmetry, and beauty of Zakir's improvisations, compositions, and flawless execution. This is drumming at the highest level of art and soul.

The soulfulness of Ustad Sultan Khan's accompaniment, combined with Zakir's breathtaking soloing, created some of the most beautiful and exciting music I have ever experienced. At one point, I was so overwhelmed with emotion that tears flowed from my eyes for at least five minutes. Amazing.

At 12:00 noon, mridangam maestro Dr. T. K. Murthy performed an incredible set in the South Indian carnatic style. He displayed a mastery and knowledge of rhythms that would baffle most Western drummers. Such rhythmic devices as metric modulations, implied metric modulation, rhythmic illusions, and beat displacement that Western drummers have been experimenting with in the past few years have been a part of the basic knowledge and abilities of South Indian drummers for centuries. They take it much further than we can imagine.

At 1:30 P.M., Ustad Gulam Zaffar Khan performed a set on a North Indian drum called a dholak. This is a folk instrument that isn't usually played in a virtuosic manner. But Ustad Gulam Zaffar Khan has taken the instrument to new heights.

From 3:00 P.M. to 4:00 P.M., I closed out the second session. I started with a snare drum and a pair of brushes, humming a twelve-bar blues to accompany myself. I explained to the audience that I would represent the drumming of the US, that our percussion instrument is the drumset with the snare drum being its heart, and that our most basic song form is the blues.

After opening on the snare drum, I moved to the drumset for an extended solo that was partly composed and partly improvised. I started with Max Roach's drumset composition in 3/4, "The Drum Also Waltzes," then metrically modulated into 4/4 to play some of my

Steve and Zakir Hussain

own theme-and-variation compositions. I also included a short section of call-and-response between my voice and my feet on the double pedal. I've been studying the South Indian rhythmic vocal language called konakol, which uses rhythmic syllables to create complete rhythmic phrases. I felt a little intimidated doing this for the Indian audience, but I went for it anyway, and they responded positively.

I ended my drumset solo with some well-known South Indian rhythmic compositions called "korvais," which I've adapted to the drumset. I closed my portion of the concert by bringing just my hi-hat to the front of the stage and playing a hi-hat solo that included a few stick tricks.

The audience seemed to appreciate my efforts. Still, I couldn't help feeling inadequate next to the other musicians. When I'm in my own world of Western drumset players, I feel comfortable and at home. But in the company of the drummers of India, I truly felt like a beginner. I'm overwhelmed by their dedication to rhythmic knowledge and their virtuosic command of their instruments. On the other hand, I'm flattered to say that the people showed me a lot of respect—especially the young drumset players who touched my feet and bowed to me, the way they treat the Indian masters. I was moved by their generosity.

After I played, there was a break in the program. My new friend Sivamani, one of the top percussionists of India, took me to a local music store and bought me a ghatam as a gift. The ghatam is a South Indian clay pot drum that I'm very interested in, and the one that Sivamani gave me sounds fantastic. He and I proceeded to jam in the store for over an hour, which was a lot of fun.

We returned to the concert hall, where at 7:45 P.M. the Manipuri Jagoi Marup opened the evening session. The Manipuri Jagoi Marup are six men who perform folk dances while playing on drums that hang around their necks.

At about 8:00 P.M., the world/fusion group Shakti played an incredible concert. The band consists of bandleader/guitarist John McLaughlin, U. Shrinivas on mandolin, Selvaganesh on kanjira, Shankar Mahadevan on vocals, and Zakir Hussain on tabla.

Selvaganesh's solo near the end of Shakti's set was one of the best drum solos I've ever heard. His instrument, the kanjira, is a small frame drum that looks like a little tambourine with one jingle in it. The drum is played with one hand, and what Selvaganesh can do with it is truly unbelievable.

When playing with Shakti, Zakir Hussain has incorporated a small "drumset" into his setup. He has a small snare drum, a bass drum, and two splash cymbals that he plays with his left hand—all while playing the tabla with his right hand. He sounds like two people playing at the same time.

When Shakti finished their set, the Manipuri Jagoi Marup came back for one piece. Then Zakir told me I was up next! He wanted me to set something up so they could all come out and jam. I couldn't have been more intimidated, but I pushed through my fear, played a short solo, and then set up an up-tempo groove. Zakir joined me first. Then one by one he brought out Ranjit Barot on drumset and then Sivamani on various percussion instruments, and we all jammed and traded licks.

Eventually, John McLaughlin and the other members of Shakti came out, and we all played a Shakti tune together. I didn't know the tune, but I did catch some of the korvais (composed unison sections) that they all played, and luckily I knew a few of those. It was quite an invigorating experience.

The concert ended about 10:00 P.M. Afterwards we all went to dinner, where I sat between John McLaughlin and Selvaganesh. I was in Shangri-La talking to two of my biggest influences.

Friday, February 4 started off with breakfast at the hotel with Vikku Vinayakram and John McLaughlin. Vikku was the ghatam player in the original line-up of Shakti.

His son Selvaganesh has taken his place in the new lineup. Vikku met the members of Shakti at the hotel and then traveled to Dubai with them to sit in as a special guest.

The rest of the day (fourteen hours actually, from 12:00 noon until 2:00 A.M.) was spent at Ranjit Barot's studio. It was a day of study, teaching, and hanging out. I studied South Indian Carnatic rhythms with Mridangist Sridar Parthasarthy, who gave me a detailed explanation and demonstration of playing a rhythmic composition at different speeds within the same tempo.

Sridar took a fixed composition—a korvai—and played it in the base tempo, which is subdivided into what we

Steve and Vikku Vinayakram

would call quarter notes, 8th notes, and 16th notes.

Then he played the entire composition one speed faster using a subdivision of 5s. (That is, five subdivisions per one quarter note.) He rhythmically transposed the entire piece so that it fit within the five-note subdivision, without changing the base pulse. Then he did it in six, seven, and eight beat subdivisions, with the latter being "double-time" as compared to the original way he played the composition.

Then Sridar took it a step further, changing subdivisions as he went, while never losing the beat or changing the composition. Even though he said that his abilities are not uncommon and that most good South Indian percussionists can do this, it was a mind-blowing demonstration.

There were also some young drumset students at the studio. I showed them some of the basics of swing playing. It was interesting for them because swing is not a part of their culture—while to me it's the foundation of drumset playing.

They were also interested in how I play Indian rhythms on the drumset, which I was happy to show them.

I noticed that the Indian drumset players use mainly single strokes to play their rhythms. By studying the Western drum rudiments, I've gotten comfortable with "mixed" stickings—combinations of singles and doubles. My approach to playing Indian rhythms on the drumset is new to the Indian drummers because of the way I use rudimental and rudimental-like stickings to approximate the nuances of their rhythms and phrases.

We all were reciting compositions in the South Indian rhythmic language called konakol, which is a favorite thing for Indian drummers to do. Playing konakol rhythms on the drumset has been my passion for the past couple of years. Learning these rhythms is still done in the oral tradition in India. No books or DVDs offer the information, and there's something very cool about that.

You have to find a teacher to get the knowledge. And in India, you have to prove that you'll be a good student before the teacher will take you on. It's not just a question of "How much do you charge for lessons?" Many times, a teacher won't charge any money for the lessons, but will have the student work for him around the home. The main thing is that the teacher knows that his own work will live on in the student. I've always loved studying and learning new ideas about music, and incorporating the influence of Indian rhythms is breathing new life into my playing.

Saturday, February 5 was spent going over my notes from the lessons the day before and practicing in my hotel room. I did a little shopping and met up with Sivamani and his wife in the evening. They had traveled to Bangalore, India to see Sting play a concert that day, so we met for a late supper and had a nice time chatting and eating some great food.

Sunday, February 6 was a relaxing day. I spent the day at the hotel writing emails and practicing. Zakir returned to Mumbai after a gig in Dubai with Shakti, so we met for lunch at my hotel. We had a chance to really talk about the concert on the 3rd, catch up on what we're both doing in our lives, and enjoy some very good food. Also, Zakir instructed me in the fine art of eating with one's fingers, which is the way it's done in India.

Monday, February 7 was a travel day. My flight left Mumbai at 3:45 A.M., which is a typical time for an international flight to leave India. I had a layover in Frankfurt, Germany and then went on to Moscow, Russia. The weather in Moscow was sub-freezing, which was especially shocking after the tropical weather in Mumbai. On the way to the hotel, I stopped at the Sonor distributor to pick out drums for the gig that Vital Information was going to be playing at the premier Moscow jazz venue, Le Club. We had played there in 2003, and it was great to be back playing for very appreciative Russian audiences.

Tuesday, February 8 was spent resting, writing, and reflecting on all that had happened in the previous couple of weeks. The rest of the Vital Information bandmembers arrived in Moscow, and for the next four nights—Wednesday, February 9 through Saturday, February 12—we'll perform at Le Club. As of this writing we've just finished our first night and we're off to a very good start.

Typically, my schedule is very dense. But it's been a

Vital Information soundcheck in Moscow
Tom Coster, Baron Browne, Steve

Steve Smith Library

whirlwind couple of weeks, with no end in sight to the travel and gigging. Next up: a weekend in Salt Lake City with Buddy's Buddies, more West Coast touring with Vital Information, an East Coast tour with Buddy's Buddies, a Sonor clinic tour of Asia, a big band tour of New Zealand, and then all summer on the road with a Steps Ahead reunion featuring Michael Brecker, Mike Stern, Mike Mainieri, and Richard Bona.

But the trip to India that I've described here, which was my first, stands alone as one of the most influential and transformative experiences I've ever had. I believe that one of the best ways for Western drumset players to advance their rhythmic abilities in ways that are inherently musical and usable is to study the Indian rhythmic systems. For Westerners, they're a largely untapped resource, a highly developed wellspring of rhythmic information and inspiration.

EQUIPMENT

Steve Smith: Gear (and more...)

By Mark Griffith

There have been many steps along Steve Smith's gear evolution, and also some surprises. Steve and I talked about all of the different equipment choices that he has made throughout the years, and how those choices have related to the gigs, and the music that he has performed.

Rogers Champagne Sparkle Kit

The Rogers kit was my first, it was a gift from my parents for Christmas 1967. It had a 14x5 Snare drum, 20x14 bass drum, 12x8 rack tom, and a 16x16 floor tom. I had been taking lessons since 1964 and played for two years on a practice pad before graduating to an actual snare drum. My first snare drum was a red sparkle Gretsch snare drum that I believe my parents traded in to offset the cost of the Rogers kit. I also bought my first cymbals after I got the Rogers kit. I saved my money working a paper route and bought a 24" A. Zildjian ride and a pair of 14" Zildjian hi-hats and I still have those

cymbals! I got them at Billy Flanagan's drum shop, in Brockton Massachusetts, where I was taking lessons. The ride was a second, indicated by an "S" stamped on it, which meant that it was a new cymbal but there was something imperfect about it and would be sold at a discount; it was $65, the price is still on the cymbal. Sadly, my Rogers kit was stolen when I was a student at Berklee. I left them in the back of my station wagon, parked on the street, went to class and came back to find the car – and the drums – missing!

Slingerland White Kit

That kit had a 20x14 bass drum, 12x8, 13x9, 14x14 and 16x16 toms. I didn't have that kit very long. That was one of the kits I played with the Lin Biviano Big

Band, and it's on the 1974 recording that I made with the band. That record was a 45 RPM single for Stan Kenton's label Creative World. The two songs were "L.A. Expression" and "Love Is Stronger Far Than We." The producer was Bob Curnow; John Lockwood played bass, Barry Kiener on Fender Rhodes and the tenor soloist is Bob Malach. Bob and I were both 19 years old on that recording and Barry was only 18.

Gretsch Walnut Kit

After I graduated high school and was attending Berklee, I learned that all the great jazz drummers like Tony Williams, Elvin Jones, Art Blakey and Philly Joe Jones were playing Gretsch, so I bought a used Gretsch kit. The kit has a dark walnut wood finish and the sizes are the classic be-bop setup: 18x14 bass drum with 12x8 and 14x14 toms. The drums were custom fit with Rogers hardware because Rogers "Swivomatic" hardware was durable and easy to adjust and Gretsch hardware was not good in those days. Eventually I had the tom mount changed to a Slingerland tom mount because they also had some good hardware in the 70s. When I got that kit, I set my cymbals up really high like Alphonse Mouzon and Eric Gravatt. I had seen Eric

Gravatt play with McCoy Tyner, and I really loved that way of setting up your cymbals, I thought it looked so hip. I also used that small Gretsch kit with the Biviano band as well. I still have that kit, the finish is pretty beat up but it sounds great.

Fibes Acrylic "Shower Door Finish" Kit

Shortly after that, I bought a Fibes kit. Looking back that was probably a Billy Cobham influenced choice, though I was studying with Alan Dawson at that time and Alan was closely associated with Fibes. I bought those at Rayburn Music in Boston. It wasn't a big kit like Billy's. That set consisted of a 22" bass drum, 13" rack tom, 16" floor tom and a 14x5 snare. I used that kit around Boston in the mid-70s. At that time, I was co-leading a big band called the Steve Smith/Joe Casano Big Band. That band was an outgrowth of me playing in the Bridgewater State College Big Band while I was still in high school. We played the standard Basie and Buddy arrangements that big bands played at the time. Joe Casano was the lead trumpet player in the Bridgewater College band. We enjoyed playing together and were motivated to continue playing big band music on a regular basis. In fact, Joe Casano still has a Boston-based big band called Mike and Joe's Big Band, co-led with his son Mike, who is an excellent drummer.

Gretsch-Pearl "Gadd" Hybrid White Kit

I also became very influenced by Steve Gadd in my Berklee years, which were 1972-76. I had heard about a kit that Gadd had created to make many of the recordings he was doing at that time and I created an identical kit to his. It was a white 20x14 Gretsch bass drum, a 13x9 rack tom, and 16x16 floor tom with a Slingerland double tom mount on the bass drum. Those were augmented with 8, 10, 12 white fiberglass Pearl Concert Toms and I had bottom heads added to them. That is what I had heard that Steve Gadd had done, so I went with the "full Gadd setup." I used that kit to gig around Boston. In 1975-76 I was in a "Top 40" band that bassist Neil Stubenhaus led called Ecstasy. Neil was a good musical mentor for pop music. He would loan me James Brown and Meters records and give me detailed instruction of what to listen for and then we'd use those ideas on the gig. I also used the "Gadd kit" in 1977 on Gil Goldstein's first record called *Pure As Rain*. Jeff Berlin played bass on that, and Bob Moses and I split the drumming duties.

The Mongrel (Walnut and White) Gretsch Kit-

I got the gig with Jean-Luc Ponty in October 1976. I put together my two Gretsch kits, the little bebop walnut kit, and the bigger drums of the "Gadd kit." For the first few months with Ponty I played the white 20" bass drum, a 12" walnut tom, a 13" white tom, a 14" walnut tom and a 16" white tom. That's the mongrel Gretsch kit you can see me playing on the video of Jean-Luc playing on the show called *Soundstage* that's now on YouTube. At the end of the first tour with Jean-Luc he asked me to buy a big "Billy Cobham kit," meaning he wanted the look, and sound, of a big double bass kit on stage. That's when I bought my first Sonor kit.

My First Sonor Kit-

I bought my first Sonor kit in January of 1977. The configuration was two 24" bass drums, 12", 13", 14" rack toms, with 16" and 18" floor toms plus a deep snare. They had an orange-colored wrap. That was the only large, double bass kit the U.S. Sonor distributor had in stock, so I went with the flow and bought an orange kit. I decided on Sonor drums because Jack DeJohnette and Bernard Purdie both played Sonor and I loved their playing and recorded drum sounds. I knew Bernard played Sonor drums on the Aretha and King Curtis records and I saw him

do a Sonor clinic at Wurlitzer's in Boston. I was really impressed with the way that the drums sounded in person. I went to my local drum shop to buy them, the Carl Goodwin Drum Shop, and Carl organized that I could pick out the drums from the warehouse of the U.S. Sonor distributor, Charles Alden Music, which was based in Massachusetts. That was the kit that I played for the rest of my time with Jean-Luc, including his album *Enigmatic Ocean*. I also played that kit on tour with Ronnie Montrose and my first year with Journey, which

included the Journey *Evolution* album. By 1979 I stopped using the kit but I kept it in storage for many years and finally sold it to a collector.

The Sonor Phonic Jazz Kit

I got so into Sonor drums, that later in 1977, I also bought a used Sonor Phonic jazz kit with an 18" bass drum and 12" and 14" toms, the same configuration as my Gretsch walnut kit. I bought both of those jazz kits from the Carl Goodwin Drum Shop, they were his kits. Carl was the house drummer at The Playboy Club in Boston and played there six nights a week. That club closed in 1977 and he no longer need both kits. Now the Boston Four Seasons Hotel is where the Boston Playboy Club used to be.

A unique feature of that particular Sonor jazz kit is there is no finish on the outside, it's just the plain beechwood. All Sonor drums, in those years, were made of beech but they usually had some kind of finish on the outside, but on this kit the inside and the outside look the same. I still have that kit and it sounds amazing!

The White Sonor Kit

I liked my orange Sonor kit but in 1979 I wanted to change to a white kit. I think white kits look great and they work well with stage lights. My tech at that time, Jim McCandless, had designed a "T-bar" rack system that had mounts for my cymbal stands and mic stands. There was a T-bar on either side of the drum riser. That was one of the earliest "rack" designs that predates the Paul Jamieson designed Jeff Porcaro rack. I played the white Sonor drums in the studio, with the riser and the T-bars, on the Journey *Departure* album.

The 1980 Oak Veneer Sonor Kit

In 1979 Journey toured Europe with Pat Travers as the opening act. Tommy Aldridge was Pat's drummer and he was a Sonor endorser. Tommy and I visited the Sonor factory during that tour and I became an official Sonor endorser as a result of meeting Horst Link, the owner of Sonor drums, his son Oliver Link, and Karl-Heinz Menzel who just started working at Sonor in 1977. I ordered a huge kit from Sonor, it's what people today refer to as a "shell pack." The drums are made of beechwood with an Oak Veneer finish and I still have them and play them, in various configurations, to this day. The set consisted of two 24" bass drums, a 20" bass drum, 6", 8", 10", 12", 13" rack toms, 14", 16" and 18" floor toms and a 14x5.5 seamless Ferro-Manganese Steel snare drum. I've never used all of the drums at the same time, but would change up the configuration for whatever I needed.

Those drums are on the *Captured* live album. For the tour I used two rack toms in 13" and 14", and two floor toms in 16" and 18". I used those drums on the *Escape* album with an added 10" rack tom and I used that same setup on the *Frontiers* album. I also used them on the first two Vital Information albums and the two Tom Coster albums. Those are fantastic sounding drums and you can see them on many of my *From the Practice Room* videos on my YouTube channel.

Steve with his tech Benny Collins

I put those drums in storage when I got the big red Sonor kit in 1981. I didn't use the Oak Veneers again until I started making the Tone Center albums in 1997. I used them on the Tone Center albums *Vital Tech Tones, GHS, The Strangers Hand, Count's Jam Band* and more. The most common setup that I used for those recordings was with the 20" bass drum, 8", 10", 12" racks and 14" and 16" floor toms.

The BIG Red Sonor Kit

For the 1981 Escape tour, I got a large set of Horst Link Signature drums. The toms were square sizes: 8x8, 10x10, 12x12, 14x14 rack toms and 16x16 and 18x18 floor toms. They sounded good, though not quite as good as my standard size Oak Veneer drums, but they looked great for the live show. The shells were made of beech, with a Bubinga interior ply and I had Sonor deliver the drums without an outer veneer, so they would be ready to paint. Jonathan Cain (keyboard player for Journey) and I decided to have our instruments painted a matching red and they were painted by an autobody shop in Oakland, California.

The drums were a little hard to play because I was sitting very low, with two 24" bass drums, with the deep rack toms on the bass drums, so I had to angle the rack toms at a pretty steep angle, but I made it work.

After the Escape tour I had those drums refinished in a sunburst finish, and I used them for a short time with Journey but they weren't one of my favorite kits, so I put them up for sale at a drum shop in Scottsdale, Arizona. They sold the drums, and then the drum shop went out of business, so I never got paid for them. I don't know who bought them, or where they are now. Every once in a while, someone contacts me saying that they have my

old "Candy Apple Red Sonor kit!" I know that they can't have that kit, because when it was sold it wasn't red, it was sunburst.

As an aside, I should mention that there was a Sonor ad that had me in front of a big yellow double bass kit. They were beautiful drums, but they weren't mine. The kit was on display at the Frankfurt Musikmesse and I used it for some clinics in Europe.

The Sonor Rosewood Kit

For the 1983 Frontiers tour I decided to return to traditional sizes and used a double bass Sonor Rosewood kit. The drums were made of beech with a beautiful Rosewood finish on the inside and outside. I integrated four Simmons pads into the kit, two on each side. I also used a 22" K Zildjian ride instead of my 24" A Zildjian ping ride. Zildjian USA had just started making K's and I loved the sound right away, though in comparison to the K's Zildjian makes now, those early models were quite heavy, which worked with Journey's music. I settled on a tom setup that I continued to use for many years: three rack toms and two floor toms. In 1983 Paul Jamieson made me a customized Radio King 14x7 snare that remained in my setup for many years.

The Sonor Lite Scandinavian Birch Kit

After the Frontiers tour I embarked on my first tour with Vital Information during the Fall of 1983. I used a double bass Scandinavian Birch kit; it was my first Sonor Lite birch kit, which sounded fantastic. Sonor was responding to requests to make lighter drums, as Sonor drums were known to be very heavy. The kit had two 22x17 bass drums, 10x9, 12x10, 13x11 rack toms, 14x15 and 16x17 floor toms, I used my Jamieson 14x7 snare and had two Simmons pads to my left. Behind me was a small gong and wind chimes. From the Frontiers tour I used the same 22" K ride and a UFIP Ice Bell, and added K crashes plus a 20" A Zildjian flat ride, as a left-side-ride, which worked extremely well for some of the fast tempos we played on that tour. You can see that kit in the bonus footage of the *Steve Smith Part One* DVD. I had our concert at Cain's Ballroom in Tulsa, Oklahoma on November 18, 1983 recorded and filmed, there are a few songs from that show on the DVD.

"Drums Du Jour"

After I left Journey in 1985, I started playing a smaller set-up that had one bass drum, two rack toms, and two floor toms. When I toured, many times I played Sonor "loan" kits that were available for Sonor endorsers in different parts of the U.S. or in different countries around the world. Sometimes these loan kits were provided by rental companies and they arrived at the gig pretty beat up. Touring drummers generally refer to these kits as "drums du jour." For example, the drums on the Steps Ahead live album and video *Live in Tokyo 1986* were a Tokyo based loaner kit. I brought my cymbals, a Noble and Cooley snare, a set of Simmons pads and a huge rack that allowed me to trigger Simmons sounds on the kit.

White Sonor Lite Kit

On the back of the Vital Information *Fiafiaga (Celebration)* album I was pictured playing my new, in 1987, White Sonor Lite's which was made of birch. The setup was a 20" bass drum, three rack toms in 8", 10", 12", a 13" tom to my left, and two floor toms 14" and 15". I used those drums on

Sonor Designer Kits

When Sonor started making the Designer drums, I had a blue Designer kit that I kept mainly on the West coast, and a green kit on the East coast. Both sets had 8", 10", 12", 14", 16" toms and there were two bass drums for each kit, a 20" and a 22". The green drums were maple and the blue drums were birch. I used the green kit when I played with Buddy's Buddies on the Hudson Music video *A Salute to Buddy Rich* and on the *Buddy's Buddies* studio record, and the blue kit on the Hudson Music video *Drumset Technique/History of the U.S. Beat*. Those drums all sounded good and I

the Steps Ahead albums *N.Y.C.* and *Yin-Yang*, and on tour with The Jazz Explosion Super Band and Ahmad Jamal, which he wasn't happy about because I was checking them on the airlines as excess baggage. Ahmad wanted me to play drums du jour, or whatever kit was at the club, which I didn't want to do. Those are great sounding drums that I still have.

Red Sonor HiLite Exclusive Kit

In 1988 Sonor sent me a beautiful birch HiLite Exclusive kit with copper hardware. The bass drum was 22" and the tom setup was 8", 10", 12" rack toms, 13" tom to my left and 14" and 16" floor toms that were mounted on a stand. I used those on the Vital Information album *Vitalive!*, and the Journey album *Trial by Fire*.

couldn't tell much difference between maple and birch. The most I can say about the difference is the birch drums had a shorter decay and the maple drums were a little more resonant. I did a lot of touring and recording with both of those kits and eventually sold them as Sonor introduced newer kits.

The Sonor SQ2 Kit

The next significant kit after the Designer drums was an early version of the SQ2 drums. Sonor asked me to play the kit at the NAMM show in Anaheim at an event with Thomas Lang and Jojo Mayer. The drums are made of maple, the finish is Silky Oak and the hardware is black chrome. The bass drum is 20x20, the rack toms are 8x7, 10x8, 12x9, each drum is one inch deeper than the previous drum. The floor toms are 14x14 and 16x16.

The 14x5 matching Silky Oak snare is an especially good sounding snare drum. I didn't think I'd like the 20x20 bass drum but once I played it, I was blown away with the sound. The kit doesn't have a tom mount on the bass drum, which I prefer, but I've gotten used to having the toms mounted on stands with this kit.

You can see this SQ2 kit in the live footage shot at the 2006 Modern Drummer Festival which was also the live footage used in my Hudson Music video *Drum Legacy-Standing on the Shoulders of Giants*. It's also the kit I used for my solo drumset album *The Fabric of Rhythm,* which is included with this book as a download. The toms are setup with Remo black dots top and bottom à la Tony Williams. Those drums sound amazing and have beautiful melody and tone.

Steve Smith 30th Anniversary Sonor Kit

2007 was my 30th anniversary of playing Sonor drums. The company wanted to do something special to commemorate my commitment to Sonor. Karl-Heinz Menzel, the president of Sonor at that time, asked me to come to the factory in Germany and the two of us would design the kit. At that time Sonor had stopped making beech drums, so that was my first idea, I wanted my drums to be a throwback to the classic beech Sonor drums. Karl-Heinz and I experimented with the thickness of the plies and the overall

thickness of the shells. He would ask someone at the factory to make a 20" bass drum with thin plies and one with thick plies. A few hours later someone would bring in the two drums. I'd put on the Remo heads I liked and then I would play the bass drums. Karl-Heinz would turn around and go to the other end of the room and listen. Then he would play and I'd listen, without looking at the drums. We determine the 20x16 bass drum with thin plies had the richest tone and the deepest fundamental. We used this process with all of the drums and ended up with thicker tom shells in classic depths, the rack toms are 8x8, 10x8, 12x8 and the floor toms are 14x14 and 16x16. The kit also included a 12x5 beech side-snare. I wanted a woodgrain finish and we settled on Birdseye Amber, plus I wanted slotted tension rods and T-Rods for the bass drum. I also wanted a heavy steel 14x5.5 shell for the snare drum with the classic 70s style lugs. That snare drum stayed in the Sonor catalog for many years. Sonor made 100, numbered, Steve Smith Signature kits and they all sold out in the first year of production. I did a world clinic tour and played over 50 clinics to promote the kit. The dealer had to buy a kit to get the clinic so I

Steve Smith Library

Sonor Vintage Kit

I do have one of the newer Sonor Vintage kits made of beech. You can see me using this kit on YouTube doing a clinic at the 2017 PASIC and playing *Mercy, Mercy, Mercy* at the PASIC concert with The Airmen of Note Big Band. Plus, it's the kit on the cover of my *Pathways of Motion,* book/video. I really love the Sonor Vintage drums. The sound is very warm, round and big. The bass drum is 22x14, 12x8 rack, the floor toms are 14x12 16x14 and the wood snare is 14x5¾.

Sonor White SQ2 Journey Kit

The kit that I used with Journey from 2016-2019 is a white SQ2 kit

played a different kit at each clinic and they all sounded amazing! I still have two of those kits. One is at the Sonor factory which I use when touring in Europe and the other one is with my cartage man Kris Castillo in New Jersey when I tour the east coast or play NYC. I also had Sonor make an 18" bass drum for that kit, which I use when I play jazz gigs in NYC. Every time I sit down and play my 30th Anniversary kit I'm reminded how special that kit sounds and feels.

Here is a video of my Sonor 30th Anniversary tour: https://www.youtube.com/watch?v=INPA6RsWyPk

with black chrome hardware. I went back to standard sizes for the bass drums: 22x14. The bass drums are made from thin beech plies, like we used on my 30th anniversary bass drum. The toms are medium ply maple and modeled after my Silky Oak SQ2 set. The three rack toms are 8x7, 10x8, 12x9 and three floor toms are 14x14, 16x16 and 18x16. The main snare is my steel 14x5.5 Steve Smith Signature snare, the de-tuned snare to the left of my hi-hat is based on a 14x5¾ Sonor Vintage snare, but with modern hardware. Next to that snare is a third snare drum that is 12x5. With this setup I had a lot of

I have to mention that I can go years without asking Sonor for a new kit. I have never been one that asks for a new kit every year or feel I need a new kit for every tour. I did at least three Journey tours with my original Sonor Oak Veneer kit. And all of the most recent Journey tours, from 2016-2019 I've used the same kit. But occasionally Sonor will call and suggest I use a new kit and I am happy to oblige them.

options for melodic fills with six toms and various orchestrations between the three snare drums.

When coming up with a kit for Journey 2016, I decided that I wanted to try the three-floor tom, "triangle" set-up that Billy Cobham and Tony Williams used when I first saw them in the 70s. Now I'm used to three floor toms and I love playing that setup.

Over the years I've often used white kits. The look great under lights as

Steve Smith Library

Steve Smith Library

Sonor Jungle Kit

As soon as Sonor introduced the Jungle Kit in the 90s, I took to that setup immediately and used it on various jazz gigs. I found the perfect application for the Jungle Kit in 2001 when I started playing with percussionists from India. I needed a kit that I could setup to be as low-volume as possible. The original Jungle kit came with a 16x16 floor tom as the bass drum, a 10" rack tom and a 13" floor tom. I used a 12x5 snare drum, Zildjian flat rides, small splashes and 12" hi-hats. I played the kit with brushes and my Vic Firth Tala Wands and I could play with tabla maestro Zakir Hussain, for example, and not blow him off the stage with volume. I recorded the album *George Brooks Summit* with Zakir sitting a few feet in front of me and there was no problem with excess drumset level. Another recording I made on one of my early Jungle Kits was "Mad Tea Time, Part One and Part Two" a song with Summit that included a duet with Zakir Hussain. That

they change color with different lighting and in general, I think they look cool. My Slingerland's were white, my second set of Gretsch's were white, my second Sonor kit was white, the Sonor Lite's are white, my new SQ2's are white and my Vintage drums are white marine pearl!

Sonor ProLite Kit

I also have a maple Sonor ProLite kit with a woodgrain finish, which you can see and hear in some of my *From the Practice Room* videos. They are made in Germany, are the least expensive of the German made drums, and sound fantastic. I've used that kit on many gigs.

Steve Smith Library

Steve Smith Library

song appears on the album *Modern Drummer Magazine presents Drum Nation*. For many years, when I performed a Sonor drum clinic, I always had a Jungle Kit in addition to the main kit. Having two kits at a clinic gave me different playing options and let people know how good a Jungle Kit can sound. I still enjoy performing on my Jungle Kit from time to time.

Jay Blakesberg Courtesy Of Zildjian Cymbals

CYMBALS

I have always played Zildjian Cymbals, and remain my choice in cymbals. My first cymbals were a 24" Zildjian ride, and 14" Zildjian hi-hats. I knew about Paiste because of John Bonham and Ian Paice, but Paiste didn't have much presence in the U.S. When I got to Berklee, I did discover the Paiste 602 Flat Ride from Roy Haynes' playing on Chick Corea's *Now He Sings, Now He Sobs* recording. I couldn't find a 602, so I bought a 2002 Flat Ride because the ECM drumming concept was popular during my years at Berklee and I associated the Paiste Flat Ride with that concept and sound. At that time Zildjian did not offer a flat ride.

When I toured with Jean-Luc Ponty, I had a setup that did include a couple of Paiste cymbals mixed in with my Zildjians. In 1977, I went to Europe with Jean-Luc, and we played in Zurich, Switzerland. A Paiste rep named Alex Bally came to the gig and invited me to visit the Paiste factory. I left the factory with a bag of cymbals and became a Paiste endorser for a short time. I was excited about the fact that a company wanted to give me free gear and I liked the way some of the cymbals sounded. Unfortunately, I could never find a Paiste main ride that I liked, so even for the brief time I played Paiste, I used a 24" Zildjian Ping ride. I saw Lenny White use one, and it sounded great, so I bought one.

Shortly after I joined

Journey in 1978 Lennie DiMuzio offered me a Zildjian endorsement, and because I had been playing Zildjian cymbals from the start and preferred Zildjian's, I was thrilled, and I became a Zildjian endorser. Armand Zildjian and Lennie DiMuzio had seen me play with The Lin Biviano Big Band in 1974 using my old K's and A's, but I think they saw me as a "local Boston drummer" and didn't offer me an endorsement at that time. Plus, the endorsement concept was different in those days. You had to prove yourself as a player and as a drummer that would have a long career before a company would offer you an endorsement.

Up until 1982, I used that 24" Ping ride as my main ride. That ride is on all of the Journey records from *Evolution* through *Frontiers*. My crashes were usually 18" and I was using all A's. In 1982, Zildjian USA started making K's, so I started using a 22" K ride with Journey, Vital Information and other groups I was playing with at that time. Throughout the years, whenever Zildjian developed a new cymbal line, I would use them. I have played A Custom's, Z's, K Constantinople's, Kerope's, and in 2016 when Zildjian developed the Avedis cymbals they were the perfect cymbals to use on the 2016-2019 Journey tours. They are as great as the original A's that I had in the 60s, and better than my A's of the 70s and 80s. I have two 22" Avedis rides in my rock setup now, the ride to my left has three rivets, and the ride to my right has no rivets. I've also used them on jazz gigs and they sound great, though my favorite jazz rides are the 22" Renaissance and the 22" Peter Erskine "Left Side Ride."

SNARES

I've never really been a big snare drum collector, though I do have some wonderful snares. Going back to the early 70s, I loved the Fibes snare drum I owned, it was really crisp. Buddy Rich had a Fibes snare that he loved, it's on the cover of the *Rich in London* record, so I knew that I was in good company. When I was young, I also had a Rogers wood snare that I liked, it was a Powertone, not a Dynasonic.

In the early 80s with Journey, I had some Radio Kings that Paul Jamieson customized and they sounded great. One was 14x5 and the other was 14x7. They didn't sound anything like the original Radio Kings, it was whatever Paul did to them that made me love the sound.

MD: Do you remember what he did to them.

SS: He redid the bearing edges, installed a Sonor strainer/throw-off, mounted a Shure 57 inside the drum with the

Steve Smith Library

Italian pop records. The drum has a beautiful rich tone and a very short decay with no ring at all.

Jeff Ocheltree made me some very heavy steel shelled snares that really knocked me out. So, when Sonor asked me to make a signature snare drum, to go with my 30th Anniversary kit, my snare was modeled after the Jeff Ocheltree snare. It's fairly easy to find a snare with good high end but rare to find a snare that has good high end and plenty of low end too. Jeff's snares have both highs and lows, which for me, makes them the ideal snare drums.

My 40th Anniversary Sonor Snare is

May internal miking system and put a beautiful sunburst finish on the shell. Those drums sounded very current for that time. They had the very deep, low-pitched snare sound of the 80s. I donated the 14x7 Jamieson Radio King to the Rock and Roll Hall of Fame when I was inducted in 2017.

It was also popular in the 80s not to play rimshots for backbeats, so on most of the Journey records I'm playing the snare drum dead center and without rimshots, producer Roy Thomas Baker (producer of Queen, Journey, The Cars) insisted on that. Through the years, I've used Sonor metal drums of various depths. One of my favorites is the 14x4 Bronze Sonor snare, that drum really pops. There is also another Sonor snare that I favor and it's a maple 14x5 Artist Series with a Scandinavian Birch woodgrain finish and gold hardware. The rims are single flanged with vintage tension rod clips.

In the early 90s I bought two 1920s Ludwig Black Beauty's. One is plain black, with no engraving, and one has the classic scrolling, they both sound great. Noble and Cooley made me a few solid ply drums in the 80s that sound very good. I have a 14x5 Solid snare that was one of my, "go to" recording drums. Solid was short lived company owned by Bill Gibson, the drummer with Huey Lewis and the News, and John Craviotto. That was the snare favored by Corrado Rustici when he hired me to play on numerous

essentially modeled after the Sonor Vintage Snare. The drum uses a 14x5¾ beech shell, rounded bearing edges with eight vintage Sonor Bowtie style lugs and Mountain Burl veneer inside and out.

HEADS

MD: Have you always used Remo heads?
SS: I always gravitated towards clear Remo Ambassador heads. That is the sound on all of the Journey albums and, in general, most of the albums I've recorded. It's only been since about 2005 that I started outfitting some of my kits with Remo clear CS Black Dots, top and bottom, with a higher tuning to get that melodic Tony Williams sound. I do occasionally use coated Ambassadors which is a classic sound. For the bass drum my preferred head is

the Remo Powerstroke 3 with a Black Dot. I started using Fiberskyn Diplomats on my main snare in the early 2000s and even used them on the 2016-2019 Journey tours. I discovered those heads hearing Jeff Hamilton use them. They work great with brushes, but they also sound great with sticks on a metal snare drum. I like the fact that they are a little darker sounding than a coated Ambassador. On a metal snare drum, the Fiberskyn Diplomat head can help a bright drum sound a little darker.

When I first joined Journey in 1978, I was playing really hard. I broke sticks and cymbals, and dented heads. I hadn't fine-tuned my technique. But through years of working on, and refining my technique, now I don't dent heads, break sticks or cymbals and I get a bigger sound. When using the thin Fiberskyn Diplomat head on my snare, on the 2016-2019 Journey tours, I didn't pit them or break them. I got five or six shows out of each snare head, but by then they were stretched out, losing some tone and need to be changed.

MD: If you only changed your snare heads after five or six shows, how often did you change your tom and bass drum heads?

SS: Very rarely. The 18" floor tom, and the 12" snare have never been changed. We changed the bass drum heads once in the four years, just to change them. I changed the 8, 10, 12, 14 and 16 maybe twice during each six-month tour.

MD: When I saw you with recently with Journey it looked like you were changing sticks a few times for specific songs.

SS: On "Lights" I used the Steve Gadd sticks, and on "Who's Crying Now" I used the Jojo Mayer sticks. There was something about the way that those sticks felt that worked for those songs. I like the way a new pair of sticks feel in my hands, so I usually end up giving my signature sticks away after one or two shows and then picking up a fresh pair for the next gig.

In high school and Berklee I used 5A's and 7A's. I do remember using Regal JC Heard sticks at one point, but

> "I like the way a new pair of sticks feel in my hands, so I usually end up giving my signature sticks away after one or two shows and then picking up a fresh pair for the next gig"

by the time I joined Journey in 1978 I was using Vic Firth 2B's. After leaving Journey I started using lighter sticks. I used Vic Firth SD9's, then the Harvey Mason signature sticks, and eventually wound up with a Vic Firth 5A. When Vic Firth asked me to design a signature stick in the late 80s, I wanted one based on a 5A, but with a tip that was elongated based on a Jack DeJohnette Sonor stick and an Elvin Jones stick from Frank Ippolito's Professional Percussion Center NYC. We eventually came up with a signature stick that met all of my requirements, is perfectly balanced and sounds great on both drums and cymbals.

Lastly, I've always liked the feel of DW pedals, I've used their pedals going back to early Journey. I don't like the heavy double chain pedals but the pedals based on the original DW5000 with the thin chain, or the nylon strap, and the light footboard.

Regarding endorsements, I play exactly the gear that I enjoy playing and I'm fortunate to have long relationships with all of the companies that I endorse, apart from the one misstep with Paiste, which I chalk up to the fact I was a 22-year-old kid on my first world tour. I have stayed with every company that I've endorsed for my entire career, starting with Sonor drums, Zildjian cymbals, Remo heads, Vic Firth sticks, to DW pedals, Puresound snare wires, Cympad Cymbal Optimizers and Gruv-X percussion products. I have also had a long relationship with Rob Wallis at Hudson Music that dates back to 1987 when Rob Wallis and Paul Siegel were DCI video. And my relationship with *Modern Drummer* Magazine has been a large part of the public support I've received over the years and has helped immensely with my visibility as a working musician. With live performances with various bands and artists, clinic tours organized by the companies I endorse, videos, DVDs and books from Hudson Music and the support of the readers of *Modern Drummer*, I been fortunate to have a career that is multifaceted which includes performing as a member of a group, session musician, sideman, bandleader and educator. It's all added up to a very rewarding life in music.

Steve and Friends

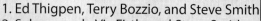

1. Ed Thigpen, Terry Bozzio, and Steve Smith
2. Selvaganesh, Vic Firth, and Steve Smith
3. Dennis Chambers, Steve Smith, Vinnie Colaiuta, John DeChristopher, and Lennie DiMuzio in the background
4. Steve Smith and Narada Michael Walden
5. Steve Smith and Freddie Gruber
6. Steve and Pete Magadini
7. Steve, Jack DeJohnette, and Zakir Hussain
8. Steve and Roy Haynes
9. Steve and Steve Gadd
10. Vital Tech Tones: Scott Henderson, Steve, and Victor Wooten
11. Steve and Billy Cobham
12. Steve Smith and Alex Van Halen
13. Steve and Charlie Watts
14. The Electric Miles Band: Jeremy Pelt, Steve Cardenas, Randy Brecker, Lonnie Plaxico, Vinny Valentino, Paul Bollenback, Shane Theroit and Steve

15. Jazz Legacy in Moscow: Baron Browne, Steve, Mark Soskin, Andy Fusco, Walt Weiskopf

16. Armand Zildjian, Vinnie Colaiuta, Steve Smith, Peter Erskine, Steve Gadd, Louie Bellson, Ralph MacDonald, and Larrie Londin

17. Brian Bennett, Steve Smith, Clem Cattini, and Bobby Graham

18. Steve and Larry Coryell

19. Steve and Kenny Aronoff

20. Ahmad Jamal and Steve

21. Tommy Aldridge, Horst Link, Steve, and Oliver Link at the Sonor Factory 1979

22. Dave Weckl, Steve, Peter Erskine

23. Steve and Anthony Jackson

24. Baird Hersey and The Year Of The Ear 1975 Top row: Len Detlor, Tommy Guralnick, Steve Smith, George Garzone, Ernie Provencher Front row: Scott Breadman, Tim Sessions, Kenny Mason, Mark Harvey, Arnie Clapman. Standing: Baird Hersey

Steve and Friends

25. Arnel Pineda, Steve and his wife Diane
26. Phil Collen, Steve, Rick Allen, Ross Valory, Joe Elliott
27. Zakir Hussain and his wife Toni, with Steve
28. Bill Evans, Mike Mainieri, Steve, Tom Kennedy, Randy Brecker
29. Buddy's Buddies: Steve Marcus, Mark Soskin, Andy Fusco, Steve, Baron Browne
30. Steve Khan, Tony Levin, and Steve
31. Ronald Shannon Jackson and Steve
32. Vic Firth and Steve Smith
33. Vital Information: Frank Gambale, Baron Browne, Tom Coster, Steve
34. Steve Houghton, Louie Bellson, Armand Zildjian, Steve Smith
35. Dennis Moody, Steve, Bob Malach, Mike Stern
36. Dave Liebman, Steve Smith
37. Isabel and Ron Spagnardi and Steve
38. Thomas Lang, Jim Kilpatrick, Remo Belli, Louie Bellson, and Steve Smith

Steve and Family

1. Steve with his mother Lorraine, Charlie Watts, and Steve's dad, Bruce.
2. Steve and his wife Diane
3. Steve and his son Ian
4. Steve and Ian
5. Steve Smith Christmas time 1956
6. Steve and Diane
7. Steve's daughter Elizabeth Spina, Steve, and son-in-law Dustin Spina
8. Ian Smith with his dad.

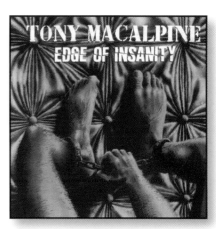

THE SONGS

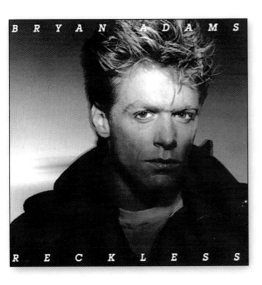

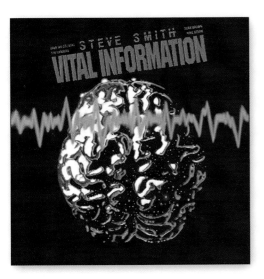

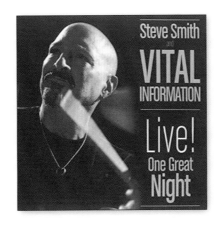

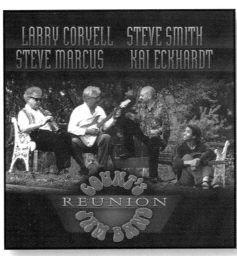

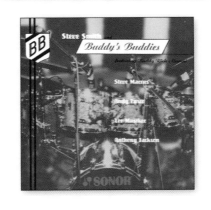

Transcriptions

By Terry Branam

Steve's Thoughts on...

By Mark Griffith

Steve Smith is the living embodiment of what it is to be a modern drummer. Regardless of the musical style he is playing in, his drumming IQ is on the absolute highest level. Smith's presence is large whether he is leading his own groups, playing as a member of a band, or as a sideman for the greats. Rooted in tradition, his playing style is on the cutting edge while always staying true to the lineage of the instrument.

Smith's evolution on the drums has been one of enormous growth and depth. He immerses himself in whichever style he takes on, spanning everything from stadium rock, bebop, fusion, prog-metal, organ trios and Indian classical music to name a few. Not only is he an eternal student of the drums, but also an important and influential educator. Defining contemporary drumset technique and the U.S. drumming style, he has set a path to follow for the students of today and tomorrow. Steve Smith is a true Legend of the drums, and his impact on today's drumming scene is unmistakable.

MUSIC KEY

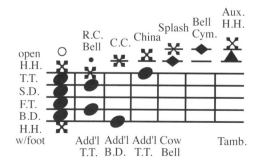

Jean-Luc Ponty "Enigmatic Ocean, Pt. II," *Enigmatic Ocean*

Ex. 1 Steve plays an aggressive fusion groove on the intro of "Enigmatic Ocean, Part II." The active snare drum ghost notes give the beat a sense of urgency. (0:00)

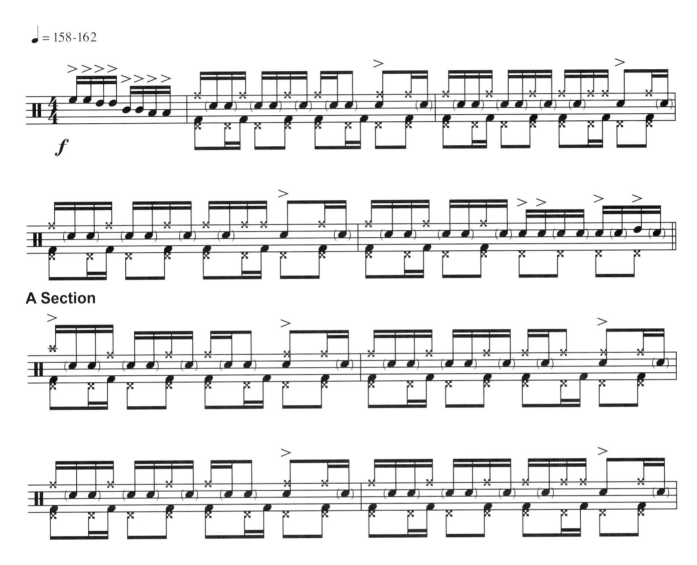

Ex. 2 He keeps the intensity high while handling the rhythmic figures and changing meters at the end of the A section. (0:24)

Ex. 3 The groove on the bridge (before the solos) changes things up, as the ride cymbal bell syncs up with the bass drum, the left hand anchors the time with backbeats. (0:50)

Ex. 4 On the solo trading section, Steve fills the spaces with ghost notes while playing upbeats on the ride cymbal bell. (1:13)

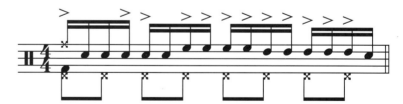

Steve's Thoughts on…
Jean-Luc Ponty "Enigmatic Ocean, Pt. II" *Enigmatic Ocean*

Damn that's fast! That was my "fast-fusion" approach that had developed by playing with Jean-Luc since October of 1976. We recorded this in the summer of 1977. I remember because it was the summer that *Star Wars* came out. I was 22 years old, recording *Enigmatic Ocean* and staying at The Holiday Inn that was on the same block as Grauman's Chinese Theater in Hollywood. I saw *Star Wars* seven days in a row because it blew my mind!

We had rehearsed for a week prior to the recording sessions, Jean-Luc had handwritten charts, there were no demos,

no click tracks… It was just "here are the charts." We rehearsed and came up with our parts. Jean-Luc had the whole album sequenced and conceptualized in his mind. To this day, it's the only record that I have ever recorded in the same sequence exactly as it appears on the record. We recorded live in the studio, solos and all. I had very little studio experience at the time, it was actually the first album I ever made. I was hanging on by a thread at that session, just trying to stay out of everybody's way and play my best. It was a great experience.

Journey "Lovin' You Is Easy," *Evolution*

Ex. 5 Smith's funky groove playing and creative beat design join forces on the song "Lovin' You Is Easy". He plays a broken pattern on the ride bell that matches up with Neal Schon's rhythm guitar part and answers with tom hits at the end of the bar. The hi-hat takes over in the verse, and quarter note accents on the bell of the ride bring contrast to the chorus. (0:00)

Verse

Chorus

Steve's Thoughts on…
Journey "Lovin You is Easy," *Evolution*

That's a really groovy and funky beat that never gets mentioned. I like the opening groove with the bell on the ride cymbal and toms, it's rhythmic and melodic. For the verses the same rhythm is played on closed hats. There is a cool groove for the chorus and

that song, from my point of view, has a Led Zeppelin inspired bridge. "Lovin You is Easy" was always a fun tune to play live with the Gregg Rolie era of Journey. We would always stretch out on the ending, which I loved.

Journey "La Do Da," *Captured*

Ex. 6 The drum solo on the live version of Journey's "La Do Da" starts with a heavy shuffle groove on the floor tom with some double bass triplet rhythms interspersed underneath. Smith plays dazzling linear combinations around the drums and introduces a melodic element with the toms. (2:27)

Steve's Thoughts on…
Journey, "La Do Da-Drum Solo," *Captured*

My solo on the *Captured* album is a good documentation of the solos I was playing on the Journey tours in the early years. I liked the shuffle tempo and feel of "La Do Da" and it felt like the perfect set-up for a drum solo. I liked to keep the tempo of the song and the "hook," or theme, of the shuffle rhythm played on the floor tom, which is what Aynsley Dunbar played on the original recording of

that song. Generally, in the first part of the solo I'd play in a triplet, swinging feel and develop melodic jazz-like figures but played with a rock attitude. I'd go back to the floor tom/double bass drum theme and then improvise in sixteenth notes, play the triplet theme and then improvise in sixteenth note triplets, that way the solo would build in note density and excitement.

Journey "Escape," *Escape*

Ex. 7 Steve confidently drives the band with a four-on-the-floor groove on Journey's "Escape." He adds spice with ghost notes on the snare drum in the intro and verse. He plays a tasteful over-the-barline phrase on the hi-hat during the interlude between the verses. (0:06)

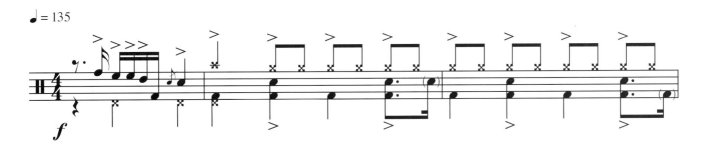

Verse

Interlude

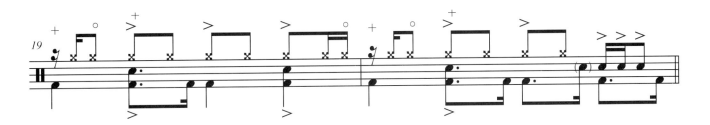

Ex. 8 He catches the guitar rhythms on the snare and hi-hat on the instrumental section after the second verse, then grabs the unison band accents with hi-hat barks. (1:21)

Ex. 9 This lightning-quick fill lands at the end of the guitar solo. (4:13)

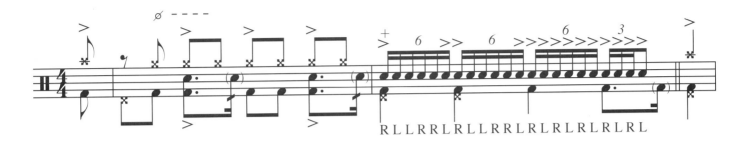

R L L R R L R L L R R L R L R L R L R L

Steve's Thoughts on…
Journey "Escape," *Escape.*

This was originally two separate tunes, and we couldn't quite get either of them developed into an entire song. We decided to join the two ideas to make one song, a sort of *mini-suite*. The groove was fairly up-tempo, and I enjoyed coming up with orchestrations and punctuations while keeping the underlying quarter-note pulse. That idea developed after playing some gigs with AC/DC opening for us. They had a song called "Problem Child" that we all loved. On that tune they kept the groove going while Phil Rudd hit these up-beat accents with his snare and a cymbal, but the bass drum never changed. As a group we watched them and noticed, on a few tunes, they used that idea of keeping a headbanging groove going while playing accents over the pulse. Their relentless groove made them a hard act to follow! We in Journey ended up incorporating that idea on some of our songs. You can hear that on

"Escape." I am catching the hits, but never stopping the pulse of the bass drum. I used that idea on "Where Were You" and "Dead or Alive" too. In "Escape" you can also hear that I set up some of the figures with "big band" type fills. I play a set-up figure, stop, leave some space, then the band figure comes in. It was natural for me to orchestrate the music like that from my years of big band drumming. (The fill into measure 13 of the 1st part of the transcription and measure 16 in the 2nd part of the transcription.)

MD: When I watched you on this last tour, I never realized how many Journey tunes that you played four on the floor.

SS: And it increased as time went on. There are quite a few four on the floor tunes on the *Frontiers* album, Steve Perry really liked that "quarter-pulse" feel, as he called it.

Journey, drum solo from "Where Were You?" *Escape Tour 1981: Live in Houston*

Ex. 10 Near the end of the extended drum solo from the song "Where Were You?" featured on the live video from the *Escape* tour, Steve breaks into a double-time fusion groove that is packed with ghost notes. He fires off fast double bass and tom combinations as the solo peaks and finishes with triplets from the snare drum to the cymbals.

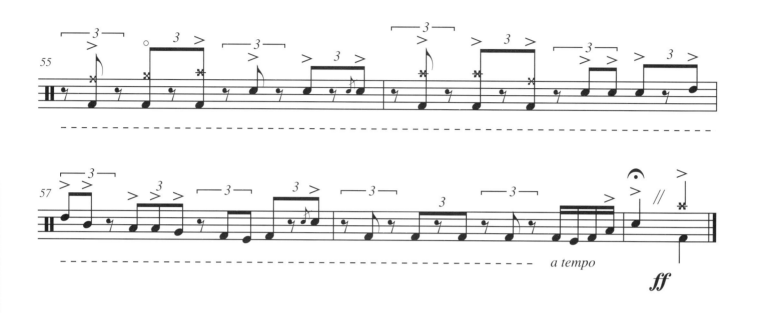

Steve's Thoughts on…
Journey, "Where Were You-Drum Solo," *1981 Escape Live* DVD
(originally aired on MTV.)

I haven't listened to this in probably 30 years or so, and I know that you love it. This solo came out of the end of "Where Were You." I kept the tempo of the song and feel of the groove going. In a rock environment I think that the people can more easily relate to a drum solo that continues on as the song fades out. I played some interesting melodic ideas with the toms on top of the groove. I also introduced some polyrhythms by working off a quarter-note triplet. After the break, I kept the same tempo but come back with a half-time groove, which then became a double time fusion groove à la Narada or Cobham.

(*Laughing*) This is clearly before I studied with Freddie Gruber because I am holding the left stick way in the back and digging the stick tip into the snare drum head. The end groove on the bell is sort of a combination of rock, fusion, and Latin with those bell rhythms. I hear a lot of Cobham paradiddle inspired ideas, and I'm doing a ton of the Narada-Bozzio type hand/foot/double bass drum combinations. This is the type of playing that I first started developing with Jean-Luc Ponty. I didn't have a chance to play like this in any Journey song, so I pulled it out in my solo!

That was a big drum set, and I was really getting around on it, which was not easy with those deep toms mounted on 24" bass drums. From my perspective today, I am physically working very hard, harder than necessary, but I didn't learn that until later. In those days it was "louder and harder is better!" Ever since late 1978 I had played a solo off of the shuffle groove of "La Do Da" in Journey, and I was trying to come up with something different. In 1981 I wanted a new solo that would work in context with the band and the show, and I came up with the idea of soloing after "Where Were You." That solo was a little different every night. I wasn't planning the solos out back then, I gave myself a starting point and then improvised and followed the thread of what ideas and phrases came out that night.

Journey "Frontiers," *Frontiers*

Ex. 11 Smith approaches the groove on "Frontiers" with an inventive four-measure pattern. The "one" might feel elusive on first listen, but the snare drum anchors the time with a solid backbeat on count four. (0:03)

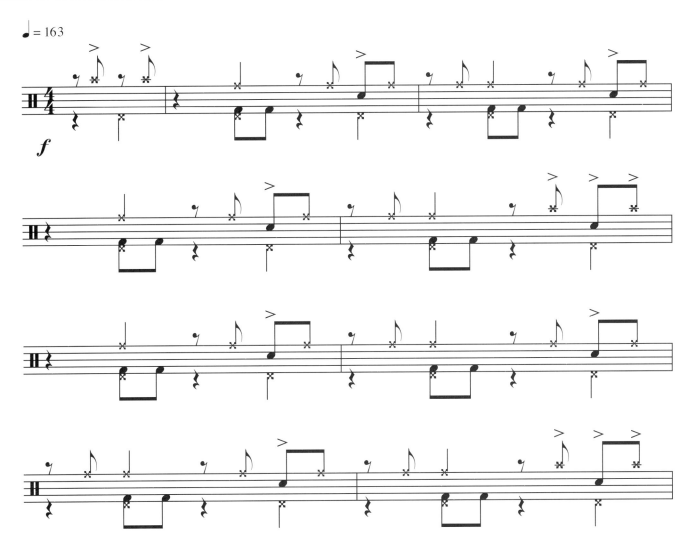

Ex. 12 He plays another interesting pattern in the verse that integrates an offbeat bell hit. Smith maintains a sense of groove despite the tricky syncopation. (0:27)

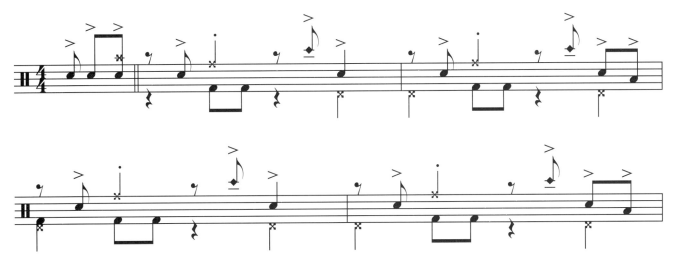

Ex. 13 The groove continues to evolve into the chorus with snare drum hits that land on the "and" of one and on beat four. (1:02)

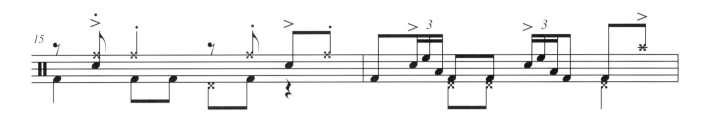

Steve's Thoughts on...
Journey "Frontiers," *Frontiers*.

That tune was written from my drum beat. I was working on some coordination stuff, and came up with a groove that incorporated the bell of my ride cymbal and a UFIP Icebell. The Police were probably an influence on this groove. They were coming up with some rhythmically sophisticated music that was being accepted by millions of people, so we wanted to experiment with that too. It's a little hard to hear where "one" is in that tune. The crashes at the beginning of the tune (and throughout the intro,) if you count with an 8th note double time feel, are on the "and" of three and the "and" of four. That tune took some rehearsing and we never played it live back then. We did play it on tour in 2017 when we occasionally played an evening of the complete *Escape* and *Frontiers* albums.

Journey "After the Fall," *Frontiers*

Ex. 14 Steve plays a skipping hi-hat groove on "After the Fall" with finesse and a relaxed feel. (0:00)

Ex. 15 He embellishes the fill that leads into the first chorus with ghost notes. (1:25)

Chorus

Ex. 16 This fill sets up the third verse. (2:12)

Ex. 17 Here is another slick fill that introduces the last chorus. The snare drum rolls on beat four into the downbeat. (2:50)

Ex. 18 Steve locks in with Randy Jackson's groovy slap bass line on the outro with an open hi-hat accent on the "a" of beat four on the first measure of the two-bar phrase and a snare and tom unison on beat four of the second measure. (3:59)

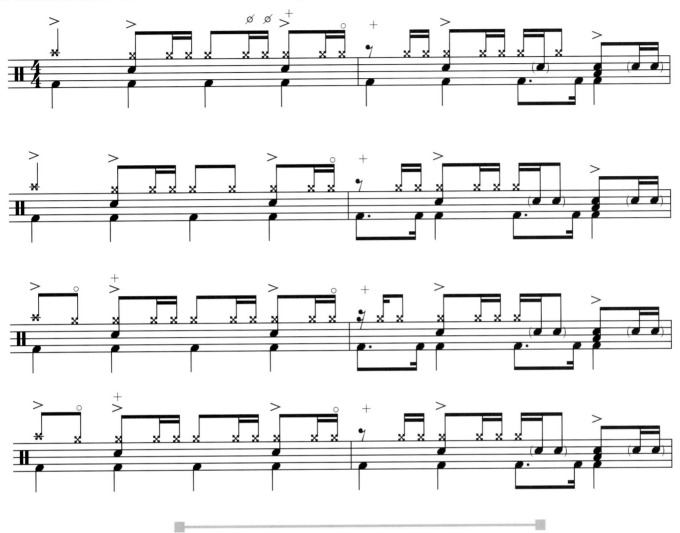

Steve's Thoughts on…
Journey "After The Fall," *Frontiers*

That tune was a problem, we couldn't get a good take on it. I love (Journey bassist) Ross Valory, and I love playing with him, but Ross just couldn't get the right groove for that tune. I suggested that we bring in Randy Jackson for that one tune. Randy and I had done session work together and were playing in Tom Coster's band. I opened a can of worms when I suggested that. That's when Steve Perry and the guys in Journey first met Randy and they all fell in love with him. I think that's

one of the best Journey tracks that we ever recorded. There is no big wall of guitar on that track, and the keyboards are pretty transparent, so you can really hear the drums, bass and vocal. Perry's performance is pretty incredible and super soulful. I got into a lot of detail and my beat evolves over the course of the song. Also, I worked out fills in the breaks that start simple and get a little more sophisticated as the song progresses.

Journey "Back Talk," *Frontiers*

Ex. 19 The drums kick off the song "Back Talk" with a strong Bo Diddley style tom-tom beat. (0:00)

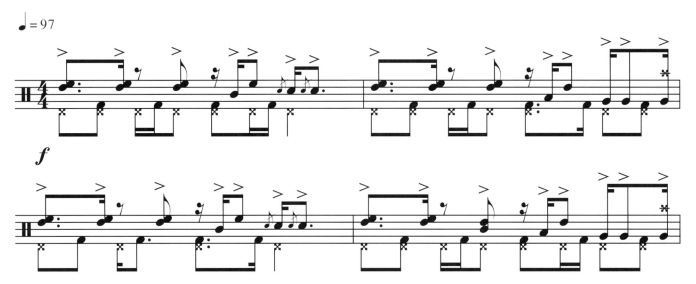

Ex. 20 He adapts the groove in the chorus to catch the guitar accent on the "and" of beat three on the second measure of the phrase. (0:39)

Ex. 21 The energy kicks into high gear during the guitar solo as Steve escalates the beat to a double-time feel on the ride cymbal. (1:57)

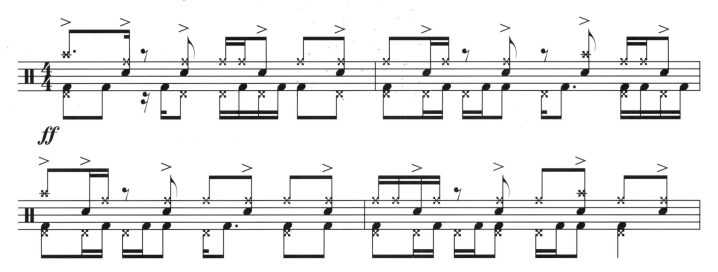

Steve's Thoughts on…
Journey "Back Talk," *Frontiers.*

That is another tune that started with some beats that I created. It's kind of a "Bo Diddley beat" vibe, but there are some twists in there so it's not a straight Bo Diddley beat.

We wrote as a group and if I came in with a groove, Neal would find a guitar riff, and Steve Perry would come up with a melody and we were off and running.

An important component of Smith's playing is his uncanny ability to deliver big, expressive drum fills on rock ballads that become integral parts of the song. Here are a few examples:

Bryan Adams "Heaven," *Reckless*

Ex. 22 Steve runs down the toms with triplets going into the bridge of Bryan Adams' number one hit song "Heaven". (2:17)

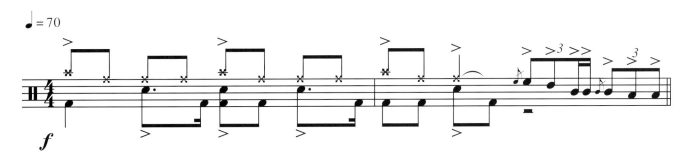

Ex. 23 The fill before the guitar solo breaks things up with a 32nd note skip going into beat four. (2:47)

Ex. 24 Snare drum accents add variety as he travels down the toms before the last chorus. (3:01)

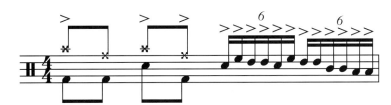

Ex. 25 As the song fades out, Steve plays a massive sixteenth-note triplet fill. (3:42)

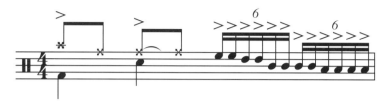

Journey "Faithfully," *Frontiers*

Ex. 26 On Journey's "Faithfully," Smith answers the piano and guitar melody in the interlude after the choruses with lyrical tom fills. (1:25)

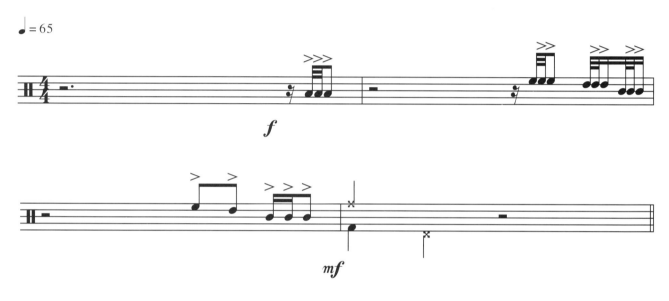

Ex. 27 Here is another phrase on the second interlude. (2:50)

Ex. 28 He plays a decisive fill going into the song's ending sequence. (3:13)

Journey "Open Arms," *Escape*

Ex. 29 Before the choruses of the iconic ballad "Open Arms," the drums step out and play a signature fill. (0:58)

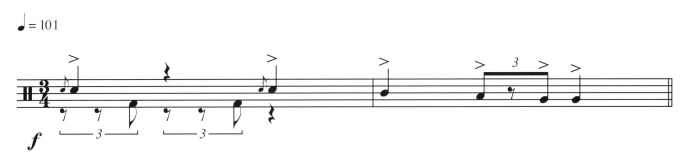

Ex. 30 Smith develops the idea by adding just one additional note before the second chorus. (2:26)

Journey "Mother, Father," *Escape*

Ex. 31 Steve announces the first chorus of "Mother, Father" with a stately fill. (1:03)

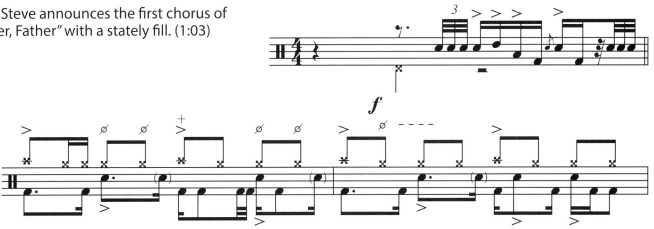

Ex. 32 He throws in a couple of 32nd notes at the end of the tom fill into the pre-chorus that add momentum into the transition. He compliments the idea by echoing the same rhythm on the bass drum at the beginning of the next measure. (3:04)

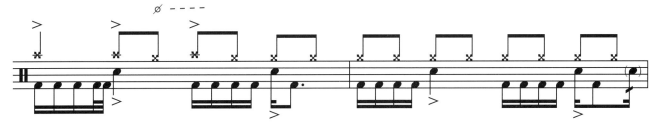

Ex. 33 An intense snare and crash fill precedes the final chorus. (4:17)

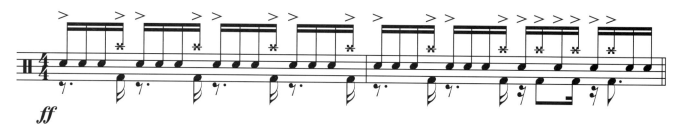

Ex. 34 The drums are featured near the end of the song, and Smith shines with more creative, dramatic fills around the kit. (4:44)

Steve's Thoughts on...
Those "signature ballad fills" from Bryan Adams "Heaven" and Journey's "Faithfully" "Open Arms," and "Mother Father."

With those fills I was consciously letting the drums resonate, letting the reverb between the attacks be heard, and giving each note its full value. Sometimes I would imagine playing in a stadium and how the drums would resonate in a huge space. I made sure the drums were tuned very melodically and with five toms I had a good melodic range. As we were writing the Journey songs, I would experiment with different fills so by the time we recorded them, for the most part, I knew exactly what I was going to play in each fill.

The session for "Heaven" happened at the last minute for me. In 1984 Journey was on tour with Bryan Adams as our opening act. We all had a day off in NYC and Bryan went into the Power Station to record "Heaven" for a movie soundtrack. Mickey Curry started the session but had to leave before the song was finished, he had a prior engagement

with Hall and Oates. Bryan knew I had the day off and called me at my hotel and I came down to the Power Station, learned the song and started tracking with Bryan's band. Bob Clearmountain, who was engineering and producing, had his own Ludwig kit in the studio. The kit was similar to my setup with three rack toms and two floor toms, I sat down and didn't adjust anything. Bob tuned the kit between takes, which I thought was unusual but cool, and in a short time we had the song. Originally, we played longer on the ending and Bob asked me to play more fills. The final triplet fill you hear near the end of the song, is a fill that Bob edited to happen sooner on the fade. Of course, in those years, he was cutting 2" tape, but for a good engineer, that was not difficult. "Heaven" is the only song that I've played on that was an actual #1 Billboard hit!

Vital Information "Looks Bad, Feels Good," *Vital Information*

Ex. 35 Steve rides the open hi-hat and accents the band figures on the bass drum on the A section of "Looks Bad, Feels Good". (0:01)

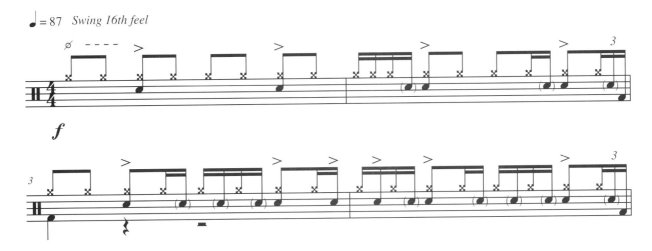

A Section

Ex. 36 Extended fills at the end of the A section bring up the energy, before going into the solos. (1:08)

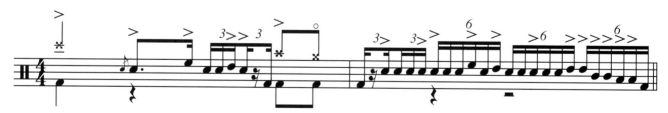

Ex. 37 The fill before the sax solo creates forward motion with accents that land on the upbeats of the triplets. (3:20)

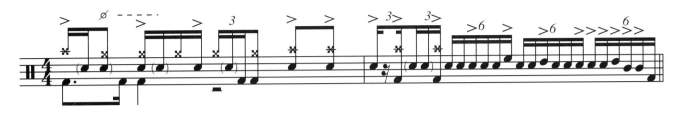

Steve's Thoughts on…
Information "Looks Bad Feels Good," *Vital Information.*

That is a Tim Landers composition and one of the earliest songs that we played even before we were Vital Information. To me that had kind of a Miles Davis feel from the era when Miles' band was Mike Stern, Al Foster, Marcus Miller, and Bill Evans. They had some tunes that had that *swunk* (swinging funk) feel like "Fat Time" from *The Man With The Horn.* Billy Cobham had already recorded "Looks Bad…"

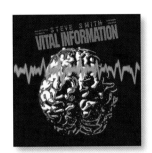

and I was hoping that a lot of people hadn't heard his version, but that didn't influence my wanting to do the tune. It was Tim's tune and we loved playing it. On that first Vital Info album both Dean Brown and Mike Stern played guitar and their interaction is amazing. In fact, that entire group played with a creativity, freshest and interplay that was remarkable.

Vital Information "Novato," *Global Beat*

Ex. 38 Steve plays a groove made of accented rolls and flams on the intro of Vital Information's "Novato." (0:00)

Ex. 39 He maintains the rudimental beat as the band enters, and the time signature shifts to a 10-beat cycle. When the song hits the A section, Steve moves to the hi-hat and plays some subtle accents inside of the open and closed cymbal pattern. (0:29)

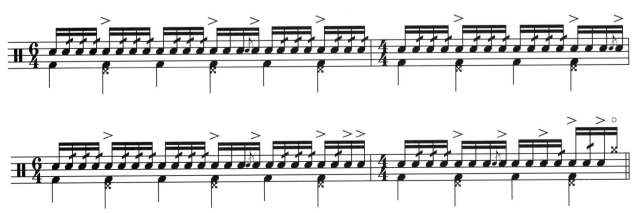

A Section

Steve's Thoughts on…
Vital Information "Novato," *Global Beat.*

I've been listening to *Global Beat* recently, because the Wounded Bird label has just released a four CD set called *Steve Smith & Vital Information - The Complete Columbia Recordings* with the first four Vital Info albums. I had a serious home studio built in 1983 with a 32 input JH-600 MCI board and a JH-24 2" tape machine. I would experiment in my home studio in the town of Novato, California, and *Global Beat* was the first album that I made there. I never became a good engineer but I could record my drums enough to document my ideas and play keyboards to them. I came up with the idea for "Novato" with the snare drum/bass drum groove with the open doubles on the snare and all the

keyboard parts, which I ended up playing on the album. I presented my ideas to Vital Information bassist Tim Landers and together we completed the song. During the early 80s I was deep into Nigerian artist King Sunny Adé and Juju music. I got to see him perform live and it was mesmerizing. That's where the cowbell rhythm on "Novato" comes from and I've used that rhythm on a number of my Vital Info tunes. Two San Francisco residents originally from Africa played on *Global Beat* and they added great parts using various hand drums, talking drums, shakers and vocals; Prince Joni Haastrup from Nigeria and Kwaku Daddy from Ghana.

Vital Information "Blues to Bappe I," *Global Beat*

Ex. 40 Smith lays down a laid-back swing feel on the intro of "Blues to Bappe I." (0:00)

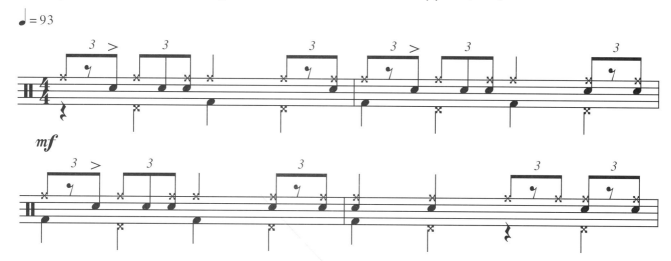

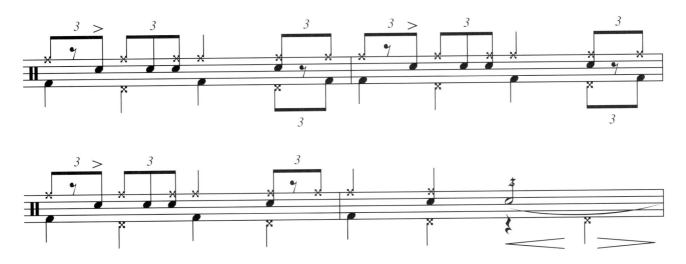

Ex. 41 He plays a Latin-jazz mambo groove on the B section. (1:53)

Ex. 42 This double-time phrase from the guitar solo ends with groups of two played between the snare and bass drum in the triplet rate under the jazz ride cymbal beat. (3:47)

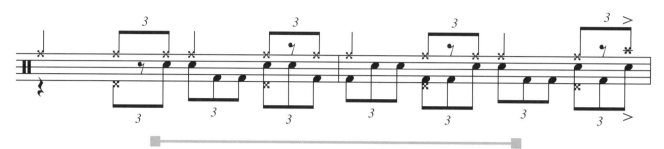

Steve's Thoughts on…
Vital Information "Blues To Bappe I," *Global Beat.*

That's a good example of me playing a tune as it was written. Vital Information saxophonist Dave Wilczewski wrote that tune with all of the hits and accents and I played the tune as he wrote it. Now that I listen to my performance from the perspective of 35 years later, I am playing the setups and accents as though I was in a big band. If I were to play that tune today, I would be much more subtle with the accents. *Global Beat* was the first Vital Info album that Tom Coster played on. Before Tom was in Vital Info the lineup was drums, bass, sax and two guitars. For me Vital Information has always been personality driven, meaning, if there is a musician I want to work with, I'll ask them if they want to play in the band. That's a different concept from my experience with Jean-Luc Ponty, for example. Jean-Luc had a sound in mind and he hired players to help him achieve that sound. The sound of Vital Information changes with each personnel change and each line-up has a distinct character. When Vital Information was coming together, I was inspired by playing with both Dean Brown and Mike Stern on guitars, and later Eef Albers stepping into Mike Stern's place. There was no one keyboard player I gravitated to, as a result the first two Vital Info albums do not have a keyboard player, except for the little bit of piano that I played on them. That changed after I moved to the San Francisco Bay Area and met Tom. We really connected. First of all, we have the same birthday, August 21, though 13 years apart. Both of us grew up as jazz players but spent time playing in successful rock bands, Tom with Santana and me with Journey, which of course, was an off-shoot of Santana. I was playing drums in Tom's band and it was natural that I asked him to play in Vital Information. He became a key member of the group and stayed for 28 years and left when he decided to retire from the music business. Tom plays a great solo on "Blues to Bappe I" over an Elvin Jones type feel before we transition into a double time swing

feel for Mike Stern's solo. Tom brought in Armando Peraza to play congas and bongos on that song. Tom had played with Armando in Santana but Armando's pedigree goes all the way back to the bebop era and recordings and performances with Machito, Charlie Parker and Buddy Rich. Armando's bongo playing behind Dave Wilczewski's solo on the fade at the end of the song is sublime.

MD: Many of these older Vital Information tunes are being re-released, can you tell me about the Vital Information four CD set that is being released in 2022.
SS: The Wounded Bird label licensed the four Vital Information albums I made for Columbia in the 80s. They are the first four Vital Information albums that I made and have been out of print for many years. The four CD set is called *Steve Smith & Vital Information: The Complete Columbia Recordings* and will be issued on CD only. I searched my storage unit and found ¼" unmastered, safety copies, of all four albums. My mastering engineer, Jim Brick of Absolute Audio, had the tapes baked and transferred onto digital. He did such an amazing job with the new mastering of the music that they sound far better than the original releases. It's been an interesting process for me to listen very closely to each of the first four Vital Information albums. When I listen to all four albums in sequence, they tell a story and document an important time in the development of my musical concepts. A key voice throughout all four albums is saxophonist Dave Wilczewski. Sadly, Dave died of cancer in 2009. Dave's playing on all four albums is soulful, expressive, creative and powerful. I feel fortunate that we have embodied some of his legacy in the early music of Vital Information.

The first album, called *Vital Information*, was recorded in January of 1983 shortly after the Journey *Frontiers* album was recorded. We got together in Warren, RI to record at a studio called Normandy Sound. They had an apartment above the studio and we all lived there for the two weeks we spent recording and mixing. The album is a wonderful documentation of the earliest incarnation of the group with bassist Tim Landers, saxophonist Dave Wilczewski and myself contributing the compositions. We recruited our guitarist friends Dean Brown and Mike Stern to complete the group. We had all played together before and you can really hear the uncanny empathy and interaction of all the players. We recorded the album very quickly with each song only taking one or two takes. I used my double-bass Oak Veneer kit and the playing is more on the rock side of jazz.

After the 1983 Journey *Frontiers Tour*, in the Fall of that year Vital Information went on an extended tour of the USA to promote the first album. This was the first time I took a group on the road and that was a serious "trial by fire" learning experience. Mike Stern was touring with Miles Davis so I called Eef Albers to take his place on the tour. I needed a "bop 'n' roll" guitarist and Eef, who I had played with in the Dutch band Focus, was the perfect choice. That band was on fire every night, we were on a mission! We played the songs from the first album and came up with new music during the tour. As soon as the tour concluded, we went back to Normandy Sound and recorded *Orion*, the second album. The music that we came up with on tour was quite diverse, so we ended up recording with a rock concept for Side One, then I changed to a small be-bop kit and we recorded Side Two, with a loose jazz approach. On Side One you'll hear that I used Simmons toms on three songs. I had integrated Simmons toms into my live Journey setup and decided to use them on the more rock-oriented songs on *Orion*.

For the third album I had a concept in mind; a "world-beat" album that added percussion and more international beats. I was checking out Reggae, Afrobeat and Afro-Caribbean music and wanted to combine those ideas into an instrumental jazz concept. The result is *Global Beat*. That album was the first that I recorded in my home studio, Neverland, and was the first Vital Info album that Tom Coster played on. I still had the core group of Tim Landers, Dave Wilczewski and Dean Brown and we added some fantastic guest musicians for that album. We had Mike Stern, Ray Gomez and Barry Finnerty contribute on guitar, Andy Narell on steel pans, plus percussionists Mike Fisher, Brad Dutz, Prince Joni Haastrup, Kwaku Daddy and Armando Peraza. I feel this is truly one of the most enduring recordings in the Vital Information catalogue. Plus, I found two bonus tracks recorded for the album but left off the original version because of the time limitations of an LP. The bonus tracks are "Jave and a Nail Revisited" which is a drumset/percussion duet with myself and Mike Fisher and "Forget Me Not," a composition by Tim Landers and I that features some excellent solos from Tom Coster and Mike Stern.

The fourth Vital Info album, *Fiafiaga (Celebration)*, continues some of the concept of *Global Beat,* but the biggest change is, I had Dave Weckl's long-time collaborator Jay Oliver engineer and produce the album. I was intrigued by Dave Weckl's recording approach of using a computerized foundation to record to, which led to me asking Jay Oliver to produce. Playing "perfect" tracks was a tough transition for me but I wanted to go through the process and stay current with the recording concepts of 1988. By that time the basic line-up of Vital Information was starting to change. Tim Landers played bass on some of the album and we used computer bass for a couple of tunes. On most of the *Fiafiaga* album, Kai Eckhardt played bass. Lenny Castro played percussion and Frank Gambale makes his Vital Information debut on the album. The original recording of Tom Coster's "The Perfect Date" is on *Fiafiaga*, that became a Vital Info standard that remained in the book for many years. I am very pleased that Wounded Bird has stepped up and released these newly remastered albums together in one collection.

Tony MacAlpine "Agrionia," *Edge of Insanity*

Ex. 43 Steve contributes his drumming brilliance to Tony MacAlpine's Shrapnel release *Edge of Insanity*, and further displays his versatility as he steps into the arena of instrumental prog-metal. He constructs a groove on the A section that fits the contour of the guitar melody as he switches between the hi-hat and ride cymbal. (0:00)

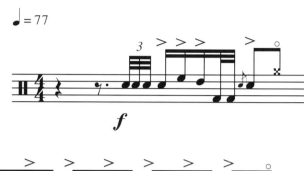

Ex. 44 This drum fill section interacts with Billy Sheehan's bass playing going into the guitar solo. (1:44)

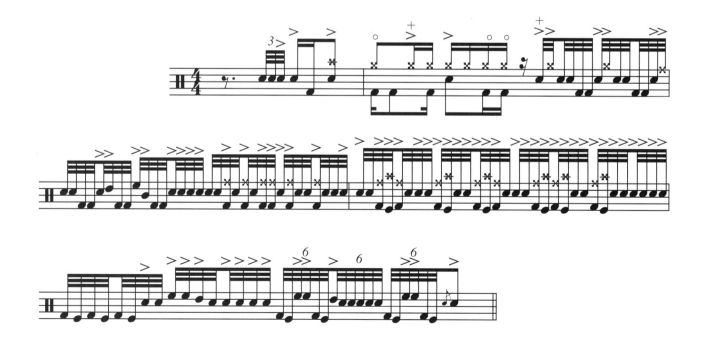

Steve's Thoughts on...
Tony MacAlpine "Agrionia," *Edge of Insanity.*

That intro fill is the same fill that starts "Mother, Father," which (as I've said) is a total Narada cop. Mike Varney called me to ask me if I was interested in doing some records for his label Shrapnel Records. Tony had a great demo of this record where he played every instrument on the recording. I learned the songs and drum parts from his demo and then put my own spin on them. Tony came out to California, from western Massachusetts where he was from, and he and I rehearsed at my home. He was a young kid who had just been signed to Shrapnel Records and *Edge of Insanity* was his first album. He and I recorded the entire record in a day and a half with just drums and guitar, no click, no bass. Billy Sheehan came in and overdubbed all of the bass parts, which are amazing. Then Tony added more guitar and the keyboard parts. Tony's a great guy and a super talent.

Edge of Insanity was the first "metal" album that I played on. To me playing metal was no different than playing with Journey or even some of the music I was making on the early Vital Information albums. The drumming wasn't different, it was the sound of the drums and guitar and the overall vibe of the music that was different. The year that I played on *Edge of Insanity*, 1986, I had just joined Steps Ahead, made the Vital Information *Global Beat* album, was out doing a lot of clinics and generally working like crazy. In 1987 I was awarded my first *Modern Drummer Readers Poll* Award for #1 All-Around Drummer. The public had responded and was starting to see me as more than "the drummer from Journey." Also, in '87 my DCI videos *Steve Smith Part One* and *Part Two* came out, which did well. I went on to win that award five years in a row until I got a message from MD's Ron Spagnardi that I was disqualified from winning All-Around Drummer again in order to give some other drummer a chance. At this point I have a wall full of thirteen various *Modern Drummer* Awards and I am very proud of each one of them!

Steps Ahead "Lust for Life," *N.Y.C.*

Ex. 45 Steve sets up the groove on Steps Ahead's "Lust for Life" with a light cross-stick groove. The bass drum, snare and floor tom rhythms answer Tony Levin's bass line. (2:55)

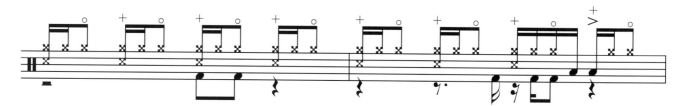

Ex. 46 The drums play sparse percussive fills that interact with the bass before settling into a four-on-the-floor sixteenth-note beat to support the saxophone solo. (1:40)

Saxophone Solo

Ex. 47 When the solo reaches the B section, Steve switches to an upbeat ride cymbal groove. His left hand plays subdivisions on the hi-hat, and he hits the floor tom as a backbeat on beat four. (2:49)

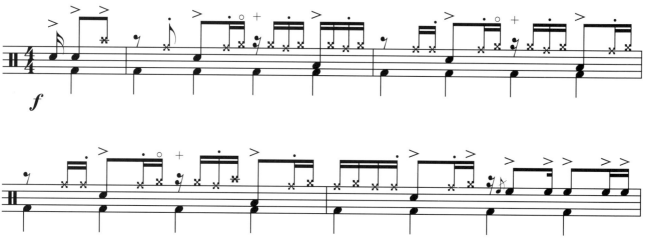

Steve's Thoughts on...
Steps Ahead "Lust For Life." *N.Y.C.*

That is a great song by Norwegian saxophonist Bendik. *N.Y.C.* is the first album Steps Ahead made when Mike Mainieri reformed the group after Michael Brecker left to pursue his solo career. Bendik is playing tenor sax, Tony Levin is playing a Chapman Stick, Steve Khan is playing guitar and Mike Mainieri is on vibes. We were tracking

with a Synclavier, which required me to be very precise. This was a live performance with the Synclavier, so it was a new way of playing. I was coming up with melodic tom parts, leaving a lot of space and interacting with the musicians all in real time. The composition has so much soul, it's one of my favorite Steps Ahead tracks.

Steps Ahead "Absolutely Maybe," *N.Y.C.*

Ex. 48 On the intro of "Absolutely Maybe," Steve flows around the kit with a loose, improvisational approach while stating a half-time feel. (0:00)

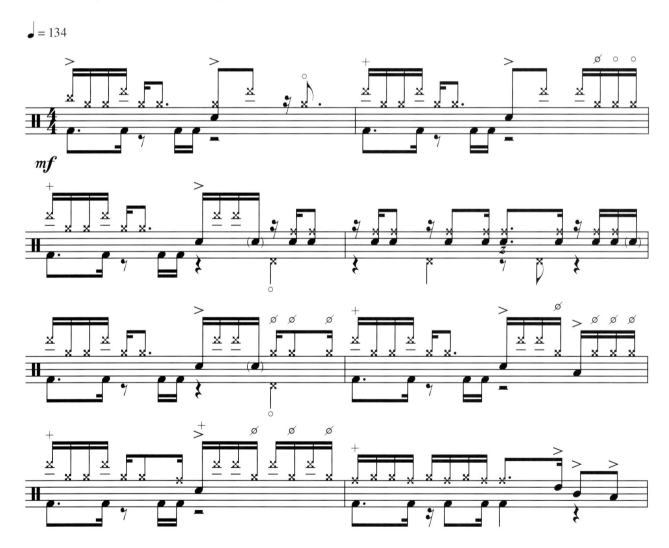

Ex. 49 He creates an interesting over-the-barline phrase in the guitar solo with a dotted eighth note spacing. Snare drum drags connect the bass drum and stepped hi-hat notes. (1:31)

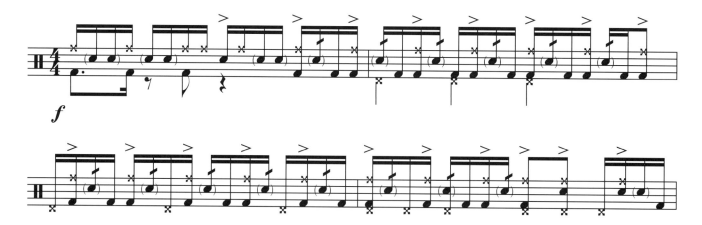

Ex. 50 The song decrescendos to the end, and all of the instruments drop out except the drums. Smith plays with a light touch, while the ride cymbal and snare drum chatter with fast strings of sixteenth notes. He closes out the tune with a cluster of sforzando snare drum accents. (3:34)

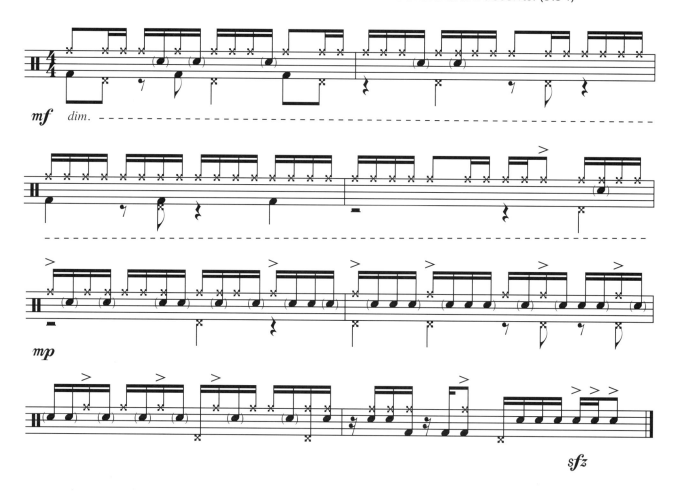

Steve's Thoughts on...
Steps Ahead "Absolutely Maybe" *N.Y.C.*

Another Bendik composition played live with a computer. Mike Mainieri is playing acoustic piano on this track, Bendik on tenor, Tony Levin on bass and Steve Khan on guitar. This is my version of a loose Jack DeJohnette approach, while playing with a click and keeping the orchestration of the parts very spacious yet precise. My kit had three rack toms, two floor toms plus a left-side floor

tom. I also had a closed hi-hat on my right and a 12" china/8" splash stack to my left. The ride cymbal was a dark Istanbul ride that I bought in Turkey while on tour with Randy Brecker. While playing I was conscious of playing with a "stereo" approach using both sides of the kit while keeping it feel loose, spacious and interactive.

Steps Ahead "Taxi," *Yin-Yang*

Ex. 51 A crisp sixteenth-note funk groove serves as the foundation for the A section of "Taxi." The hi-hats are nuanced with dynamics, textural accents, open notes, and doubles. (0:33)

Ex. 52 On the breakdown before the B section, Steve plays expressively on the hi-hats and picks the energy back up with a fill around the drums. (1:07)

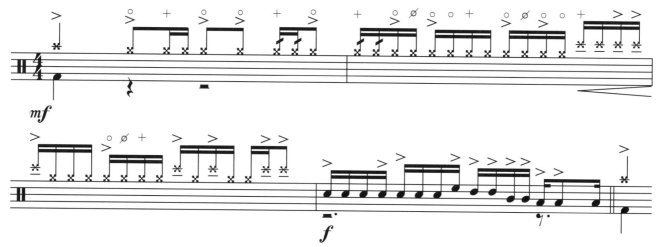

Ex. 53 After the band trails off on what appears to be the end of the song, Smith comes in strong with a fill into the final A section. (2:50)

Steve's Thoughts on...
Steps Ahead "Taxi." *Yin-Yang*

Bendik wrote the song and programmed a lot of samples into the computer, and again, the band played live with the Synclavier. I had to double some of the samples as we tracked, so I wrote them into my chart. The drumming isn't remarkable but the groove is serious and I love the sound of my kit on

this. Jeff Andrews was in the band on this album but it sounds like it's computer bass on this track. This is grooving with a machine and being somewhat free to improvise within the confines of playing with a computer. It's possible.

Vital Information "Cranial #1: Right Now," *Show 'Em Where You Live*

Ex. 54 A fast triplet fill kicks off "Cranial #1: Right Now." Steve plays an intriguing groove that straddles the line between half-time and double-time feels. (0:00)

Steve's Thoughts on…
Vital Information "Cranial #1 Right Now"
Show 'Em Where You Live

This type of groove implies both double time and half time at the same time. That type of open groove gives the soloist a lot of room to play and is interesting because it doesn't have a static 2 & 4 on the snare. Al Foster played grooves something like this with Miles Davis. Check out the opening groove that Al plays on "Come Get It" from the Miles album *Star People*. The Cranial's were all live jams in the studio, some worked and some didn't. I would come up with a drum beat and then the other band members would improvise. We'd record for a while and hopefully find a few minutes of magic and that would be it. The late 90s into the 2000s was a creative period for Vital Information. Bassist Jeff Andrews joined around '93 and we made *Ray Of*

Hope. Once we finished the album, most of it felt too commercial to me. I wanted to change directions and go back to roots, like the The Meters or Booker T. and the M.G.'s as a jazz group. I asked Tom Coster to play the Hammond B3 and accordion, which were his original instruments, and I asked Frank Gambale play a hollow-body jazz guitar. We made *Where We Come From*, which I was very happy with. Then bassist Baron Browne came on board and the band got into a deeper groove and we were on a creative high. The next studio album was *Show 'Em Where You Live*, which is a very strong album, start to finish. We were touring a lot and recording regularly. That band was a powerhouse, we had fun and made some very good music.

Vital Information "Seven and a Half," *Live! One Great Night*

Ex. 55 Smith plays a solo melodic drum pattern in 15/8 time to start Vital Information's "Seven and a Half." When the band enters, the drums settle into a tight funk groove. (0:00)

RLRRLLRLRRLL

Ex. 56 He fills at the end of this phrase by subdividing the 15 into six groups of five sixteenth notes. (0:48)

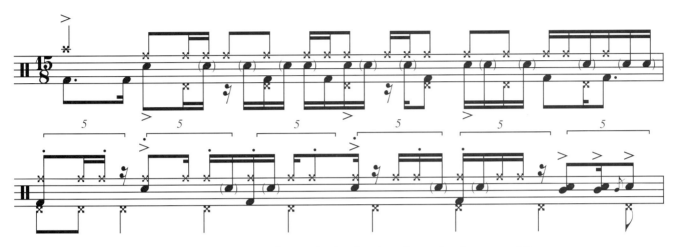

Ex. 57 Later in the song, the drums return to the melodic rhythm from the intro, and Steve utilizes his Indian rhythmic sensibility and plays a tihai cycle across the bars of 15. (1:30)

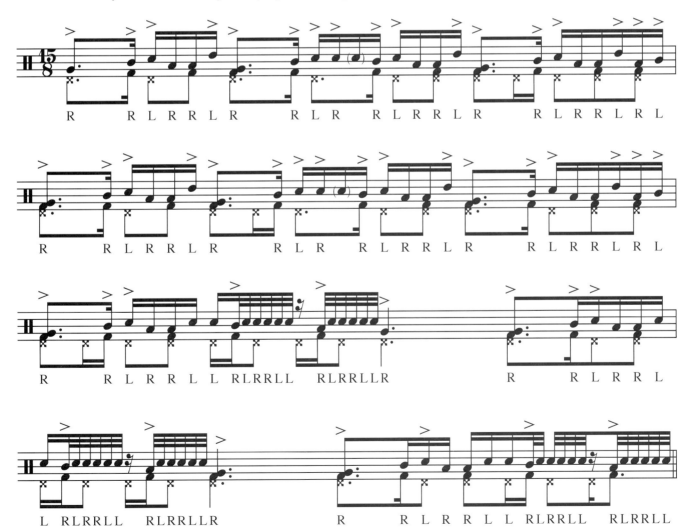

Ex. 58 This drum break has Smith once again tapping into the Indian rhythmic vocabulary as he expands and contracts the accented phrases within the time. The note groupings seem to start and stop in unexpected places yet make perfect sense within the framework of the meter. (5:20)

Steve's Thoughts on…
Vital Information "Seven and a Half." *Live! One Great Night.*

I came up with a groove that was based on a Mridangam beat that I had heard Trichy Sankaran play. I played with Trichy a couple of times and I learned one of his compositions called "Talavadya Kacceri in Khanda Eka Tala" from his album *Laya Vinyās* so I could play it with him live. His composition is in five and there is a short section where Trichy played a very funky "five-groove" on the Mridangam. I came up with a way of playing the groove on a drumset and started to mess around with it. Eventually I turned it into a groove in 15. The

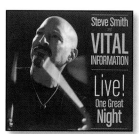

Indian musicians that I had been working with called "Seven and a Half." I felt like my seven-and-a-half groove was melodic and had a "hook." In Vital Info fashion, I played the groove for Tom Coster, Baron Browne and guitarist Vinny Valentino, who had just joined the group. Collectively we came up with the song "Seven and a Half" while writing/rehearsing at Vinny's family lake house in upstate New York. "Seven and a Half" became the most requested and most popular song on *Live! One Great Night!*

Buddy's Buddies "Ya Gotta Try," *Buddy's Buddies*

Ex. 59 Steve plays the stop time melody of "Ya Gotta Try" with great precision and drive. He sets up the accents with a big band attitude within the small group setting. (0:54)

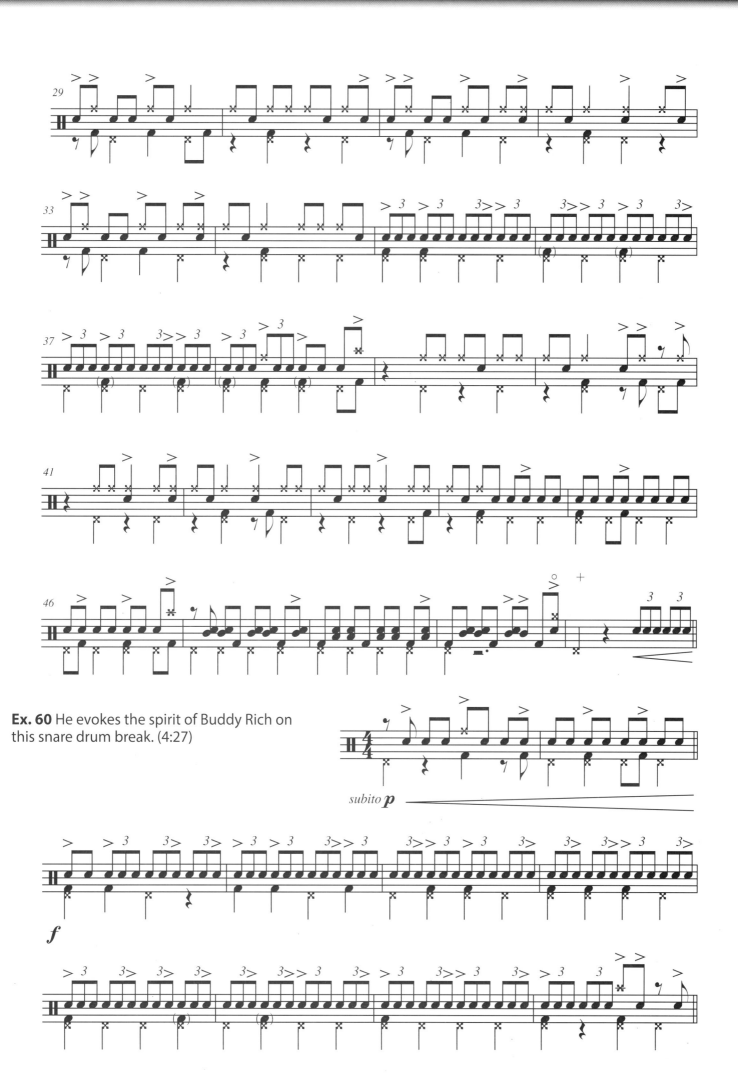

Ex. 60 He evokes the spirit of Buddy Rich on this snare drum break. (4:27)

Steve Smith and Buddy's Buddies "Ya Gotta Try," *Buddy's Buddies*

That is my take on playing the up-tempo barnburner that was a Buddy Rich staple. When I played with the Buddy Rich Big Band or Buddy's Buddies, I am playing the arrangements and performing with the musicians on the bandstand. I'm not trying to channel Buddy, just play music. Bobby Shew, the great lead trumpet player that played on Buddy's original recording of "The West Side Story Medley," called me to play in his Buddy Rich Tribute big band. He said to me, "I need a drummer that can swing a big band and play an extended solo." That sums up my approach to Buddy's music. The *Steve Smith and Buddy's Buddies* record came out of my touring with The Buddy Rich Big Band. Cathy Rich and Steve Arnold asked me to be involved with Buddy's Buddies, which was a small group that played quintet versions of charts associated with Buddy Rich. Andy Fusco (alto sax) and Steve Marcus (tenor and soprano sax) also thought that I would be the right guy to be involved, so we played some shows and it was a good fit. The first incarnation of the band was actually with Steve Marcus, Andy Fusco, Will Lee (bass) and Joel Weiskopf (piano) for the Buddy Rich tribute concert (and Hudson

Music video) called *A Salute to Buddy Rich*. In 1999 I was deep into producing and playing on jazz/fusion albums for Mike Varney's label Tone Center. I pitched Mike on recording the Buddy's Buddies album, which was not a fusion record, and he agreed. The idea for the album was that everyone in the band had to be a Buddy Rich alumni, except me, of course! We recruited Anthony Jackson on contrabass guitar, who had played with Buddy's small group at the club Buddy's Place in NYC. In fact, in 1974 I went to Buddy's Place and saw Buddy with Anthony and the group that made the album called *Very Live at Buddy's Place*. Pianist Lee Musiker, who had also toured and recorded with Buddy, came up with some excellent re-imaginings of Buddy's charts. We made the record in New York live to two-track, which helped with the album budget. That was the session that I met you on, because I had asked you to write some cool historical liner notes for the album. When I took the band on the road we had Baron Browne on bass, Mark Soskin on piano along with Marcus and Fusco. We toured for six years and recorded two live albums at Ronnie Scott's Jazz Club in London.

Steve Smith, Scott Henderson, Victor Wooten "Crash Course," *Vital Tech Tones*

Ex. 61 The drums play a splashy rock groove to open up the song "Crash Course." Smith brings in the guitar and bass riff with a powerful flam accent fill that spans the kit. (0:00)

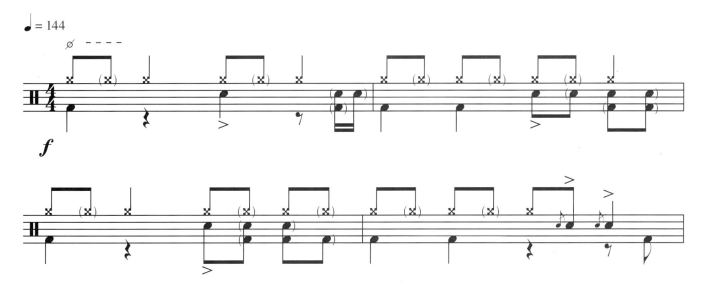

Ex. 62 He channels the great Tony Williams by playing fast triple strokes on the open and closed hi-hat over a half-time snare drum backbeat on the A section. (0:45)

Ex. 63 At the end of the song, Steve opens-up over the band figures with a barrage of ideas and shapes. He builds the solo all the way to the end of the song, adding excitement with each new phrase. (5:44)

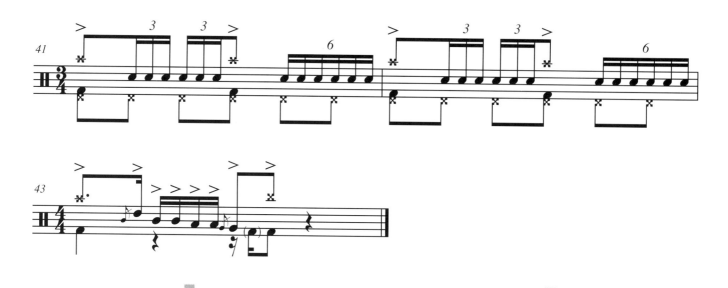

Steve's Thoughts on...
Steve Smith, Scott Henderson, Victor Wooten, "Crash Course." *Vital Tech Tones.*

In 1997 Mike Varney knew that there was a market for high energy jazz-rock fusion in the style of Mahavishnu or Return to Forever, and he decided that he would make records for that audience. Mike called me and asked if I had the opportunity to put together a rock-fusion trio with guitar, bass, and drums, who would I ask to record? I said Scott Henderson, because I loved playing with Scott in the Players band with Jeff Berlin way back. I had also just "discovered" Victor Wooten through hearing his first solo bass record called *A Show of Hands*. He was already in the Flecktones, but as an individual artist he wasn't yet well known, but I thought he was incredible. I called Scott and Victor and both agreed to get together and make an album.

Scott, Victor and I wrote, recorded, and mixed the record in my home studio in nine days. Basically, we wrote, recorded and mixed a song a day until we had a complete album. I had a number of drum grooves prepared and we wrote using those. Scott had some tunes and we reworked Coltrane's "Giant Steps." Scott's solo on "Giant Steps" is incredible, you can really hear his deep knowledge of jazz harmony on that. *Vital Tech Tones* sold very well and that's how the Tone Center label got off the ground.

After *Vital Tech Tones*, Mike asked me if I had any other ideas, and I did! The next Tone Center record I made was with Frank Gambale and Stu Hamm, and then I made one with Tom Coster and Larry Coryell. That process of making albums for Tone Center continued until 2005. The last one I made was *Flashpoint* with Dave Liebman (sax,) Aydin Esen (keyboards,) and Anthony Jackson (contrabass guitar,) it was a very creative period for me. I played on, and produced, sixteen albums with various groups for Tone Center. In 2009 Tone Center released a *Best of Steve Smith* CD that is a very good cross-section of the music I made for the label.

"Crash Course" is a jazz/fusion power-trio playing in the style of The New Tony Williams Lifetime. The song is modeled on the feel of Allan Holdsworth's "Fred" with the double time jazz ride beat on the hi-hat, with a rock bass drum and snare underneath. When I saw Tony play "Fred" live I was knocked out, I'd never seen any drumming like that before. The way he played the hi-hats was very relaxed and the hats were super-loose and undulating. The rock aspect of the drumming was all underneath the jazz feel. It's still an untapped concept in fusion drumming. The Billy Cobham funk/fusion approach is widely integrated into the fusion drumming lexicon but not this Tony Williams concept.

Steve Smith, Scott Henderson, Victor Wooten "Everglades," *Vital Tech Tones*

Ex. 64 The drums and bass start the song "Everglades" with a second-line feel over mixed meters. The time signatures switch from 6/4, to 7/4, back to 6/4, then 8/4. Steve makes it all feel comfortable with a swinging pocket and a thoughtfully constructed part. (0:00)

Ex. 65 After the guitar solo, Smith takes a ride on the bumpy terrain with a drum solo over the odd-meter vamp. He stretches out over the barlines and delivers an incredible performance that is truly worthy of his legendary drumming status. (5:34)

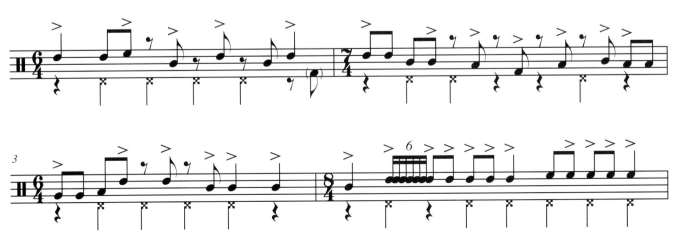

Steve's Thoughts on...
Steve Smith, Scott Henderson, Victor Wooten, "Everglades" *Vital Tech Tones.*

That's odd-time second-line swamp funk. I came up with the basic drum vamp, then Victor came up with his bass part and Scott put harmony and a melody to it. The main vamp is 6/4+7/4+6/4+8/4. Vic and I solo over the odd-time and Scott wanted something rhythmically a little easier to play over so we came up with a 6/4 groove. I love the melodic vamp that Scott and Vic came up with for my drum solo, it made soloing in 27/4 a lot easier!

In the early years of Vital Information, I wrote entire tunes. I wrote the harmony, melody, came up with the groove and brought the tunes to the band. I was composing from the piano. But as the years went on, that got more and more tedious and emotionally painful for me because of my keyboard limitations. When music computer programs came out, I started using them for writing, and I wrote quite a few tunes with that approach, but I found I was spending more time on the computer and much less time on the drums. I decided to focus my attention on coming up with interesting drums grooves and presenting those to the people I was working with. Today, players call that "writing drum parts," and that makes sense, but at that time it was not a typical way of coming up with songs in a jazz setting. I had such a good experience creating grooves and basing tunes around them in Journey, that I introduced that concept to the Vital Information group in the early 90s and it worked well. Tom Coster took to it right away because he had the group writing experience with Santana. When I talked to writer Joel Selvin about that he called it "a San Francisco hippie way of group writing." I introduced that way of writing to a lot of jazz musicians that had never done that before, and after some initial skepticism from some, it worked. Using this approach, some of the musicians I've written songs with are Scott Henderson, Victor Wooten, Frank Gambale, Stu Hamm, Tom Coster, Jeff Andrews, Baron Browne, Howard Levy, Larry Coryell,

Jerry Goodman, George Brooks, Prasanna and Vinny Valentino. One reason it works is because I can take the ideas that they improvise to my grooves and help shape those into finished pieces of music. That's where I combine an arranging and producing overview to the raw material and help nurture the ideas to a satisfactory end result.

Steve Smith, Larry Coryell, Steve Marcus, Kai Eckhardt "Scotland," *Count's Jam Band Reunion*

Ex. 66 The 17/8 meter of Larry Coryell's jazz/rock tune "Scotland" shifts subdivisions every other measure through a two-bar phrase. The first measure is divided as seven groups of two and one group of three, and the second measure is five groups of three and one group of two. Steve creates a drum part that feels natural inside of the odd meter. (1:12)

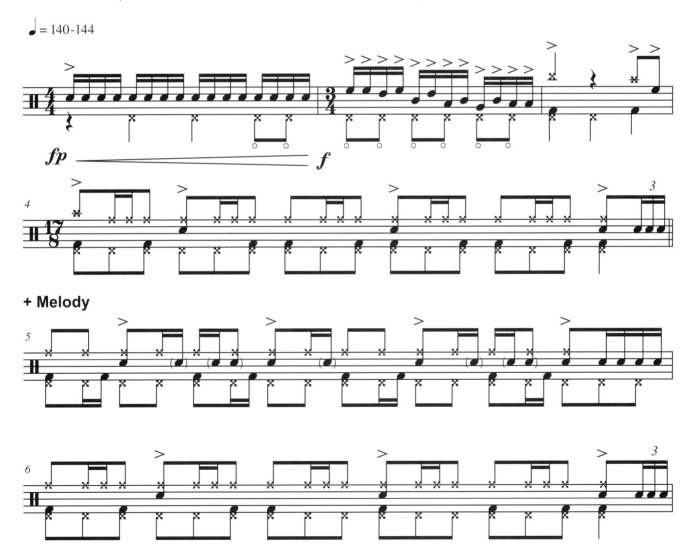

+ Melody

Ex. 67 Smith rides upbeats on a China stack through Larry Coryell's guitar solo. The pattern overrides the meter and crosses through the barline as the subdivisions change through the measures, providing a steady pulse through the asymmetrical 17/8 phrase. (3:15)

Steve's Thoughts on...
Steve Smith, Larry Coryell, Steve Marcus, Kai Eckhardt, "Scotland," *Count's Jam Band Reunion*

I had been working with Steve Marcus with Buddy's Buddies and after lots of on-tour discussions I learned that Steve had a deep history with Larry Coryell in the early days of jazz/rock in the mid-late 60s. After working with Larry on some projects I came up with the idea having a Coryell/Marcus reunion. In the 60s Marcus was known as "The Count" and his band was called Count's Rock Band, hence the album name *Count's Jam Band Reunion*.

"Scotland" is an older Larry Coryell composition that he and Steve Marcus

recorded in 1972 on Larry's album called *Offering*. I thought we could re-record and update the song and we got a very good result. After a free-time intro, "Scotland" is in seventeen, which is phrased (using Indian terminology) first as Eight and a Half and then Six and 2/3rds. The Eight and a Half part is played with straight 8ths and the Six and 2/3rds part is played with subdivisions of three. Each measure is seventeen with different phrasing, the end of one measure sets up the next. Challenging and fun!

Jerry Goodman, Howard Levy, Steve Smith, Oteil Burbridge "Caliente,"
The Stranger's Hand

Ex. 68 Steve handles the A section of "Caliente" with a fluid groove that catches the syncopated rhythms of the melody while anchoring the time as the signature switches from 7/8 to 4/4 and back. (0:15)

Ex. 69 He plays drum fills over the unison band hits in the first half of the B section, and seamlessly transitions into a groove while the bass solos through the second half. (0:59)

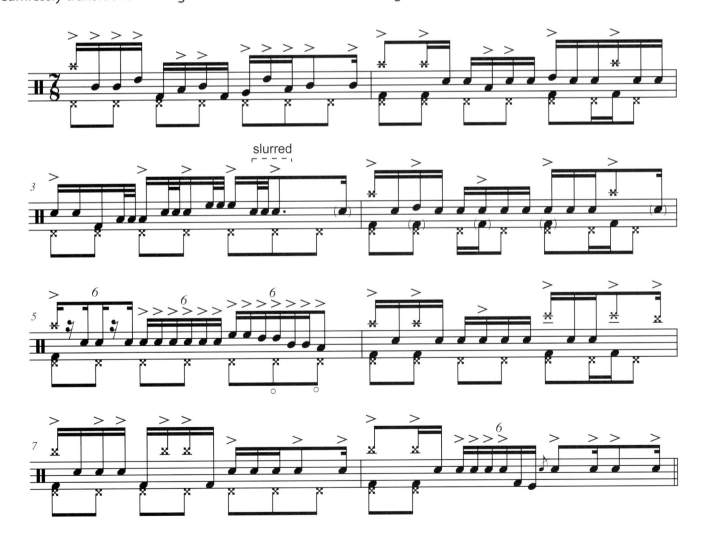

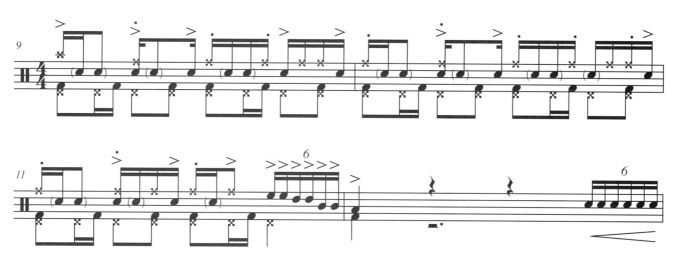

Ex. 70 The band plays a vamp in 7 and Smith takes the spotlight once again with a fiery drum solo. His supreme facility and control on the instrument is evident as he pulls out all the stops on this command performance. (5:22)

Steve's Thoughts on…
Steve Smith, Howard Levy, Jerry Goodman, Oteil Burbridge, "Caliente," *The Strangers Hand*

The Stranger's Hand album was the most unusual and interesting line-up of all the Tone Center albums I produced. Violinist Jerry Goodman I knew from the Mahavishnu Orchestra but it wasn't until I worked with Victor Wooten that I became aware of Howard Levy and his work with Béla Fleck and the Flecktones. Howard is a remarkable multi-instrumentalist being a virtuoso on both harmonica and keyboards. When I asked Victor Wooten to recommend a bassist for this line-up, he immediately told me about Oteil Burbridge. "Caliente" is a Howard Levy composition essentially, but not always, in seven. I was reading a chart and Howard tracked the keyboard first and then overdubbed harmonica. I really pushed myself on the drum solo, always trying to go beyond what I had recorded on previous records, though on the song itself, I was playing pretty over-the-top, which was part of the Tone Center ethos. Mike Varney told me his production concept for Tone Center Records, which was the antithesis of the "smooth-jazz" records that were popular during that time, "When you record for me, throw in everything you know, and when you get to the kitchen sink, keep on going!"

Jerry Goodman, Howard Levy, Steve Smith, Oteil Burbridge "Glimmer of Hope," *The Stranger's Hand*

Ex. 71 Steve plays a well-crafted part on the intro of the Mahavishnu-inspired song "Glimmer of Hope." He starts with crashes and tom runs over the 11/8 meter with subdivisions of 4+4+3. When the band settles into the A section, the subdivisions of the 11/8 meter change to 3+3+3+2 then briefly switch back to the 4+4+3 feel at the end of the phrases. (0:00)

A Section (3 + 3 + 3 + 2)

(4 + 4 + 3)

Steve's Thoughts on…
Steve Smith, Howard Levy, Jerry Goodman, Oteil Burbridge, "Glimmer of Hope," *The Strangers Hand*

Jerry Goodman brought "Glimmer of Hope" to *The Stranger's Hand* sessions. This is straight out of the Mahavishnu concept. In the opening, I outline the figures by filling in on the toms modeled after Billy Cobham's orchestration of the piece "Hope" on the Mahavishnu album *Birds of Fire*. Similar in concept to Larry Coryell's "Scotland," Jerry uses two different ways of phrasing the same time signature, in this case, eleven. In some sections there are three measures of Three and 2/3rds and then one measure of Five and a Half.

What Three and 2/3rds means is, the subdivision of the beat is three 8th notes and there are three beats

of three 8th notes and the next beat only has the first two of the three beats, hence 2/3rds. Five and a Half is subdivided in 8th notes and there are four beats of 8th notes and when you get to the fifth beat, there are three 8th notes. The Indian musicians say "five and a half" in the rhythmic phrase of 1, 2&, 3. Once I worked out the math of the song, we rehearsed for a while, got comfortable with the various ways of playing in eleven and worked out the arrangement. For the Stranger's Hand group of musicians, playing in odd-times was natural and in a short while we recorded our final take of "Glimmer of Hope."

Steve Smith, Prasanna, George Brooks "Katyayni," *Raga Bop Trio*

Ex. 72 "Katyayini" is an Indian Carnatic-style duet between Smith and Prasanna playing guitar. Steve plays a melody around the drums with mallets over inverted doubles on his feet. The left foot travels between the bass drum pedal to the hi-hat and back, creating an ostinato underneath. (0:00)

(Snares off)

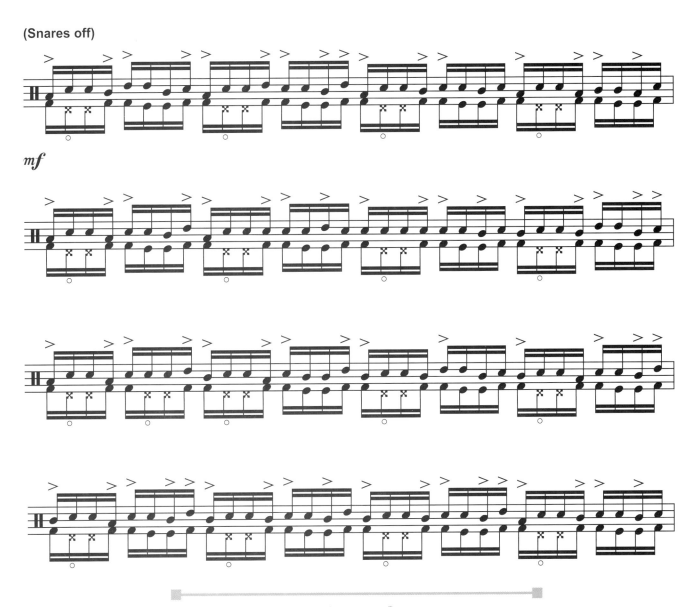

mf

Steve's Thoughts on...

Prasanna, George Brooks, Steve Smith, "Katyayini" *Raga Bop Trio.*

This is based on traditional Carnatic (South Indian) music that is generally played by two musicians; a melodic instrument and a drum. That's a full band in India. We did this with electric guitar and drumset, which is unique and not typical. I came up with a double-bass-drum/hi-hat foot ostinato for my feet, and I played mallets on the toms and snare with the snares off. Again, it's my version of a Mridangam groove but on a drumset with five toms. There are tihai's on this that don't resolve to beat one. In Carnatic music if the melody doesn't start on one, the tihai's resolve to the beat where the melody starts. That was beyond what I had played before so Prasanna calculated the tihai's and taught them to me.

Katyayini is in 8/4 and if you count (while listening to the song) you'll hear that the tihai is 3x7 which starts of the & of beat 5 and resolves to the & of 2, which is where the melody starts. Before we started the Raga Bop Trio with George Brooks on sax, I had played quite a few duo gigs with Prasanna. I learned a lot from playing with Prasanna. The entire Raga Bop Trio experience was a deep learning curve as it was a trio without a bass player. We toured extensively and it was a challenge to play in a way that covered my basic function as a drummer plus added extra low-end that filled in some of the sonic space a bass would occupy. I found myself playing less cymbals and more toms with that group.

Mike Corrado

Mike Corrado

Rick Malkin

Rick Malkin

Mike Corrado

Robert Knight

Mike Corrado

Steve Smith Library

Mike Corrado